Loss and Grief

*Also published by Palgrave

Loss and Grief

A Guide for Human Services Practitioners

Edited by

Neil Thompson

Consultant editor: Jo Campling

palgrave

First published 2002 by
PALGRAVE
Houndmills, Basingstoke, Hampshire RG21 6XS and
175 Fifth Avenue, New York, N.Y. 10010
Companies and representatives throughout the world

PALGRAVE is the new global academic imprint of
St. Martin's Press LLC Scholarly and Reference Division and
Palgrave Publishers Ltd (formerly Macmillan Press Ltd).

ISBN 0–333–96328–8 paperback

This book is printed on paper suitable for recycling and made from fully managed and sustained forest sources.

A catalogue record for this book is available from the British Library.

Library of Congress Cataloging-in-Publication Data

Loss and grief: a guide for human services practitioners/edited by Neil Thompson.
    p. cm.
    Includes bibliographical references and index.
    ISBN 0–333–96328–8 (pbk.)
1. Loss (Psychology) 2. Grief. I. Thompson, Neil, 1955-

BF575.D35 L665 2002
361'.06–dc21   2001059053

10 9 8 7 6 5 4 3 2 1
11 10 09 08 07 06 05 04 03 02

Printed and bound in Great Britain by
J. W. Arrowsmith Ltd., Bristol

For Ben-Joshua

Contents

Foreword

Western culture teaches a mixed message. On the one hand it teaches that children have to lose the immunity they received from their mothers, in order to develop the antibodies, the strength to resist illness in adulthood. It teaches that children have to lose the comfort of their home, to go to school to gain the strength they need to meet new challenges. It teaches that children gain new skills, such as interpersonal relations, by losing the self-assurance they had in old skills. Yet, at the same time, outside of the above, Western culture teaches that losses, even the discussion of losses, should be avoided. Western culture pretends that losses can be avoided, or at least delayed unendingly. As Goldman (1981) has pointed out, whenever there is an emotional event that is likely to happen – a marriage, a child birth, graduation from school, a new job – we think of the event often, perhaps continuously. Yet even though the death of someone close to us is a highly emotional event that has a 100 per cent chance of happening, we never allow ourselves to think of it.

The Buddhists teach us that the acceptance of the fact of loss is the beginning of spirituality. We want to make sense of a world that seems not to make sense, a world full of losses. 'Why me?' As Becker said, spirituality 'is an expression of the will to live, the burning desire of the creature to count, to make a difference on the planet because he has lived, has emerged on it, has worked, suffered, and died' (1975, p. 3).

Living, including the dying phase of it, is a lonely spiritual journey. Many will find an appropriate spiritual path through the teachings of the major religions. Others do not find the traditions meaningful. But, even those who find help in religion still must walk the path alone. The story of Abraham and Isaac still applies. We have to make our decisions alone. This loneliness of decision-making about things that matter most, is what I mean by the spiritual journey of life. Elsewhere, I have written that 'Spirituality refers to the ability of the human person to choose the relative importance of the physical, social, emotional, religious, and intellectual stimuli that influence him or her and thereby engage in a continuing process of meaning making' (Morgan, 2000). The most that the great teachers of philosophy and religion can offer us is suggestions. We must do the choosing, and live in conformity with our choices.

We could not survive in the contemporary world without two contradictory things. The first is the need to build walls around ourselves. We would not survive in school, at work, sometimes even at home, if we were to allow others to see how truly vulnerable we are. Yet, at the same time, we cannot survive unless we have social support. Unless we feel safe enough to take a few bricks out of the walls to allow one or two others to enter in. That is social support.

Social support, the essential backdrop of the spiritual journey of life, comes in many ways. It comes through the strength of the family staying together in good times and bad. It comes through the organizations of religions. It comes through friends made in the family, school and workplace. It comes anywhere an experience is provided 'which validates the worth of the person and offers them a caring presence when they are troubled' (Jaco, 2001).

Social support also comes through this book that Neil Thompson has prepared for us. These chapters are excellent guides to those who work with those seeking help, because they have become aware of the losses of life. It is a privilege to work with others in such situations. They have taken a chance on us to allow us to enter into their vulnerability. A book such as this one gives us some of the many tools that we need to merit the trust that others place in us.

JOHN D. MORGAN
King's College Centre for Education
about Death and Bereavement,
London, Canada

Preface

Loss and grief are fundamental aspects of human existence, basic building blocks of our life experience. The traditional emphasis in the literature base on loss and grief has been on death-related losses. Such literature has also tended to have a major psychological focus. This book differs from that traditional literature in two major respects. First, while fully acknowledging just how important death and dying are both for individuals and for society more broadly, the focus here is a much wider one. The book incorporates much discussion of issues relating to death and dying but also includes coverage of the other loss arenas that are very powerful factors in shaping our lives. These arenas include adoption and substitute care; divorce and separation; old age; disability; ill-health; and the justice system. Second, the book recognizes the importance of a theoretical understanding of loss and grief, but is critical of much of the established wisdom on these topics. The book therefore presents a range of theoretical perpectives which seek to go beyond the narrow focus of the traditional literature.

Although quite wide in its scope, the book is, of course, not comprehensive in its coverage. To state that the field of loss and grief is enormous is perhaps something of an understatement. Clearly, then, we cannot hope to cover the whole field in one volume. However, it is to be hoped that the breadth of coverage here will be sufficient to help readers appreciate the significance of loss across the various arenas in which it manifests itself and to encourage further reading and exploration of those aspects of loss not covered here.

The book seeks to provide a firm foundation of theoretical understanding to underpin professional practice. It is my hope that this foundation will be of use and value to a wide range of professional workers in what can be referred to as the 'human services' – social workers and social care staff; nurses and other professions allied to medicine; doctors; counsellors; youth and/or community workers; advice workers; mediators; police officers; and so on. Indeed, any workers whose role brings them into contact with issues of loss and grief should find something of value here.

Dealing with loss and grief is challenging work, as it often involves working with the extremes of pain and dread, in both those that we seek to help and indeed in ourselves. No one is beyond the reach of the hand of loss and the grief it brings. We cannot avoid it and so the challenge we face is to prepare ourselves as much as we reasonably can. I present this book and the important insights of each of the contributors as one part of what we need to face that challenge.

NEIL THOMPSON

Acknowledgements

Of course, the first people I should thank are the contributors who have provided such rich insights into the complexities of loss and grief. I am indeed very grateful to them for being prepared to share their knowledge and understanding. I have been very fortunate to have such a wide range of contributors to draw upon, and to have received such high-quality writings from so many different people across academic, professional and geographical boundaries.

Although all contributors have played an important role, I would like to thank two in particular for their special contributions to the project overall. First, I would like to acknowledge the important role of Denise Bevan, long-standing friend and colleague. Denise was kind enough to read many of the chapters in draft form and to offer helpful comments. I have also benefited from the very many discussions I have had with her about loss and grief over the years. The depth of her understanding and the quality of her insights have been a source of not only considerable learning but also inspiration. Second, Sue Thompson has contributed not only Chapter 11, but also so much more. She has offered helpful comment on many of the chapters in draft form and, as always, has been a major source of support in so many different ways. I am very much indebted to her for her part in bringing this project to fruition and indeed for the so many other positives she brings.

I would also like to thank the various colleagues in the International Work Group on Death, Dying and Bereavement who have played so important a role in establishing such a positive basis for learning and living in a context of considerable loss and grief. They bring a very human face to a topic of study that can be very cruel and painful.

Jo Campling was very helpful in shaping this project in what turned out to be a much more lengthy gestation period than is usually the case. I am grateful to her for that and for continuing to be such a reliable source of advice and guidance. Catherine Gray and Jo Digby at the publishers have continued to be very helpful and a pleasure to work with, something I appreciate very much. I am also delighted to thank Judy Marshall for her excellent copyediting.

This book is dedicated to Ben-Joshua Jaffee. I would like to thank him for his insights, his commitment and his friendship.

The Contributors

Adam Anderson is a doctoral candidate in Clinical Psychology in the Psychology Department, University of Memphis, USA, where he conducts research on the predictors of traumatic reactions to loss, and the mechanisms of change in psychotherapy and psychosocial intervention. He is currently completing his doctoral dissertation and works as an intern at the Brigham Young University Counseling and Career Center.

Denise Bevan is a senior social worker at St Rocco's Hospice, Warrington, UK. She has extensive experience of working in the human services as a nurse, community care worker and social worker, with a major focus on loss-related issues. She also has experience of teaching, researching and writing about loss and grief.

John Dawes is an Honorary Research Fellow, School of Law, Flinders University, South Australia, and also teaches in the Department of Social Administration and Social Work. A social worker, he was head of the SA Department of Correctional Services from 1982 to 1993 and was SA's inaugural Public Advocate. He is a member of the International Work Group on Death, Dying and Bereavement.

Suki Desai is a senior lecturer in social work at the University of Wolverhampton. She has worked as a social worker in mental health settings and is a founder member of the Leicester Black Mental Health Group. She was involved in the setting up of the Mental Health Shop, an advocacy project for black people with mental health needs.

Jeanne Katz qualified as a social worker before training in medical sociology. Since 1990 she has taught several courses at the Open University, most notably 'Death and Dying'. Her recent research focused on older people dying in residential and nursing homes. She edited *Death, Dying and Bereavement* (Sage, 2000, with D. Dickenson and M. Johnson) and *Grief, Mourning and Death Ritual* (Open University Press, 2001, with J. Hockey and N. Small).

Brynna Kroll is a former family courts' welfare officer and now lectures in the Department of Social Work at Exeter University, where she specializes in child and family social work. She has published in the areas of divorce and contact, from the child's perspective, and is the co-author of *Parental Substance Misuse and Child Protection* (Jessica Kingsley, 2002).

Margaret Lloyd is Senior Lecturer in Community Care at the University of Sheffield. Prior to her academic career she was a social worker. She is particularly interested in the maintenance of a holistic approach, including loss counselling, in mainstream settings. She has undertaken empirical research around dying and bereavement, and in community care implementation for people with Parkinson's disease.

Bernard Moss is a Learning and Teaching Fellow and Principal Lecturer in Social Work and Applied Social Studies at Staffordshire University. His teaching interests include studies in death and dying; bereavement studies; divorce and mediation. He has a developing interest in exploring the links between spirituality, faith communities and human services.

Robert A. Neimeyer holds a Dunavant University Professorship in Psychology at the University of Memphis, where he maintains a clinical practice. He has published 17 books, including *Meaning Reconstruction and the Experience of Loss* (American Psychological Association), and *Lessons of Loss: A Guide to Coping* (Brunner Routledge). He is Editor of the journal *Death Studies*, and a member of the American Psychological Association's Task Force on End-of-Life Issues.

Gordon Riches lectures in sociology at the University of Derby. Along with Pam Dawson, Bereavement Co-ordinator of the London Borough of Bromley, he has researched the impact of a child's death on marital and family relationships. He is particularly interested in exploring the ways crisis affects social networks and identity transformation.

Mary Romaine is the Director of BAAF Adoption and Fostering in Wales – BAAF Cymru – an independent organization developing services for children and young people in foster care or being adopted. Prior to this Mary was a consultant working in Kent, developing social care services for people affected by HIV and Aids.

Bob Sapey is a lecturer in applied social science at Lancaster University. He worked with disabled people as a social worker for many years before moving into social work education. His publications focus on health and social care practice issues regarding disability and the use of information technologies. He is co-author, with Michael Oliver, of the second edition of *Social Work with Disabled People*, published by Palgrave.

Dame Cicely Saunders is recognized as the founder of the modern hospice movement, having founded St Christopher's Hospice in 1967. She holds qualifications in nursing, social work and medicine. Awards include the British Medical Association Gold Medal for services to medicine, the Templeton Prize for Progress in Religion, the Onassis Prize for Services to Humanity, the Raoul Wallenberg Humanitarian Award and the Franklin D. Roosevelt Four Freedoms for Worship Medal.

Sue Thompson is an independent social worker and practice teacher and a Director of *Avenue Consulting Ltd* (www.avenueconsulting.co.uk). She has extensive experience in the human services as a nurse, social worker and care manager. She is the author of *From Where I'm Sitting*, a training manual for staff working with older people (Russell House Publishing, 2002).

Neil Thompson is a Director of *Avenue Consulting Ltd* (www.avenueconsulting.co.uk) and Visiting Professor at the University of Liverpool. He is the author of numerous books, including *People Skills* (2nd edn, Palgrave, 2002), *Promoting Equality* (Palgrave, 1998) and *Theory and Practice in Human Services* (2nd edn, Open University Press, 2000). He is a member of the International Work Group on Death, Dying and Bereavement.

Jeremy Weinstein worked as a social worker before moving to South Bank University, London, to teach on the social work programme. He is currently Course Director for the postqualifying MSc in Social Work, and also a UKCP registered psychotherapist and a BAC accredited trainer, with a small private practice as a Gestalt psychotherapist working with individuals and organizations, also as a researcher.

Introduction

Neil Thompson

In this introductory chapter my task is to set the scene for the book as a whole. I begin by discussing the significance of loss for the human services before providing an overview of theories of loss, drawing comparisons between traditional and contemporary perspectives. This overview paves the way for an account of a model of loss and grief which is proposed as a basis for developing an understanding of the complex interplay of factors that contribute to experiences of grieving and mourning. This model is not presented as 'the answer', in any definitive sense, but rather as a framework for drawing together some of the strands of recent developments in loss theory and beginning to develop a more sophisticated understanding than traditional theoretical perspectives allow.

The significance of loss

This book recognizes the importance of establishing the significance of loss and grief as major factors underpinning so many aspects of human services practice. It is based on the premise that life is characterized by movement, change and development – and therefore by transitions, losses and grief. Without an understanding of loss and related issues, practitioners in the human services can be seen to be at a distinct disadvantage in terms of making sense of the complex situations encountered, as loss and grief are such pervasive and influential factors in human behaviour and interactions. Without such an understanding, we also run the risk of exacerbating difficult situations for people experiencing a grief reaction by failing to be able to appreciate what they are going through.

The first aspect of loss and grief that it is important to recognize is that loss is a broad concept and does not relate solely to losses brought about by death. There is an extensive literature base that addresses death-related losses (for example, Corr *et al.*, 1997;

Dickenson *et al.*, 2000), and such texts demonstrate clearly and effectively just how important death-related losses are in relation not only to the psychology of the individual (that is, how individuals respond at a personal level to bereavement), but also to the role of loss issues in relation to culture and society more broadly (Howarth and Jupp, 1996; Field *et al.*, 1997). However, we should not allow the importance of such issues to distract us from recognizing the significance of other forms of loss – that is, forms of loss that are not directly death-related.

A second important aspect of loss to recognize is its relative 'invisibility' in the dominant theoretical underpinnings of human service professions. Textbook after textbook on work in the human services generally or within the specific disciplines (social work, nursing, counselling, youth and community work, proba- tion and community justice and so on) attaches little or no significance to the role of loss and grief in people's lives, in the problems they encounter or the challenges they face. This is not to say that there is no theoretical foundation on which we can draw. On the contrary, there is an extensive literature base of theory and research that we can use to inform our thinking. My point is that this literature has tended to remain within the domain of specialist work and has had a relatively small impact on mainstream thinking. It should also be noted that, where the specialist literature does filter through, it tends to be the tradi- tional, often fundamentally flawed, theory which features, with an almost total neglect of more contemporary theoretical work which offers a more developed and sophisticated approach. This distinc- tion between traditional and contemporary theories is one to which I shall return in more detail below.

The third aspect I wish to emphasize is the importance of drawing out the implications of loss and grief for practice across the human services. It follows that, if issues relating to loss and grief tend to be neglected in the theory base, they are also likely not to attract the attention they deserve within the practice field. This can be seen to apply in particular to those losses that are not death-related, as these generally do not have the same level of recognition associated with losses involving death. This is because we have sets of rituals that come into play at the time of a death (Zulli, 1998), and these rituals give a very clear signal that we are dealing with loss and grief. Other losses, however, tend not to have such rituals associated with them, and so awareness of the grief being experienced by the person or persons concerned tends to be at a much lower level.

Theories of loss

As mentioned above, there is a well-established theory base relating to loss issues. However, an important aspect of this book is that it seeks to go beyond the traditional, well-established theory base. This is for a number of reasons, not least the following three:

- traditional theories can be criticized for 'psychological reductionism' due to their neglect of the phenomenological and structural dimensions (to be explained below);
- contemporary developments (meaning reconstruction; dual process; disenfranchisement and so on) have yet to receive the widespread attention their insights deserve;
- links with other theories such as crisis intervention, stress theory and so on are rarely made and yet, as I shall argue below, there is much to be gained by examining the overlap and interlinking themes and issues across these diverse theoretical terrains.

Let us consider each of these in a little more detail.

Traditional theories: strengths and weaknesses

Perhaps the best-known theoretical approach to loss is what has come to be known as the 'stages model', a perspective closely associated with Elizabeth Kübler-Ross, a key figure in the development of loss theory (Kübler-Ross, 1969). Kübler-Ross wrote of five stages that dying people were understood to go through: denial, anger, bargaining, depression and acceptance. This model was later extended to apply to grieving more generally and was adapted in a number of ways.

This has proven to be a very influential approach and has had a major impact on practice and training. However, it has also come in for considerable criticism. For example, Corr *et al.* (1997) summarize Kastenbaum's (1995) evaluation in the following terms:

> One serious and thorough evaluation of this stage-based model raised the following points: (1) the existence of these stages as such has not been demonstrated; (2) no evidence has been presented that people actually do move from Stage 1 to Stage 5; (3) the limitations of the model have not been acknowledged; (4) the line is blurred between description and prescription; (5) the totality of the person's life is neglected in favor of the supposed stages of dying; and (6) the resources, pressures, and characteristics of the immediate environment, which can make a tremendous difference, are not taken into account. (p. 153)

This basic model has much in common with work developed by Colin Murray Parkes (Parkes, 1996). He described grief in terms of 'psychosocial transitions'. He too favoured a stages approach, dividing the process up into four such phases: shock and numbness; yearning and searching; disorganization and despair; and reorganization.

By contrast, the work of William Worden (1991) sought to move beyond the stages approach and preferred to regard grieving as a matter of achieving 'tasks' (parallel with the well-established idea in developmental psychology that human development involves achieving certain tasks – for example, the task of making the transition from childhood to adulthood). In particular, he wrote of four tasks, namely:

- *To accept the reality of loss.*   The shock of a major loss can leave us feeling that the situation is unreal. The first task, therefore, is to take on board the fact that the loss has actually happened.
- *To work through to the pain of grief.*   The second task is to acknowledge and begin to work through the pain caused by the loss.
- *To adjust to an environment in which the deceased is missing.*   A significant loss is likely to bring with it other changes in our environment, and so this task involves making the necessary changes to adapt to the new situation.
- *To emotionally relocate the deceased and move on with life.*   This involves allowing ourselves to invest emotional energy in new relationships.

This was a more flexible and adaptable approach in so far as it moved away from the rigidity that had come to be associated with the stages approach. For example, the tasks do not necessarily have to be completed in a particular order.

A further approach to loss and grief, although this time not one directly associated with death-related losses, is that of attachment theory. Closely associated with the work of John Bowlby (Bowlby, 1951, 1988), this approach focuses on the 'attachments' that children make and the importance of these for the development of identity and a sense of security. The basic argument is that a child who lacks secure attachments (for example, to parents) is likely to have emotional difficulties in establishing a secure sense of self, forming relationships and so on. The breaking of attachments (or 'affectional' bonds) involves losses that can have a significant bearing on the child's psychosocial development. According to this theory, then, the nature and development of such attachments are key factors in human development that can have a profound impact on our adult lives.

The earlier formulations of attachment theory have been heavily criticized for gender-biased assumptions which reinforce patriarchal gender roles and also for not taking account of cultural differences across groups. However, more recent texts have at least begun to address these criticisms of an unduly narrow approach (see, for example, Howe, 1995 and Howe *et al.*, 1999).

The traditional approaches in general can often be criticized for the narrowness of their approach to loss, and, in particular, for neglecting two very important dimensions – the cultural dimension (of shared meanings) and the structural dimension (of social relations in general and power in particular). This means that such approaches can be criticized for their 'psychological reductionism'. That is, they reduce complex, multilevel phenomena to the simple level of individual psychology. In so doing, they omit consideration of some very important issues and attach an inordinate amount of significance to the psychological dimension.

Fortunately, we have a growing literature base that can help us to rectify this imbalance and draw attention to the underrepresented cultural and structural dimensions. We shall discuss some of the issues arising from this literature in the next section.

Developments in loss theory

Recent years have seen the development of a number of new approaches and perspectives relating to theories of loss and grief. Here I present an overview of some of those key developments in order to illustrate some of the ways in which our understanding of these complex issues has moved on. The discussion is, of course, neither comprehensive nor exhaustive. It should be seen as an introduction to contemporary developments in the theory base rather than a definitive statement on them or an attempt at theory development in its own right.

In 1995 Margaret Stroebe and Henk Schut presented a paper at a conference in Oxford in which they outlined what they termed a 'dual process approach' to loss (Stroebe and Schut, 1995). In essence, this approach seeks to explain grief reactions in terms of two concurrent processes or 'orientations'. These are described as 'loss orientation' and 'restoration orientation'. The former refers to what is traditionally seen as a grief reaction and is characterized by sadness, anger and so on. Restoration orientation, by contrast, is characterized by attempts to rebuild our life, to move on as far as we reasonably can.

While traditional theories would approach these two orientations in chronological terms (that is, with loss orientation leading gradually towards restoration orientation), Stroebe and Schut are at pains to emphasize that they see them as concurrent processes – both featuring in the lives of grieving people, with a degree of movement backwards and forwards between them.

Indeed, this latter point is a key feature of the theory. We do not move gradually from one orientation to the other, as if part of a natural healing process. Rather, we oscillate between the two, with one dominating at any given time but yielding to the other before too long. At certain times we may be heavily immersed in sadness and feelings of loss, while at others we feel more able to look at what we need to do to move on and rebuild our lives or those parts that the loss has disturbed or destroyed.

Stroebe and Schut argue that it is likely that loss orientation will predominate in the early stages of a period of grief and that restoration will gradually gain ascendancy over time. However, this is not a simple transition from one to the other. It also means that, even a long time after restoration has established itself as the dominant orientation, loss orientation can still re-emerge temporarily (for example, as in the well-established phenomenon of feelings of sadness and loss recurring at key times such as anniversaries).

This approach therefore offers a significant advance on earlier approaches in so far as it:

- recognizes that there is no one 'grief process', but rather complex interactions between two opposing orientations – it therefore avoids the tendency to oversimplify;
- helps to explain why grieving is so often characterized by tension, given the impact of the opposing tendencies of each orientation – that is, it shows why grieving is not a smooth, linear pathway that we follow stage by stage;
- lays the foundations for developing a more sophisticated understanding of broader social aspects of grief – for example, cultural and gender differences, as these can, in part, be explained by different emphases in relation to the two orientations, with some cultures placing more value on open expressions of grief (moaning and wailing) and others less so (stiff upper lip).

Perhaps the most important aspect of dual process theory is that it moves us away from the narrow, psychologistic approach which presents grieving as a (largely biologically-based) natural process and alerts us to the complex web of psychological, cultural and sociopolitical factors which interact to make loss experiences far more complex than traditional approaches would have us believe.

Another important perspective that has emerged in recent years is that of meaning reconstruction theory (see, for example, Neimeyer, 2001b). In brief, this theory is premised on the fundamental argument that, when we experience a profound loss, we also experience a loss of meaning, a potentially deep-going disruption of our lifestory. Accordingly, the process of grieving can therefore be seen as one of making sense of the loss – answering to our own satisfaction the practical, existential and perhaps spiritual question of why it happened and reconstructing what our life means, particularly those aspects of our life directly affected by the loss. In effect, through grieving we are struggling to integrate the significance of the loss into our lives after our previous meaning system has been disturbed.

For example, imagine a situation where someone regularly meets a close friend for a coffee on a Saturday morning, always meeting in the same place at the same time. If the close friend were to die (or otherwise become unavailable to us, for example through moving away or falling out), not only would that friend be lost as a friend, but also what Saturday mornings mean would be lost. The grieving person would have to construct a new way of handling Saturday mornings because what they previously meant will no longer apply. This is a small example, but would of course be but one example across a whole host of meanings that would be lost in such a situation, creating a wide range of adaptations needed to our meaning system.

I shall say little more about this theory at this stage as Chapter 3 is devoted to this topic. I shall therefore restrict myself to making the important comment that, although dual process theory and meaning reconstruction theory have developed independently of each other, they are highly compatible and offer considerable scope for further development through a combination of their respective insights. For example, it could be argued that there are (at least) two aspects of meaning reconstruction – seeking meaning by looking back on the loss experience and its impact on the frameworks of understanding that are part of our identity and sense of personal well-being (which can be equated with loss orientation) and seeking meaning by looking forward, attempting to rebuild our lives and the meaning systems which also contribute to our ontological security – our sense of being comfortable with who we are and how we fit into the world. This has much in common with the 'progressive-regressive' method of existentialist theory (Thompson, 1992; 1998a).

Meaning is also a significant aspect of the next theoretical development I wish to introduce, that of 'disenfranchised grief'. This is a concept developed by the American sociologist Kenneth Doka. It refers to experiences of grief which are in some way not socially accepted, and which may therefore be more difficult to deal with because of a lack of social support or the benefits of established rituals (Doka, 2001).

Experiences of grief can be disenfranchised in the following ways:

- *The griever is disenfranchised.* Some people are often assumed not to grieve (for example, people with learning disabilities – 'They don't understand') or to be used to grieving (for example, older people – see Chapter 11 in this volume). The people in these categories of disenfranchisement may therefore have their grief go unrecognized, because of stereotypical assumptions.
- *The relationship is disenfranchised.* Some forms of relationship are subject to social disapproval, in some quarters at least – gay relationships, for example. The break up of a long-standing relationship can be painful enough when that relationship is openly acknowledged, but where the relationship is either a socially stigmatized one or a secret one (where one or both partners is married, but not to the other), the lack of openness, social support and/or comforting rituals can add significantly to the difficulties experienced.
- *The loss itself is disenfranchised.* Some forms of loss are, in themselves, disenfranchised. For example, the loss associated with perinatal death tends to receive far less attention and recognition than other deaths of infants. In addition, many losses that are not death-related may be disenfranchised because of the strong tendency to associate loss primarily with death. The losses involved in adoption would be a good example of this – see Chapter 8 in this volume.

The concept of disenfranchised grief is an important one, as it helps to establish the *social* basis of loss and grief. That is, it shows that grief is not simply a psychological matter and has important social dimensions. In particular, it shows that an individual's response to a loss is partly shaped by the social context in which the loss takes place. It also serves the very important purpose of helping to sensitize us to the range of losses that can so easily go unrecognized if we stick too rigidly to narrow conventional views of the nature and scope of loss in human existence.

Walter (1999) adds further dimensions to our understanding of loss. First, he builds on the work of Klass *et al.* (1996) by exploring the importance of 'continuing bonds' and, second, he examines the issues relating to what he refers to as 'policing grief'. I shall explore each of these in turn.

The 'continuing bonds' thesis is another important contribution to the critique of traditional models of grief. Part of the established wisdom is the notion that an important part of grieving is the 'letting go', relinquishing our relationship with the deceased person. This has become part of what Walter (after Wortman and Silver, 1989) refers to as 'clinical lore' – the practice wisdom that has grown up over the years, based on theory and research, but not necessarily consistent with them. The notion of letting go can be seen as an oversimplification of Worden's (1991) fourth task, that of 'relocating' the deceased. Of course, relocating does not necessarily mean letting go of the relationship, but rather redefining it in the new context of the loss.

Klass *et al.* (1996) emphasize the importance not so much of letting go, but of actually holding onto the relationship – being able to feel that there is still an important relationship even after the loss has occurred. Grieving, it is argued, is not so much a process of severing ties as one of maintaining those ties despite the loss. Walter (1999) comments on the well-established assumption within 'clinical lore' that it is necessary to work towards letting go and, in the following passage, shows how dangerous such an uncritical assumption can be:

> In 1996 I published an article [Walter, 1996] in which I argued that the purpose of grief is not to break the bond with the dead but to integrate the dead into the survivor's ongoing life. Hardly a new thesis as far as the scholarly literature was concerned and yet I subsequently received a sizeable mailbag from bereaved people who had somehow or other stumbled across this scholarly article, many of them expressing relief that what they had felt all along had at last been legitimated. These people had received counselling and read umpteen books on bereavement, yet nowhere had they received permission to find a place for their dead. Everywhere the message they heard was 'Let go. Leave behind. Move on.' (p. 106)

Here we encounter another approach that challenges the traditional wisdom and, once again, we find that there is a need for a much broader, more sophisticated approach than clinical lore and the traditional literature on which it is based allow for. As McGee (1995) comments:

> Current models of grief are not well equipped to incorporate change and growth among people who do not accept 'move on,' or let go of the past. Perhaps we need additional models. ... holding on to grief might be the most growth-producing, liberating experience of all. (p. 18)

Walter's second topic, that of the policing of grief, also gives us cause to question parts of the established wisdom. His basic thesis is that loss and grief have implications not only for those who are directly affected, but also for society more broadly, and so it is not surprising that there should be social mechanisms in place for 'containing' and regulating grief. He cites Rosenblatt (1997, p. 36): 'I know of no society in which the emotions of bereavement are not shaped and controlled, for the sake of the deceased, the bereaved person, or others' (Walter, 1999, p. 119). The important point to emerge here is that we have another example of the need to move beyond a narrow, individualistic focus and take on board wider social issues if we are to develop an adequate understanding of loss and grief.

This fits in with the point made earlier about the relative neglect of cultural and structural factors in traditional approaches. PCS analysis (Thompson, 2001a) is a framework that can be applied to counter this traditional emphasis on the individual at the expense of the social. Originally developed as a framework for understanding discrimination and oppression, PCS analysis can also be used to appreciate the complexities of loss and grief. The basic idea is that it is important to address three different, but interrelated levels if we are to avoid the trap of narrow, psychological reductionism. These levels are:

P – The *personal* level relates to the individual and his or her, feelings, attitudes and actions and so on.

C – The *cultural* level relates to the sphere of shared assumptions and meanings, the discourses that help us make sense of our lives and give us a framework of values, beliefs, codes and so on that become part of our individual and group identity.

S – The *structural* level relates to the structure of society and the complex network of power relations and social divisions (class, race, gender and so on) that underpin it.

The basic premise of PCS analysis is that social reality is based on the interactions of these three levels. An individual's actions (the P level) will be strongly influenced by the ideas, values, taken-for-granted assumptions and shared meanings that are part and parcel of the cultural context (the C level). These shared meanings and so on will, in turn, be largely shaped by the power relations at the S level. For example, the loss experiences of individual men and women will be partly shaped by the specific and unique experiences of the individual concerned, but will also be influenced by cultural norms and expectations about gender (in terms of how men and women are socialized to respond in subtly but significantly different ways – see Chapter 5 in this volume), and the patriarchal power relations on which such gender norms are based. To focus exclusively or even primarily on the individual level is therefore to over-simplify a complex picture and to fail to address the role and significance of cultural and structural factors.

In many respects this book is partly an attempt to counter the traditional overemphasis on the individual level and to draw attention to the importance of wider social issues such as class (Chapter 4), gender (Chapter 5), race and ethnicity (Chapter 6) and so on. However, it should be noted that the emphasis here on the need to address the cultural and structural issues is *in addition to* the importance of the personal level, and not *instead of* it. The aim is to provide an holistic overview as far as possible rather than replace one skewed view with another.

Stress, crisis and loss

The subjects of stress, crisis and loss each have an extensive literature base, but, for largely historical reasons, these have tended to overlap and interconnect to a very limited extent only. Literature relating to stress has a very strong empirical tradition and a major focus on the workplace (that is, stress has been researched and theorized primarily as *occupational* stress – see, for example, Arroba and James, 1987). The crisis literature, by contrast, has tended to focus on mental health issues, with a strong psychodynamic influence (see, for example, Caplan, 1961). And, as I have already mentioned, the loss literature has tended to concentrate mainly on death-related losses.

These three subject areas do none the less have a great deal in common in a number of ways, including the psychological processes involved, the social contexts which play a part in shaping our responses, and the problems that arise for individuals, groups, families and organizations. To develop a coherent and comprehensive approach to these three areas that incorporates the major insights of the relevant disciplines would, of course, be a major task, more suited to a life's work than one part of a chapter within an introductory textbook. However, to sketch out some of the possible linkages and interconnections within an overall framework is a more realistic aim for present purposes, and so it is to this that we now turn.

Developing a model of loss

An important concept that has emerged from postmodernist thought is that of 'dedifferentiation'. Basically, this refers to a breaking down of artificial barriers between academic (and professional) disciplines (Hollinger, 1994). For example, there is a significant overlap between microsociology and social psychology, and yet attempting to work across the two disciplines can be very difficult because of the differing traditions, assumptions, priorities and so on. However, in the human services crossing such barriers is an essential part of working with the theory base which draws upon a number of different academic disciplines – dedifferentiation is therefore a concept that can potentially be of great value to staff in the human services.

It is also an important concept in terms of the model I am presenting here. This is partly because the model draws on a number of different academic disciplines, and partly because the areas of academic knowledge explored here (stress theory, crisis theory and theories relating to loss and grief) have their own boundaries that have grown up over the years, keeping researchers, theorists and practitioners in one topic area relatively isolated from those working in others. For example, I feel it is significant that, when teaching students about the interconnections across these three topic areas, a common response is one of surprise – surprise at how much overlap there is but how unaware they had been of the interrelationships between concepts, themes and issues. What follows, then, is an exercise in dedifferentiation.

Pressure and stress

Human existence is, of course, characterized by a range of demands made upon us. Each day brings new challenges or pressures. These pressures are part of our everyday lives. As such, they can be either positive or negative. Pressures can be positive in motivating and stimulating us, bringing us satisfactions (for example, job satisfaction). However, pressures can also be experienced negatively, leading to distress, tension and possibly ill-health or other problems (Thompson *et al*, 1994; 1996).

The amount and/or nature of pressure can therefore be very significant in terms of whether it is experienced as positive and life-enriching or negative and life-impoverishing. In this regard, the definition of stress offered by Arroba and James (1987) is particularly apt: 'Stress is your response to an inappropriate level of pressure' (p. 3). This enables us to distinguish between pressure and stress. Pressure is neutral, in the sense that it can be either positive or negative, depending on the circumstances. Stress, by contrast, refers to situations where the pressure, due to its nature, amount, duration – or a combination of the three – is doing us harm in some way (in terms of our health, relationships, psychological well-being, capabilities and so on).

Another important point to note in relation to this definition is that stress is seen as our response to an inappropriate level of pressure – it therefore has a *subjective* dimension, based on our perceptions. What makes this important is that, amongst other things, it means that what one person experiences as stressful will not necessarily be experienced as stressful by others. We cannot therefore have a standardized approach to stress – we must always take into account the subjective dimension in terms of the perceptions of the individual concerned (Thompson, 1999).

These comments are very relevant across the human services. This is because practitioners in these areas are regularly dealing with people who are encountering levels or types of pressure that are leading to stress. It is for this reason that we should be aware that stress is not simply a matter of *occupational* stress, but also applies to individuals, families, communities and so on, in any aspects of their life, rather than just the workplace.

I have argued previously (Thompson, 2000a) that social work can be characterized as helping people respond to 'existential challenges' – the demands made upon us as part and parcel of being human, such as coping with change, transition and loss. This argument can be extended further to the human services as a whole. For example, health care staff will find that they are often, if not always, dealing with people experiencing the existential challenges associated with illness, disability and loss.

Pressure, then, can at times lead to harmful stress, but how does this relate to crisis theory and crisis intervention?

Crisis

Crisis intervention is a therapeutic approach which has its roots in mental health but which has been used much more broadly across the human services (Aguilera and Messick, 1986). It is based on the idea that a crisis is an upset in a steady state, a moment where our usual coping resources are overwhelmed and we are forced by circumstance into developing new ways of coping.

'Homeostasis' is the term used to describe the steady state. It is a term used in a similar sense to how the term 'thermostat' is used in a heating system. Just as a thermostat regulates heat output in a central heating system, homeostasis refers to the individual's ability to regulate coping responses to the pressures he or she experiences. The temperature in a heating system will go up and down slightly, but will be kept within certain upper and lower limits. Similarly, our ability to cope will go up and down slightly over time, but will generally stay within certain range – that is, while homeostasis is maintained. A crisis is said to occur when something happens to us that cannot be dealt with by means of our usual methods of coping, and thus homeostasis breaks down.

The notion of crisis is very significant for the human services. This is because change becomes more likely at the point of crisis. In periods of homeostasis the motivation to make significant changes to our lives is likely to be low. However, at times of crisis, we are far more likely to be prepared to engage in a process of change, perhaps partly in an attempt to re-establish a degree of stability.

A crisis is, by definition, short-lived, as it does not take long to establish some form of homeostasis. We may return to our previous level of functioning and thus 'get over' the crisis, or we may not be able to manage to do so, functioning at a lower level of coping, having thus been weakened by the crisis. However, the other possibility is that we may actually benefit from the crisis, learning and growing stronger as a result of the experience. This is where the notion of 'crisis intervention' comes in – it is an approach to practice that seeks to capitalize on the energy and positive change potential generated by the crisis. The aim for the worker is not simply to restore pre-crisis levels of coping as soon as possible (what could be called 'crisis survival' – Thompson, 1991), but rather to maximize the positive potential of the crisis scenario.

Crises can occur for various reasons, but for present purposes I shall comment on just two categories of situation that precede a crisis. First, we have what I shall call 'last straw' situations. This describes the sort of circumstances where pressures have led to stress, which has then continued over an extended period, gradually straining the individual's coping abilities until eventually they are overwhelmed, resulting in a crisis. Second, we have crises brought about by a sudden and unexpected trauma. This is where an unanticipated event occurs, causing sudden and dramatic changes to a person's life (for example, a serious accident, a bereavement or redundancy). With both types of crisis there is considerable scope for human services workers to be involved in a helping capacity.

Although I have described both stress and crises in terms of the individual, it is important to recognize that such matters apply far beyond the individual. Just as the literature relating to loss can be criticized for its relative neglect of wider social factors, so too can the literature relating to stress and crisis. For example, the family context is an important aspect of situations characterized by stress and/or crisis. This applies in two senses. First, for those of us who live in families, there will be the influence of those family members with whom we share physical and emotional space. We do not simply respond as individuals in isolation. How we respond to a crisis will depend in part at least on how those around us in our family react. Also what constitutes a crisis may be family-based – that is, a whole family may reach a point where its coping abilities are overwhelmed, with the ensuing crisis affecting the whole family.

Second, even where individuals do not live in families, there remains, for the vast majority at least, the influence of their family of origin. That is, what we experience as stressors, our coping responses, and whether and how we seek support may all be shaped in part at least by the family traditions that we are likely to have internalized in growing up.

So far, then, we have seen how:

i.   human existence is characterized by demands and existential challenges that lead to pressures upon us;
ii.   in certain circumstances, such pressures can lead to harmful stress;
iii. stress (either over an extended period or as a result of a sudden trauma) can lead to our coping methods being overwhelmed, homeostasis breaking down and thus a crisis ensuing;
iv.   the crisis can leave us less well equipped to deal with future pressures (weakened by the crisis) or can actually strengthen us in terms of our ability to cope with pressures and problems in future; and

v.   the aim of crisis intervention is to attempt to maximize the positive outcomes of the crisis, rather than simply help people
survive the crisis by 'riding the storm'.

What we must now do is to relate all this to the topic of loss and grief.

Loss and grief

If we consider the scenarios presented so far, we can see that each of
them has loss implications and may therefore produce a grief
response:

- *Stress.*   When pressures reach the point that they are experienced as harmful stress, loss can become a significant feature of
the situation. People under stress can lose their health (physical
and mental), confidence, ability to relax or to work or other capabilities and so on. Such losses can then lead to a vicious circle in
which, for example, loss of confidence leads to a lower level of
ability in terms of dealing with the pressures faced. We should
also note that stress can be caused by a loss experience as a result
of the psychological and social pressures that grieving can
generate.
- *A 'last straw' crisis.*   Here loss issues can be very significant, in so
far as the losses associated with stress can lead to a cumulative
loss reaction. That is, one pressure may involve a loss and thus
feelings of grief and so on, followed by the effects of further pressures and losses, each adding to, and perhaps intensifying, the
negative feelings.
- *A 'sudden trauma crisis'.*   In a sense, this directly describes a loss
situation, in so far as it is likely that the trauma will involve a
significant loss. Examples would include the death of a loved one,
one's home being destroyed by fire or flood, or any such event
that causes a major disruption to our established life patterns.

In all these cases a common theme is the withdrawal of 'cathexis'.
This is an important term which refers to the investment of emotional energy in a person or thing – for example, through the development of a relationship (Rando, 1984). When we experience a loss,
it is as if we have encountered a loss of that investment – the emotional equivalent of a Wall Street crash, as it were. It is this that
necessitates the need for adjustment to the loss. If we have not made

an emotional investment in a relationship, then we will not feel the need to grieve for the loss.

To live at all involves making an emotional investment in different individuals, groups, processes and things. In some cases, this 'cathexis' will be relatively minor, and so the price to pay for losing the person or thing in which we have made a personal investment is similarly relatively minor. However, when we make a major emotional investment, for example through love, the cost of losing that love can be immense and extremely difficult to bear. And, of course, in such circumstances, it is not only the beloved person we lose, but also what he or she means to us, that part of our identity that the relationship formed or at least influenced, the happiness that person brought us and myriad other things. Grief, then, is indeed the price we pay for love.

Outline of the book

An important feature of this book is its diversity. I have already commented on the rather unhelpful tendency for the broad spectrum of loss issues to be narrowed down to a primary focus on (a biologically-based) individual psychology. A key aim of the book, therefore, is to reintroduce the rich diversity of issues, concepts, themes and implications relating to loss and grief, to draw it out from beneath the blanket of conformity that has tended to conceal it for so long.

This diversity is reflected in a number of ways. First, there is no uniformity of approach – different authors come from different perspectives, and no attempt has been made to 'homogenize' them as part of the editorial process, as I see this as neither workable nor desirable. Similarly, the writers come from different professional backgrounds in terms of both role (academics, practitioners and trainers) and discipline (social work, nursing, medicine, advice work, mediation and psychology). And finally, the diversity extends to the international nature of the book, with contributions from Australia and the USA as well as different parts of the UK.

The book is divided into three sections. Part One sets the scene in terms of history, theory and sociopolitical context, while Part Two addresses specific areas of experience relating to loss and grief – what I would refer to as the different 'arenas' of loss. Part Three focuses on some of the implications for professional practice and education.

Part One comprises six chapters. The first provides an introduction to the philosophy of hospice and is written by Dame Cicely Saunders, a major figure in the development of the hospice movement. The chapter identifies the key values underpinning a philosophy that has come to be recognized as a major contribution to our thinking on death-related losses. The implications of these values for responding to other forms of loss are readily discernible. Chapter 2, by Bernard Moss of Staffordshire University, addresses the vitally important role of spirituality in understanding and working with loss and grief. He outlines what he describes as a 'personal perspective' in which he explains the importance of meaning systems, including – but not limited to – religious doctrines.

Chapter 3 focuses on meaning reconstruction theory and is written by one of the leading proponents of this approach, Robert Neimeyer of the University of Memphis, in conjunction with his colleague, Adam Anderson. This chapter explores the application of constructivist psychology to issues of loss and grief and, in so doing, challenges aspects of traditional approaches to this area. In Chapter 4, Suki Desai of Wolverhampton University and Denise Bevan, a practising hospice social worker, provide an overview of the importance of ethnicity and racism as far as loss and grief are concerned. Their basic argument is, that while a focus on ethnically sensitive practice is to be welcomed, this is no substitute for a genuinely anti-racist practice in which the impact of racism is taken into account.

Gender and loss is the topic covered in Chapter 5. Here sociologist Gordon Riches, of Derby University, presents a discussion of the significance of gender in terms of how we respond to loss. He argues that differential patterns of socialization between men and women lead to different patterns of grieving at the time of a loss. The chapter is richly illustrated with examples drawn from ethnographic research. Chapter 6 has as its theme poverty and inequality and the influence of class position on experiences of loss. Written by Denise Bevan of St Rocco's Hospice, Warrington, this chapter identifies important links between loss and class status and argues that good practice needs to take account of the way inequalities in life are so often reflected in death, and indeed in other losses.

Part One has a major, but not exclusive, emphasis on death-related losses. This is partly because Part One incorporates an historical as well as sociopolitical perspective, and therefore reflects up to a point the traditional focus on death-related losses in much of the literature. This paves the way for Part Two where we note a significant widening of the focus to incorporate a number of losses that are not death-related.

Part Two also comprises six chapters. Chapter 7, by Brynna Kroll of Exeter University, explores issues relating to divorce and separation. She explores the effects of such losses on children and their carers, relating her comments to attachment theory. The chapter illustrates well the powerful emotions that can be generated and the dangers of professional staff neglecting these. Chapter 8 features a discussion of adoption and substitute care and is presented by Mary Romaine of British Agencies for Adoption and Fostering (BAAF). Here the focus is on the range of losses encountered when children are placed in settings outside their family of origin. As with Chapter 7, the ideas presented here give considerable food for thought in terms of how we work with children and young people.

Disability and loss form the basis of Chapter 9, written by Bob Sapey of Lancaster University. Common assumptions about the nature of disability and the losses associated with it are challenged in this critical perspective based on a social model of disability, as opposed to a traditional, medicalized one. The chapter warns of the dangers of oversimplifying a complex situation by relying on stereotypical assumptions. A discussion of loss issues relating to ill-health follows in Chapter 10, written by Jeanne Katz of the Open University. The chapter explores the ways in which losses and our grief reactions can lead to ill-health and, conversely, how the experience of illness can involve a number of losses, before drawing out the practice implications.

In Chapter 11, Sue Thompson, an independent social worker, examines the range of losses associated with old age. She considers the various aspects of loss and grief that can apply to older people and explores the ways in which ageist assumptions can result in poor practice by leading to situations in which practitioners fail to recognize the complexities involved. Chapter 12, on justice and loss, is provided by John Dawes of Flinders University, and relates to losses associated with imprisonment, mandatory sentencing, the forced removal of Aboriginal children from their families and deaths in custody. The chapter paints a picture of unrecognized losses and emphasizes the importance of narrative therapy as a way of understanding, and dealing with, such issues.

Part Three comprises two chapters. Chapter 13, by Jeremy Weinstein of South Bank University, explores some of the key issues relating to education and training in respect of loss and grief. The chapter examines the core knowledge, skills and values needed for tackling the vast array of issues that relate to loss and grief. Ideas for curriculum development are presented and strategies for promoting learning are explored. Chapter 14, 'A framework for working with loss' is where Margaret Lloyd of Sheffield University provides an important discussion of how loss issues can be incorporated into human services practice. The chapter tackles the thorny issue of relating theory to practice.

This, then, is a wide-ranging book, as this is what is felt to be needed – a counterbalance to the tendency to see loss and grief issues in narrow, psychologistic terms. We hope that you find it not only a source of food for thought but also a basis for high-quality practice in dealing with these complex, sensitive and demanding issues.

Part One

Loss in Context

1 The Philosophy of Hospice

Dame Cicely Saunders

'Philosophy' may seem a pretentious word to use to refer to a developing specialty, growing as it has out of an older tradition of care based in the western world on a (now less recognized) Christian heritage. Approached somewhat tentatively, however, the following definitions lead into a discussion of the basic assumptions on which a now worldwide movement is based, and point out the principles which those with widely varying belief systems can embrace.

The *Shorter Oxford Dictionary* includes two definitions which apply to the philosophy of hospice care and the specialty of palliative medicine which has developed from it over the last three decades. They are:

> That department of knowledge or study which deals with ultimate reality or with the most general causes and principles of things.

> and

> The study or general principles of some particular branch of knowledge, experience or activity.

At no time of life is the impact of an awareness of ultimate reality more pressing than when a person is facing its end, yet practical concerns and multifaceted distress may be so overwhelming as to swamp all other considerations. The essence of hospice care is the giving of a secure continuity of support that frees a patient and family to turn to their own priorities. This may be in an inpatient unit or day centre but hospice care is not restricted to buildings but comprises attitudes and skills that can be deployed anywhere.

These may be more easily demonstrated in various situations than in words expressed. Roy (1997), in an editorial, 'Palliative Care: A

Fragment Towards its Philosophy', quotes Wittgenstein's response to a friend's poem, which gave a picture of a lifetime in 28 lines: 'And this is how it is: if only you do not try to utter the unutterable then *nothing* gets lost. But the unutterable will be – unutterably – *contained* in what has been uttered.'

Much of the giving of space to turn to what is important at the end of life is in a few words, more often in attentive listening or in the way care is given. Words may indeed confuse or misdirect us from the truth of a situation.

Nevertheless, after nearly thirty years' experience in St Christopher's Hospice, its Mission Statement (1996) set out a list of core beliefs in this area. Beginning: 'St Christopher's exists to promote and provide skilled and compassionate palliative care of the highest quality', it cites five values:

> We believe that palliative care exists:
>
> - To affirm life; not to hasten death but to regard death as a normal process.
> - To respect the worth and individuality of each person for whom we may care.
> - To offer relief from pain and other distressing symptoms.
> - To help patients with strong and unfamiliar emotions. To assist them to explore meaning, purpose and value in their lives. To offer the opportunity to reconcile and heal relationships and complete important personal tasks.
> - To offer a support system for family and friends during the patient's illness and in bereavement.

These values imply an awareness of both the definitions of philosophy, as already given, as well as challenge all members of the caring team to demonstrate them in their daily work. Often pressured by multiple and complex demands, they may feel these are aims that may be impossible to achieve. But, as Winnicott is frequently quoted: 'One should not expect to be perfect, only "good enough".' Nevertheless, 'perfect' remains a challenge to continual learning from experience, and is an inspiring target.

Such experience comes above all from patients and families. Some years ago, when I was involved daily in the clinical care of patients, I contributed a chapter to Feifel's *New Meanings of Death* (1977), in which I wrote:

> Mr B. was sitting by his bed in one of the small number of single rooms at St Christopher's Hospice. Now 63, he had, for many years, been a fire-fighter in London. He had been admitted 2 weeks before with a fungating and offensive recurrence of a carcinoma of the floor of his mouth.

He had had surgery $4\frac{1}{2}$ years earlier, followed by radiotherapy and chemotherapy. His previous hospital had now decided that further treatment of this nature was inappropriate and had asked the Hospice for admission to alleviate his terminal distress. His pain was by now well controlled, and the odour, previously his greatest distress and humiliation, no longer noticeable. We greeted each other, and after he had reported that his previous symptoms were under control, we went on talking.

'What do you do with yourself all day?'

'I read a bit and watch television; my wife and daughter spend a lot of time visiting me.'

'Do you get bored?'

'No. I am contented – all my life I've been, as you might call it, succouring people, helping others; now I am on the receiving end.'

'Do you find that hard?'

'No, I don't now, life has a pattern.'

Mr B. died five days after his birthday party. His wife had prepared a small celebration and came in to find that, according to Hospice custom, a birthday cake and party had been organised by the ward. The party continued for much of the day.

I was away but was told about it afterwards by Mrs B. She said, 'Everything that went before and everything that may come after will be worth it for that day.'

Such exchanges remain in the memory. Just a few days ago I spoke to Mrs B. on the telephone: 'Yes, I remember that day and it is still true', she said.

Hospice and palliative care are demanding but bring great rewards for those who are prepared to share whatever may be given by the person facing his or her own 'moment of truth'. This represents more of a relationship than words and much more than the perennial question of what to tell, how and when. It may be the summing up of a whole life, the moment when the essential person is revealed, however weak may be the physical state.

That there should be a degree of honesty in communication may seem to be implicit in the Mission Statement but this matter should be approached with skill and sensitivity. Writing for the *Nursing Times* (Saunders, 1959) at a time when it was still commonly thought and taught that one could not expect a patient to face either the diagnosis of cancer or a poor prognosis, the title 'Should a Patient Know?' aimed to place the emphasis on being approachable enough to let patients ask – or, as often the case – tell, as and when they were ready. After the breaking of the news to one patient that death was not far off, I was asked: 'Was it hard for you to tell me that?' When I answered him positively, he said: 'Thank you – it is hard to be told but it is hard to tell too.' It *should* be hard, for the giver of such a truth must be committed to the accompanying that will be needed or, at least, be ready to ensure that there will be other appropriate support.

Not all patients want to face truth as honestly as that man, and while the principle of never lying should be upheld, there should be flexibility and readiness to tailor communication to the patients' readiness to face reality in their own way. It is a matter of both time and timing. Here too, sensitive teamwork is demanded of us. Much will be expressed in silence or metaphor or during the course of practical care.

Over the years since then it has become common practice for there to be much greater honesty in communication with patients, often together with their families. Both diagnosis and prognosis may be discussed but, because so little is remembered after one interview, various ways of supportive follow-up should be made available. Sadly, however, this is not always provided. Hospice staff often have an advantage in having more time for discussion and should not be too critical of busy outpatient departments. Here, too, the family doctor has an important role.

In the early days, such comments as: 'It seemed so strange, no one wanted to look at me' and 'When the doctor said nothing and my family said nothing, then I knew' revealed how much anxiety was suffered because of mistaken silence. My own past experience of working in this area made me realize how much courage and common sense could be mustered to face the end of life but also how much important unfinished business was left undone, because people were not expected to be able to face unwanted truths.

To take each 'value' in turn:

- *To affirm life; not to hasten death but to regard death as a normal process.*

Palliative care, now frequently deployed earlier in a mortal illness, often overlapping with active, curative treatment, is concerned with the quality of living with persistent disease. There are several scales currently in use for its measurement. To my mind, Calman (1984) produced an apt summary in suggesting it can be seen as a reflection of the degree of congruence between hopes and expectations and the reality of their achievement. Hospice care, whether at home or in a specialist unit, is usually seen as being offered at a late stage of illness. However, any visitor to a hospice day centre will see vigorous and creative life and often reluctant, if only temporary, discharge from it in order to allow for new referrals when unexpected remission occurs. In the same way, life can find enhancement to its end. Recently, a daughter who had kept watch overnight with her dying mother met me when she was on her way to breakfast. Not only did she speak of security and the discovery of unexpected family and personal strengths but she added: 'And we had fun, too.'

Few hospice workers are proponents of active voluntary euthanasia. They have seen too many achievements made up to the natural end of life and too many fears of being an unwanted burden to believe that any safeguards would avoid the loss of important moments or prevent unwarranted pressures. Although its advocates are concerned to relieve suffering, it is seen as a negative and dangerous solution to an extremely complex problem. Answers given in a National Opinion Poll give high figures for public agreement to such legislation. However, a survey of carers' memories of the last year of life of those they cared for found that few patients had asked for the hastening of a looked for end to weariness or pain by an act of euthanasia. In this 1990 study the carers of a large group of patients who had died were asked: 'Did s/he ever say that they wanted to die sooner?' and (if yes) 'Did s/he ever say that s/he wanted euthanasia?'; 24 per cent had said they wanted to die earlier but only 3.6 per cent asked for euthanasia (Seale and Addington-Hall, 1994).

The phrase used by many hospices, first published in a discussion of this subject in the *Nursing Times* (Saunders, 1976) aims to sum up this approach. It is: 'You matter because you are you and we will do all we can, not only to help you die peacefully, but to live until you die.'

● *To respect the worth and individuality of each person for whom we care.*

A working party on spiritual need held at St Christopher's Hospice summed up its discussions in the following definition (slightly edited, Austin-Baker, 1996):

> Palliative care starts from the understanding that each human being is a person, a single bodily and spiritual whole and that the proper response to a person is respect. Respect means being so open to each man, woman and child not as simply an individual but as someone with a story and a culture, with beliefs and relationships, that we give them the value that is uniquely theirs.

A readiness to listen is at the heart of respect. A hospice team is not aiming for those who come for its help and support to think as they do, but that in their own way they think as deeply as they can. People of various backgrounds and cultures have not always met this approach. The 'good death' is a person's *own* death, which may be in an unexpected fashion and demand much flexibility from a hospice team. It is sometimes difficult to give such space in a community. A ward or a day centre's social system must meet the needs of all, for patients have varying capacities to recognize and integrate their poor prognosis; to internalize their anxiety and meet a complex of social roles (Foster, 1965). Hospice has shown a capacity to interpret its values in widely different cultures, but any approach must still be modified to meet an individual's needs and there is much learning still needed here. An individual approach must be added to knowledge of a family's cultural background.

There is no call to idealize people as they approach the end of life, and certainly not to tell their stories with sentimentality – but everyone in this field of care has frequently met resilience, courage and realism to give them confidence as they welcome the next admission. Ordinary people will do extraordinary things, leaving memories to strengthen those they leave behind. There are many lessons in living to learn from the dying, not the least how to meet them on the level of personal recognition and respect.

• *To offer relief from pain and other distressing symptoms*

The extent of learning and research in this field is well illustrated in the *Oxford Textbook of Palliative Medicine* (Doyle *et al.*, 1993, 1998). The success of this first edition led to an enlarged revision in 1998. Its breadth of approach goes beyond the control of symptoms to the holistic approach which has characterized the field from its beginnings in the 1960s. This was summed up by Wall (1986) in an Editorial to mark 25 years of the journal, *Pain*, as:

> The old methods of care and caring had to be rediscovered and the best of modern medicine had to be turned to the task of new study and therapy, specifically directed at pain.

There are now many journals in the field, and research is reported both in them and in the general medical literature. For example, a recent retrospective study was prompted by public and professional concern that the use of opioids for symptom control might shorten life. The pattern of opioid use in 238 consecutive patients in a palliative care unit showed that median doses were low and those patients who received opioid increases at the end of life did not show shorter survival than those who received no increase (Thorns and Sykes, 2000). It concluded that, in such situations, the doctrine of double effect need not be invoked to provide symptom control at the end of life. Such skills are spreading widely, to include patients with diseases other than cancer.

But relief means more than the skilled use of drugs: 'And then I came here and you listened. It seemed the pain went with me talking' – said one patient. Attention to detail, understanding and concern from social workers and chaplains together with, for most patients, skilled and compassionate nursing care, bring about relief. Some problems are complex and seemingly intractable, often after disadvantaged or dysfunctional lives or years of demanding treatment. A willingness to persevere, discuss and explore will mean no one is abandoned with that devastating phrase: 'there is nothing more I can do'.

- *To help patients with strong and unfamiliar emotions. To assist them to explore meaning, purpose and value in their lives. To offer the opportunity to reconcile and heal relationships and complete important personal tasks.*

The belief that change and creative development are possible to the end, which is implicit in the above statement, has been affirmed in hospice experience countless times and illustrated in many publications. Although most people in Western Europe do not express themselves in overtly religious language, the exploring described above is carried on in a dimension that can truly be described as spiritual. A recent PhD thesis on 'The Search for Sources of Meaning and Sense of Self in People who are Dying' drew from philosophical and theological sources to illuminate a series of in-depth interviews with a number of patients. These took place in a hospice day centre, an inpatient unit and with patients being cared for at home (Stanworth, 2000). Symbols and metaphor were frequently used, as by the woman who kept her dead flowers on her locker because they spoke to her of the new life of their developing seeds.

Another patient pointed out: 'You only look at things like this when you know your time is short – only something dramatic makes you see this way.' And: 'I just feel I'm not afraid. I'm not religious, I've got no faith, but I just feel I'm going to a peaceful haven.' And another: 'My hope is that it will lead me into peaceful waters. Sailing on a calm sea. I have expended so much anger in the past and have longed to get rid of it. It seems that this tragedy has taken me on that path at last' (Stanworth, 2000).

Most of Stanworth's 25 patients had a struggle to reach such equanimity and some remained restless and wrestling to the end. She emphasizes that there is a real need for the listener to develop the reflective attention that helps to give space for such a search. More than one patient referred to their partnership with the staff. Much also goes on between patients and their families and friends that should not be intruded upon. The majority of these exchanges are likely to take place in the privacy of home. 'I've had it all out with my wife, now we can relax and talk of something else', said one man on admission. The giving of a secure space, a sense of safety and confidence, can give scope for such exchanges and will give strengths to the bereaved. We are honoured by involvement in such moments, which may come unexpectedly. Nor must we forget that the way care is given can reach the most hidden places and that this may be our main enabler of a search for spiritual peace. A patient with incontinence may be reassured by being told: 'It's the disease, not you.' Such a patient was able to say to the researcher:

> When they have to wash you from head to foot, they talk to you, and gradually you think well, why not? It's a perfectly natural thing for them to do and they talk to you all the time. They do it all the time – and all that pride, that silly male pride – gradually it disappears and you lie back and enjoy it. They do everything with such dignity and care, that in the end, you don't give a damn.

It begins to appear that the man who is dissatisfied is himself the new man – and has been there all along.

- *To offer a support system for family and friends during the patient's illness and in bereavement.*

The Hospice Movement has been fortunate from the beginning in involvement by psychiatrists, social workers and chaplains concerned with bereavement and follow-up care. Parkes' work in particular influenced the development of a bereavement service, largely composed of carefully selected and trained volunteers. The charity Cruse was founded in 1959, a year in which several publications highlighted end-of-life issues. Since then a body of literature has formed part of the growth in this field of human need (Parkes, 1996).

St Christopher's Hospice has now more than ten times as many patients being cared for at home as in the unit on any one day. The families are the main caring team, with unending demands, often resulting in much exhaustion and anxiety. The support of a 24-hour call and ready visits from a nurse specialist cannot be emphasized enough. To know that someone who has met this situation before and has both concern and expertise to offer, adds immeasurably to the capacity to carry on with a last gift of service for a loved person. A network of co-operation with all the other community services has developed, but still needs tailoring to the different situations faced. Much deprivation is often discovered through a simple request for advice on symptom control. Different ethnic groups have their specific needs and possibilities, and evidence shows these are not always addressed at all adequately (Koffman and Higginson, 2001). The needs of children (including those after the sudden death of a parent or sibling) are being recognized and addressed by imaginative projects.

The whole movement is an illustration of the possibilities of growth through loss. In one way, death is an end, yet in bereavement many have found a new beginning. The gap remains, the sense of loss may be less acute but is still there, but many who have travelled that road would not have been without the relationship being grieved over. The original hospices were places of hospitality for people on a journey recognized as important. Today's postmodern world needs some of those older values.

The challenge of the Mission Statement has to be met by a well-chosen and supported team. Many disciplines have been drawn into the Hospice since its pioneering days in the 1960s. The founding vision of care, continuing through links with those giving active treatment through home care and inpatient security when required, grew over the first few years. The home care and research teams were built up once the unit and its work had been recognized by its local community. At this stage, everything was in the process of becoming, owing its ethos to those who felt the original call to move out of the scenario of the few early charities and the National Health Service. It was not intended to remain apart, but rather that once they had begun to be demonstrated effectively, the practices and the principles underlying it should spread wherever the need for compassionate and efficient end-of-life care was called for. This first research and teaching hospice was set up, not as a model for imitation but as an example to inspire other ways of action appropriate to different settings and cultures and among patients with various diagnoses.

Early in the 1970s, workers from North America came on sabbatical visits and set up different patterns, interpreting the basic principles in a home care team in New Haven, Connecticut, with no back-up beds. This led to the widespread development of hospice in the USA. A consulting hospital team in New York had less immediate impact, but the present Palliative Care Teams are now working in this way and one is undertaking an exciting programme of education funded by a well-known Foundation. Finally, a Palliative Care Unit with consulting teams was opened in Montreal, developing an international conference now widely supported and which led to the name of the specialty.

Other countries in their turn have modified these basic patterns according to culture and resources. Developing countries, including some of the poorest, have shown much determination as they have proved how well small beginnings may influence their own health services. Many have an uphill struggle and those better financed teams can well learn from their spirit. Listening to some of these pioneers brings those in more established teams to look to their own condition as they cope with the inevitable growth of structures and contracts. The spontaneity of early days needs refreshing in continual personal and professional development. Professional associations, career structures and the recognition of the multidisciplinary specialty encourage challenges to the general field, where most patients will spend the greater part of their journey through mortal illness.

Although the hospice movement grew in the interstices of an NHS which began with neither plans nor provision for end-of-life care (Clark, 1999), it has over the last three decades been recognized as appropriate to all, except those whose sudden death leaves no need for longer-term care. The number of complaints to the health Ombudsman illustrate that this need has still to be met in all areas of health service provision.

The early Christian hospices were largely run by religious communities. A few still remain, but the secularization of this impulse does not mean necessarily that there is nothing to be learned from them. Personal commitment springs from many beliefs and cultures. Years ago, on a visiting lectureship in the USA, when St Christopher's Hospice was still being built, I was asked whether such a personal conviction was essential. As I answered, I realized that many doors had to be opened if such care were to spread widely and fulfil the wider aims. The reply was, therefore: 'No – but you need to develop a founding philosophy.'

The values listed at the beginning of this chapter come after thirty years of development, during which workers of widely divergent views have made their contribution. A statement from a small group inherited from the original steering committee, which had met for five years before the Hospice opened, included as a final statement:

> The wider spiritual dimension at St Christopher's has been built up from the creativity and growth of many of its patients and witnesses to the discovery of their own strengths by countless families; it has developed through the experiences of its staff, a community of the unlike.

A philosophy is built up in this way if its proponents continue to ask themselves whether they are truly hospitable to all those who come. Such an organization (now with over 300 staff and 800 volunteers) must work continually to select, train and support each member, cherish honesty in relationships among them as well as among those who seek their help. Only in this way can it react sensitively to the total pain – physical, psychological, social and spiritual – that brings them. People working in this field need their own outside interests and support as well as opportunities for professional growth. It is idealistic to expect every member to be so totally committed, and Winnicott's 'good enough' must constantly be remembered. We are to be neither elitist nor incompetent in management but ready to go on building this community of the unlike. 'It felt like coming home', said a nurse to me recently on returning from maternity leave. To maintain that confidence after twelve years of working in hospice care, underpins the welcome to patients and new staff that we seek to establish. We too have to search for meaning constantly and find our own sense of self if we are to establish a climate in which others can make their own quest for lasting values. Much happens without words, but somehow the hospice, itself a pilgrim, remains a haven, built up by people who still maintain their commitment to this demanding but rewarding work.

2 Spirituality: A Personal Perspective

Bernard Moss

'When I use a word,' said Alice, 'it means what I choose it to mean.'

With a deftness of touch which would be the envy of many a political spin doctor, Alice, in her own wonderland, managed to define her own terms for the discussion, thereby wrong-footing any who would seek to take her to task.

Discussions about spirituality frequently suffer from the same problem. At one end of the spectrum there are those who appear to deal with spiritual certainties with a deftness of touch which leaves their listeners gasping with admiration, albeit wishing, wistfully perhaps, that they could have just a little of what these cognoscenti have been able to experience. Others of course dismiss the whole thing as gobbledygook and psychologically flawed metaphysics which have been thankfully put firmly in their place by the postmodernist critiques. At the opposite end are those who seem to use the concept of spirituality with an Alice-like touch – it seems to have such a variety of meaning that some begin to wonder whether it has any real meaning at all, apart from giving a warm glow to those who claim to be in touch with it. It is perhaps hardly surprising, therefore, that many people who find themselves in between these two extremes wonder what it is all about. They sense, maybe, that it deserves careful attention, but where to start, and whom to trust on the journey of discovery, is a truly tricky one.

This book is exploring a range of issues dealing with grief and loss, both in the painfully sharp experience of bereavement, and also in the wider experiences of loss which characterize human existence. If part of being human is about discovering things – about ourselves, our relationships and the world in which we are set – then another

34

equally vital aspect of being human is to experience loss at a variety of levels. Stroebe and Schut's (1999) dual process model, which is explored in the introduction to this book, is in some ways a metaphor for what it means to be human. We are enriched by our discoveries and impoverished by our losses, and spend large amounts of time and energy moving in between these two orientations.

We could argue, of course, that just as we learn more from our failures than from our successes, because failure make us examine ourselves and our assumptions and forces us to discover what we need to do differently, so too with loss. It is perhaps in our experiences of loss, especially significant loss, that we face most acutely the whole question of meaning. The tortured question *Why?* which so easily falls from the lips of those facing traumatic losses of all kinds, brings us face to face with the deepest questions which both perplex and enrich the human spirit. It is the things which bring us up with a jolt which make us face the profoundest questions about what it means to be human, both individually and in community. And for many, this is the territory of spirituality – the search for meaning. Morgan (1993) defines spirituality as an 'existential quest for meaning'. He argues that: 'Human spirituality is to seek an answer to the question "How can you make sense out of a world which does not seem to be intrinsically reasonable?"' (p. 6).

In her discussion about parents who have been struggling to cope with the death of a child, Lloyd (1996) comments on: 'the frequency with which professional bodies encounter the "Why?" question ...' (p. 307). One of the themes running through this book is precisely this same question, which, at times of great crisis and loss, is thrown directly or indirectly at many people who work in human services, be they doctors, social workers, nurses, care assistants, counsellors, youth workers, leaders of faith communities and so on. People may ask for all sorts of other forms of help and support at such times which professional workers may feel much more capable of delivering. But the big question – *the really big question* – is far less easy to handle.

Another theme running through this book is the way in which contemporary human services have in many people's view 'lost their heart'. Consider, for example, social work. It is informative to note the ways in which, as a professional discipline, it has become very focused on regulation and the allocation of scarce resources, in the assessment of risk, and the completion of systematized and bureaucratized tasks. The social worker's badge of office is often the pocket calculator; the community nurse has a long list of domiciliary visits to be completed; the advice worker has the panoply of reference books (a laptop if really lucky) to calculate benefit entitlement; the probation officer has the report to be completed, and the doctor has the prescription pad. To fulfil their roles, each of these professionals will have completed a demanding training programme and each will doubtless seek to do their best within the parameters of their expertise and professional role. And each of them may well struggle with the 'Why?' question when it is asked, and each of them may feel it is best left to someone else to tackle – 'someone who knows about these things'. The assumption is that spirituality, however it is defined, is outwith the professional expertise, or even concern, of most human services practitioners. As Lloyd (1997) so aptly observes: '... a "spiritual dimension" is not generally seen as part of the liberal-thinking, politically-aware social worker's anti-discriminatory tool kit' (p. 183).

And yet, if the basic premise of this book is accepted, that the experience of loss frequently raises the question of meaning in many people's minds and hearts, then human services practitioners are inevitably going to be caught up in these painful searchings for meaning, not only with the people they are trying to help and support, but also for themselves as individuals. The questions which our service users/patients/clients/enquirers raise have an uncanny knack of getting under our skins too.

In order to make progress with this issue, however, we will have to challenge Alice, for if spirituality is no more, albeit no less, than each individual's definition of it, then it will be difficult to attain even a modest overview of the topic.

It is important to acknowledge from the outset, therefore, that for people who belong to a particular faith community, spirituality has a very specific set of defining principles which help believers to understand and make sense of their lives, including their profoundest losses. Within the multifaith and multicultural communities in the UK, there are many examples of people for whom spirituality means living in some relationship with some greater 'other' being who has a deep interest and concern for their lives. Some faith communities have special words for this – Allah; Yahweh; God, for example – others talk about the 'spirit world' in more general terms. All of them, however, would begin their answer to the question 'Why?' by seeking to relate it to the being who provides some ultimate sense of meaning and purpose. For them, spirituality is a faith-specific activity of both heart and mind, and it often contains a willingness to accept that the 'Why' question may not ever be fully answered satisfactorily in human terms alone. For example, in Islam the phrase 'Insch Allah' – 'God willing' – carries the clear assumption that

Allah knows best and that everything that happens is given its meaning by Allah, whether we understand it or not.

Alongside these approaches are other equally powerful challenges to systems and approaches which deny a spiritual dimension to our understanding the context of human experience. Thompson (1992), for example, explores the attitude of positivist social science theories and suggests that:

> Traditional theories neglect the important dimension of ontology, the fundamental issues of existence, nothingness and contingency. If we have little or no understanding of issues relating to existence and being, then our speculation about personal and social relations lacks a fundamental basis. (p. 67)

Lloyd (1997) adopted a definition of spirituality for her study of people who were dying or bereaved which suggests that:

> spiritual[ity] was defined as 'a dimension which brings together attitudes, beliefs, feelings and practices *reaching beyond the wholly rational and material'*. (p. 185, emphasis added)

She also draws on Peberdy's (1993, 2000) work with dying people where it is asserted that:

> Few (people) have an entirely materialistic view of themselves and others. People commonly say, 'I am not religious', they do not say I am not spiritual' .... Without giving it a formal religious expression there is a spiritual dimension to their living and dying. (cited in Lloyd, 1997, p. 185)

For human services practitioners, one recent definition offered by Canda and Furman (1999) adds another tantalizing dimension, where they suggest that:

> Spirituality is the heart of helping. It is the heart of empathy and care, the pulse of compassion, the vital flow of practice wisdom, and the driving force of action for service.

Apart from being a glorious essay title to set for students to discuss and critically evaluate, this statement takes the emphasis of spirituality towards the activity of those who are seeking to help. To those who are made to feel uncomfortable by the big 'Why?' question, this definition goes to the root of why people would want to help other people in the first place. In effect, it expands the great 'Why?' question to embrace the helpers as well as those seeking help, and suggests that spirituality, however unacknowledged it may be, is a driving force that brings helpers face to face with the questions posed by those experiencing pain and loss.

Canda and Furman's book explores these issues in great detail, but the very language they use in their definition can be regarded as 'heart language' in stark contrast to the assertion made elsewhere in this book that the background to the issues being raised is that in many ways the human services seem to have lost their heart – reflecting that perhaps the 'people professions' are no longer so much about people. This definition of spirituality therefore is bringing a challenge to all human services practitioners about what motivates and urges them forward in their professional tasks. In turn, this challenge is raised for those involved in training, educating and supporting front-line staff and students, with each having to ask not only, 'What about my own motivation? What am I striving for?', but also, 'What approach do I take to helping others learn for themselves about such issues?'

One final dimension deserves to be raised, a dimension which has common threads in both faith-community, and more general definitions of spirituality. This is the dimension of passion and justice. Alongside very personal and private views of spirituality, there are wider perspectives which find expression certainly in the monotheistic traditions. Here we find that a real love of the divine being, however conceived, and a real commitment to what is required of people of faith, is measured not by the fulsomeness of piety, but by the degree of zeal for truth and justice, in seeing right prevail, the captives set free and the hungry fed. (For example, in the Hebrew Bible see Isaiah 35 vv 1–10; Amos 5 vv 10–13; Isaiah 61 vv 1–4; in the Christian New Testament Luke 2 vv 46–55; and in the Qu'ran chapter 2 v.110; 148; 177; 215.)

In this passionate conviction that all deserve equality of treatment and respect, there is an underlying passionate spirituality that has an energy and restlessness that will not find peace until truth and justice prevail. Maybe if more of this spirituality had been in evidence in recent decades, some of the antipathy between social work, as just one of the human services, for example, and spirituality might have been avoided.

To gain a better insight into this fundamentally important relationship between those working as human services practitioners and the core theme of spirituality, it is worth pausing to explore a brief historical perspective. For the purposes of simplicity and illustration, social work as a formal profession will be used briefly as an example for this part of the discussion, in the hope that people from other professional backgrounds will be able to draw whatever parallels are appropriate.

Social work is a particularly important example. This is because, in recent years especially, social work has sought to emphasize its *social* nature and its commitment to social justice by moving away from what tend to be seen as liberal, individualist matters (Thompson, 2000a), perhaps making the mistake, in the process, of assuming that spirituality is an individualist matter unconnected with social concerns and a commitment to social justice. And, besides, as Brandon (2000) so aptly comments: 'The spiritual road is about living out our *uniqueness*, not our individualism' (p. 17).

The relationship between social work and spirituality throughout Europe has been one of the fascinating motifs of the last century. The 'imperative to care' which is at the heart of many of the major faith communities in Europe, has been a driving force behind many of our social welfare programmes. Indeed, the development of social work itself owes a great debt to people who saw in its outreaching activities an opportunity to give practical expression to the faith which they held.

For many more, an involvement in social care and social work has been a practical expression of a 'hard-to-define' but nevertheless important dimension to their lives, for which the term 'spirituality' is useful shorthand. Canda and Furman's (1999) suggestion that 'spirituality is the heart of helping', might have met with receptive approval in the early days of social work, but from the 1960s onwards and into the postmodern era with its emphasis upon 'deconstruction' of major overarching systems, such a claim would not only have fallen upon deaf ears – it would have been met with astonished hostility. Religious and spiritual matters were not only debunked in such circles – they were regarded as being fundamentally suspect, the smoke screen left by primitive superstition, which needed to be blown away in order to establish social work on a sound value base, with good academic underpinning which would enable it to hold its head high among other professions and academic disciplines. As Lloyd (1997) observes:

> one legacy of social work's embracing of Freudian theory in the 1950s and 1960s has been a continuing mistrust of religion and a tendency to dismiss by association the significance of spirituality. (p. 183)

Against this background, people from faith communities certainly, and people with less easily definable spiritual convictions probably, began to keep a low profile. Social work had become a truly secular activity, all the more mature for having cut its ties from any religious or spiritual past. The loss of these dimensions evoked minimal mourning, as throughout Europe in different ways the profession began to grapple with the major issues confronting it, and the huge expectations placed upon it by governments and communities. Religion and spirituality were pushed to the margins, to occupy the territory reserved for individual preference and pastimes, like playing sport, attending concerts, or rock-climbing. Such activities had nothing fundamental to say to the professional responsibilities of social workers, and woe betide anyone who tried to suggest otherwise.

Today, however, some of these certainties are now being challenged. The pendulum seems to be slowly swinging back towards an appreciation of religious and spiritual matters: indeed, such issues have been placed upon the social care agenda, certainly in the UK. Major legislation such as The Children Act 1989 requires due consideration to be given to a child's religious needs when making assessments with a view to placing them in care. The religious needs of older people have been a recent focus of a report from the Centre for Policy on Ageing, in which Howse, the author of the report:

> points to a growing movement in the US which recognises the health implications of spirituality and is trying to place responsibility for patients' religious care jointly between social care professionals and institutional religion ... some medical academics are even calling for spiritual needs assessments. ... (cited in *Community Care*, 4 November 1999)

Pushing at these boundaries still further, Zohar and Marshall (1999) invite us to 'connect with our spiritual intelligence' by moving beyond seeing ourselves as 'human doings' to the point where we can fully appreciate the spiritual dimensions of being human.

The seminal developments in anti-discriminatory and anti-oppressive practice in social work, and increasingly in the other human services, have also highlighted the richer tapestry of human needs which must be taken into account by human services practitioners when making their assessments. The multifaith and multicultural communities throughout Europe which create the context for much contemporary social care work, provide an important challenge to us all. Needs-led assessments dare not any longer ignore the religious and spiritual needs of service users, whatever their age. Nowhere is this more necessary, of course, than when dealing with people who are experiencing loss, especially when this leads to a feeling of meaninglessness and emptiness. The skill and humanity of the worker – no matter what professional role is being filled –

become just as important to the person in need as the practical out-
workings of that professional's expertise.

Part of the pendulum swing, therefore, has been some initial
attempts to address these issues as part of the education and training
for human services practitioners. In the UK, important contributions
have been made – for example, by the Central Council for Education
and Training in Social Work (CCETSW). *Children, Spirituality and
Religion* (1996) is a training pack for social work educators; *Visions
of Reality* (1998) is an important set of essays exploring a range of
key issues to do with spirituality. A recently produced training pack,
Jewish Issues in Social Work and Social Care (Barnett *et al.*, 2000) –
explores issues from a Jewish perspective.

Important though these materials are, it is still likely, however,
that many students and practitioners will use these resources principally to find out more about the people whom they are required to
assess and care for, as part of good anti-oppressive practice. It is
regarded as another area in which the social worker's awareness
needs to be raised in order to offer a more effective service.

It has only been with the important work of Canda and Furman,
however, drawing on recent developments in the US, that social care
workers and human services practitioners have been significantly
challenged to explore these issues *for themselves* as part of their professional responsibilities. And it will be here that the greatest challenge is to be found, as the question again is raised: *Is the loss of
religious and spiritual dimensions something to be applauded or regretted?*
or, still more pointedly, can the flight from self-awareness in so
many of the human services training programmes any longer be
justified? Has the point now been reached where, unless we have a
spiritual self-awareness, we are likely to do more harm than good?

It would seem, however, that for many human services practitioners the issue is still seen in the narrower context of religions and religious systems, rather than in the wider context of spirituality and
the importance of meaning in our lives. Therefore, the loss of the
influence of religious systems is still something to be celebrated and
indeed to be strived for. This is something more than the postmodernist deconstruction of religion; it goes to the very heart of a structural analysis of oppression. Much contemporary social care work
practice is based on a deep understanding of the way society is structured, resulting in many people becoming marginalized, oppressed
and devalued. Good practice, therefore, is about recognizing the
wider societal pressures at work, and seeking to find ways to liberate
people. Within this understanding, some aspects of religious practice

and attitude are to be seen in themselves as oppressive, and therefore 'part of the problem'.

One of the litmus tests of any faith community is the way it treats minority groups; another litmus test is the way it treats women, and a further one is the extent to which it values difference and diversity. On all these accounts, many of the major world religions stand condemned at the bar of contemporary sociological perspectives. Priesthood and ministry remain largely masculine activities in many religions, and even where women now have a place in the leadership, there has been a bitter struggle to achieve equality. The continuing practice of female circumcision in the name of religion – some would argue that male circumcision should also be included here – remains a deep scandal that is far more widespread than many realize. The continuing persistence of male leaders in dictating how women should live, what their role should be, and how they should treat their bodies remains deep-seated. The personal decisions about contraception, and the morally and emotionally complex issue of abortion, are taken over by the male religious decree-making machine.

The experience of gay, lesbian and bisexual people within faith communities remains deeply precarious: official and doctrinal disapproval, and at times actual condemnation, make their life of faith and sometimes their very existence fraught with fear and disquiet. Safe communities of faith and acceptance are rare oases in a blighted desert of discrimination and disapproval.

It is no wonder, therefore, that human services practitioners, faced with people who are being oppressed in such ways, will want to strive ceaselessly to achieve the loss and removal of such domineering systems which restrict and diminish the lives of powerless people. The loss of all of this will be celebrated as a victory for the dignity and value of the human spirit. Indeed, one of the ironical facets of organized religions is their capacity to institutionalize their activities, sometimes in stark contrast to the intentions of their founders. Martin Buber, the distinguished Jewish theologian, once observed that there is nothing like organized religion for 'hiding the face of God' (Buber, 1957).

By contrast, however, a study of the basic tenets of the three major monotheistic religions – Judaism, Christianity and Islam (to put them in their chronological order) – shows that there is also a deep moral imperative to regard people as precious, created and valued by divine love. Within Jewish scriptures there is a strong prophetic element which challenges and chastises organized religion for its neglect of the poor and needy and outcast (Micah 6 v. 8; Amos 5 vv 10–14 in the Hebrew Bible). Islam requires its followers to give generously of their time and money to support those in need (Qu'ran Chapter 2 v. 177). The founder of Christianity took the Jewish command to 'love thy neighbour as thyself' and elevated it to parity with the core loving of God which is at the heart of the religious experience and commitment (Luke 10 v. 27 in the Christian New Testament).

In the twentieth century many theologians within the Christian tradition in particular, struggled to articulate a 'liberation theology' which addresses the deep-seated oppressions which enslave so many people caught up in restrictive political ideologies. For such theologians (for example, Gutierrez, 1973; 1984), there is no 'apologia' possible for the way in which religion has served both to enslave people and also to confirm, and at times actively serve, the political systems which oppress. On the contrary, they argue powerfully that, at the heart of the religion, there is a prophetic proclamation of liberation in the name of the living God who is on the side of the poor and needy and oppressed, and who is fully served only through a deep commitment to emancipatory practice. Dom Helda Camara in Brazil, for example, passionately lived out this deep-seated commitment to justice for the poor as a priest in the Roman Catholic Church. This reflects the theme of passion and justice highlighted earlier in this chapter as an important dimension of spirituality.

As soon as this dimension is highlighted, the whole shape of the debate changes. Suddenly it is possible to see partnership where previously there was polarized suspicion; collaboration where previously there was hostility. If the heart of religious commitment, as experienced in the three major monotheistic religions, is a striving in the name of God / Yahweh / Allah to achieve emancipation at the very deepest levels – personal, emotional, communal, spiritual and political – then new allies have been found, and the defining boundaries have been redrawn.

Within this framework, the loss of the spiritual is to be deeply mourned, and its gradual recovery something to be celebrated, precisely because of this deep-seated imperative to work at every level for the wholeness and liberation of human beings from everything which enslaves and impoverishes the human spirit. In this sense there will be a powerful clash not between spirituality and those who are arguing passionately for, and striving ceaselessly for emancipatory practice, but rather between these two new allies on one side, and on the other side the forces of organized religion which, as has been argued earlier in this chapter, have served at times to enslave and diminish and to control. Spirituality becomes not just 'the heart of helping' but also, crucially, the very heart of the struggle for justice and emancipation.

For human services practitioners, therefore, who are involved in working with people who are experiencing loss in all its many forms, there are some important lessons to be learned. These may be stated starkly:

- Spirituality is something we all share and, if professional workers deny this for themselves, they are likely to deny it for the people whom they seek to help.
- The experience of loss – together with the loss of meaning and purpose – has a profoundly spiritual dimension to it.
- We can no more give a sense of meaning and purpose to someone else than we can eat or breathe for them. But to share that journey with them can help them feel valued, which is the first step to a regaining of purpose and meaning.
- Finally, if spirituality has the significance which is being suggested, then the first step towards achieving emancipatory practice for others is to accept the importance of acknowledging it for ourselves as human beings.

3 Meaning Reconstruction Theory

Robert A. Neimeyer and Adam Anderson

Introduction

Five years after the death of her infant daughter, Jessica, from congenital heart problems, Helen remains embittered and withdrawn, grieving intensely a loss that seemed to her inexplicable.[1] A devout Christian, she struggles to fit the tragedy of her daughter's untimely death into a belief system that she hoped would sustain her in her bereavement, but did not. As she notes, 'The only thought that comes to me is that God must have really needed Jessica to be one of his angels in heaven, because she died so suddenly and didn't show any of the symptoms of the condition she suffered from that caused her death.' Reflecting on herself, now at the age of 32, Helen notes:

> I'm much older than my actual chronological age. I've aged very rapidly. I no longer care for tedious things. I have higher standards and expectations regarding family and friends. I'm able just to cut people out of my life if they don't live up to my expectations. My only expectation from friends and family is that they be there for me when I need them. If they're not, they're out of my life.

Time itself seems to have shrunken for Helen; confronted by a painful history, and the bleak anticipation of continued loneliness, she concludes, 'I have learned that we can't live in the past, nor the future ... We must only live in the present.' Overall, she acknowledges that she finds little meaning in the life she now lives, either privately or in the occasional and unsatisfying company of others.

Contrast Helen's story with that of Ophelia, a 31-year-old mother who similarly suffered the perinatal death of her first child a few years earlier because of congenital heart problems. Speaking about her loss, Ophelia states:

> I believe that my baby Michael's purpose in life was to bring us great joy and love in the three short days he was here on earth. I believe that he helped strengthen my marriage and more importantly, my and my husband's and my family's faith in God. I come from a Christian family, but none of us were involved in church, and we've all started attending church again since his death. My husband was Catholic and I was Baptist, and we compromised and became Presbyterian and joined a church we attend regularly. I also believe that if it weren't for Michael, we would not have any children because we had decided not to have children. But after Michael came into our lives, we decided to try again. We now have Phillip, who is 4, and Grace, who is 4 months!

For Ophelia, the life lessons learned from this loss were multifaceted:

> I have greater appreciation for life and for healthy babies. I have a greater knowledge of the heart disease Michael had. And I feel I can help others who have lost a child and those who will lose a child in the future. Spiritually, I know that when I die, I will go to heaven and we will be together again. ... And I am not as afraid of dying as I used to be.

As she reflects on the fabric of her life in light of her loss, she teases out threads of consistency, braided together with new fibres of moral strength spun by adversity:

> First and foremost, I am Michael's mom. And I realized even after he died and I had no other children at the time, that I was and always would be a mother. And last, but not least, I'm a survivor. I feel that if I can survive this, I can do anything!

Ophelia clearly views her child's death as rich in significance, and describes herself as living a life charged with meaning. Her grief, while still poignant at times, serves to connect her to a common humanity shared with others, as well as to the mysteries of a universe that remains ultimately benign.

How do we understand these two quite different reactions to an objectively similar loss, against the background of broadly comparable demographic, familial and even religious factors? What processes permit the integration of loss in such a way that one's life story is enriched, rather than impoverished, by the experience? Our own attempts to address such questions have led us to question dominant models of loss that emphasize its presumed sameness across people and contexts, whether explained in terms of fixed evolutionary patterns[2] or predictable stages of emotional adjustment[3] to bereavement. Instead, we have come to believe that *meaning reconstruction in response to loss is the central feature of grieving*, and that this often-effortful attempt to reconfigure a viable self and world in light of the loss proceeds on deeply personal and intricately social levels simultaneously (Neimeyer, 2001a).

Our goal in this chapter is to sketch the outlines of this emerging approach to grieving as the emotionally resonant reconstruction of meaning, a conception that is currently being elaborated by a handful of theorists in Europe, Australasia and North America. In addition, we describe our own efforts to extend our understanding of the processes by which this occurs, offering illustrations from our ongoing work with bereaved persons, in both the psychological clinic and the research laboratory.

The meaning of meaning

What do we mean when we speak of meaning-making in the context of loss? Although this question could be answered in any number of ways, we have found it useful to focus here on the *context* of the search for meaning – whether regarding the loss *per se*, the hidden benefits or life lessons learned, or one's resulting sense of self – and the *narrative processes* used to formulate one's account of these transitions. Thus, *how* one tells the tale can be contrasted with *what* one focuses upon, and both of these factors are distinguishable from the nearly inexhaustibly varied *content* of people's meanings regarding loss, the specific interpretations they place on it as a function of their personal positioning in broader cultural discourses shaped by gender, culture, age, relationship to the deceased, mode of death and so on. In the following section, we will illustrate these core dimensions of the search for significance, and then consider how these might work together to facilitate the reconstruction of a meaningful world disrupted by loss.

Contexts of meaning

When traumatic loss confronts us with a profound disruption of our 'assumptive world' (Janoff-Bulman and Berg, 1998), that sustaining but largely unspoken network of beliefs in a predictable life, a benign universe and a worthy and resourceful self, we are faced with the onerous task of revising these taken-for-granted meanings to be adequate to the changed world we now occupy. Simultaneously we must deal with urgent questions about what this loss signifies, whether something of value might be salvaged from the rubble of the framework that once sheltered us, and who we are now in light of the loss or losses sustained. All of this questioning plays out on levels that are practical, existential and spiritual, and all of it is negotiated using a fund of meanings (partially) shared with others, making it as much a social as a personal process (Nadeau, 1997; Neimeyer, 2001a). Here we draw attention to three contexts in which this meaning reconstruction occurs – sense-making regarding the loss, benefit-finding in the experience, and identity reconstruction in its aftermath – illustrating each briefly in light of the opening vignettes of Helen and Ophelia.

Sense-making

In the wake of the tragic 1999 shooting deaths of 13 students in Columbine High School in Littleton, Colorado, two major American newsmagazines, *Time* and *Newsweek*, independently printed cover photos of weeping survivors, emblazoned with the identical headline, in a massive font: '*Why?*' A similar question arises with poignant urgency in the aftermath of many losses, particularly in the case of bereavements that are 'off time', as in the deaths of children, or when the loss is sudden, senseless or violent (Murphy *et al.*, 1998). Under such circumstances the loss seems to represent an existential violation, and survivors commonly find themselves seeking ways to assimilate the tragedy into a pre-existing framework of belief, or failing this, striving to accommodate their previously held meaning system to render it more adequate to their changed reality they confront (Viney, 1991). In the case of the deaths of children, qualitative research suggests that the former strategy, when workable, provides greater comfort to parents as they undertake the difficult adaptation to follow (Braun and Berg, 1994; Milo, 1997). The ability to make sense of the death seems especially important in early adaptation to the loss, when the ability to find some sort of explanation for a seemingly inexplicable loss promotes adjustment, at least in the short term (Davis *et al.*, 1998). However, it is worth noting that even those parents who succeed in finding provisional answers to why their child 'had to die' – in medical or spiritual terms – frequently revise these answers as the months pass, and as their search for significance leads them to ask deeper questions, or perhaps abandon the search altogether (Davis *et al.*, 2000).

Something of this search can be seen in the responses of Helen and Ophelia, both thrown into a maelstrom of questioning by the sudden death of their children, so soon after their birth. For Ophelia, the quest for meaning in the loss ultimately led to attributions of divine purpose for Michael's short life, which reaffirmed both her commitment to her marriage and her faith. Importantly, the passionate beliefs that she endorsed galvanized related actions, including renewed involvement in her church. It is also noteworthy that the active pursuit of meaning in Michael's death was not simply a private intrapsychic preoccupation, but a social and dialogical one, which involved negotiation between Ophelia and her husband about 'compromising' their differing religious affiliations, and about whether to risk having other children. It is for these reasons that a meaning reconstruction model casts in some suspicion an interpretation of 'sense-making' in thinly cognitive terms, and instead views it as an impassioned effort to find sustaining meanings that offer new and practical reorientation in our world with others (Neimeyer, 2001c). In contrast to Ophelia's success in this effort, Helen fared less well, finding little comfort or purpose in the hackneyed consolation that 'God needed Jessica to be an angel in heaven'. If anything, the unpredictability and capriciousness implied in this explanation might have further undercut her precarious sense of a future, and provided her little guidance in how she might now live her own life.

Benefit-finding

Although it seems paradoxical, the ability in the long term to find spiritual, existential and personal benefits in a loss has been found to mediate survivors' eventual adjustment (Davis *et al.*, 1998). What sort of good can come from the death of those we love? Frantz *et al.* (2001) found that 84 per cent of bereaved adults cited gains of various kinds, ranging from the strengthening of bonds with family and friends (33 per cent), and a kind of *carpe diem* philosophical commitment to live more fully or reorder priorities (20 per cent), to greater compassion for others (8 per cent) and enhanced spirituality (3 per cent). Our own ongoing data collection shows roughly comparable trends, although significantly, a higher percentage of our bereaved college student respondents (nearly 40 per cent) are unable to identify a single gain, but only losses, in the deaths their loved ones suffered. This suggests that the mining of life lessons from the vein of grief is by no means a certain outcome, and when it occurs, it is likely dependent on a host of maturational, personal and social resources.

Again, Ophelia and Helen illustrate the divergent outcomes possible for bereaved persons as they struggle to wrest gains from losses. For Ophelia, the gains are multifaceted, ranging from greater medical sophistication to a keener appreciation of the miracle of life and health. Perhaps most importantly, the emptiness wrought by her own suffering has become a place in which she can 'hold' the pain of others, responding with greater empathy and sensitivity to the unique anguish of others in similar predicaments. A further benefit is that of diminished death anxiety as a function of her renewed spirituality, an outcome observed in other groups of people who come face to face with death, such as gay and bisexual men contending with the diagnosis of AIDS (Bivens *et al.*, 1994) or grieving the loss of partners to the disease (Richards *et al.*, 1999). Helen's example, however, underscores the caution that such benefits are by no means inevitable, as she grimly acknowledges that the lesson she has learned is that 'we must only live on in the present', uprooted from a meaningful past, and steering toward no rewarding future.

Identity reconstruction

Finally, a meaning reconstruction approach acknowledges that grieving is a personal process, one that is idiosyncratic, intimate and inextricable from our sense of who we are (Neimeyer, 2001b). How we grieve is shaped by that unique fund of beliefs, practical skills, resources and relational dispositions that defines our very sense of self in social context. That is, our identity constrains our experience and expression of grief, and is reciprocally transformed by it. In Attig's (1996) apt phrase, loss prompts us to 'relearn the self' as we 'relearn the world'. Only the most peripheral of losses leave us substantially unchanged; the losses of central people, places and projects that anchor our sense of self force a (sometimes radical) reordering of the story of our lives, triggering the 're-authorship' of a new life narrative that integrates the loss into the plot structure of our biography (Neimeyer and Levitt, 2001). The result, when favourable, is 'post-traumatic growth' in the wake of post-traumatic stress, an outcome that has been observed by many who have studied how people triumph over tragedy (Tedeschi *et al.*, 1998).

Ophelia exemplifies this sort of growth, as her very survivorship becomes a badge of honour and a bulwark against the further challenges that life will bring. However, although she views herself as profoundly transformed by Michael's death, she also recognizes thematic consistencies in her sense of identity, including her remaining very much his mother. This effort to conserve meaningful roles is central to the dynamics of grieving (Marris, 1974), as a fitting counterpoint to the experimentation with new roles that the 'restoration orientation' phase of the grief process also demands (Stroebe and Schut, 1999). Thus, a progressive reconstruction of one's identity in the aftermath of loss typically includes a reorganized, but not relinquished 'continuing bond' with the deceased, which ideally is affirmed at social as well as individual levels (Klass *et al.*, 1996). Helen's more regressive identity reconstruction, by way of contrast, compounds her loss and isolation, while underscoring her 'rapid ageing' and tendency to 'cut people out of her life' if they fail to address her urgent needs. As a result, she feels disconnected not only from sources of vitality within herself, but also from life-sustaining contact with the child who God inexplicably took away, and the living others who might provide solace and new direction in the life she now leads.

Narrative processes

The deeply rooted human tendency to seek significance in suffering is at one level obvious, and the sense-making, benefit-seeking, and identity transforming dialectics described above reflect this defining characteristic of humans as a species. Less obvious are the subtle processes by which this meaning is crafted, at both individual and social levels. As we have tried to study and facilitate such meaning-making in response to loss, we have been drawn to look more closely at the forms and features of self-narratives, the ways people organize an account of events that disrupt the stories of their lives (Neimeyer, 2000a). One aspect of this work has been our attention to *narrative processes*, the distinctive *styles* of storytelling that give self-narratives their unique form, and that might contribute to the transcendence of tragedy described above.

In their research on self-narratives told in the context of psychotherapy, Angus *et al.* (1999) have identified three narrative processes, which they term external, internal, and reflexive. In our own work on grief we have found this same taxonomy helpful in describing the way people make meaning of loss in the stories they construct for themselves and others (Neimeyer and Levitt, 2001). Typically, in spontaneous accounts of their experience in the presence of confidants, people tack back and forth among these narrative forms, although different individuals often show a characteristic orientation toward one narrative process over others. In this section we outline three such narrative processes that seem to be operative in accounts of loss, laying the groundwork for a more detailed analysis of the narrative journey of a grieving college student seeking new meaning through the healing power of storytelling.

External narratives

External narratives of loss entail the concrete, typically sequential description of an event or issue. They are 'external' because they depict the outward events at hand in a clear, intelligible fashion, constructing an account of happenings as they might have been seen or heard by an observer of the death, loss or transition. However, their apparent 'objectivity' can belie the important subjectivity that gives them their most important meaning, as the very events the storyteller chooses to relate are inevitably selected because they conform to personally important themes. Thus, spoken and written self-narratives often contain implicit 'markers' (Greenberg, 1992) or 'quality terms' (Neimeyer, 2001a) that invite further inquiry and elaboration, as the person strives for greater subjective coherence in the account. The sometimes apparently straightforward, journalistic conventions of external narratives – with their emphasis on what happened when – also tend to conceal the fact that stories are told from a particular perspective, and often confer a preferred moral position on the author-as-character (Wortham, 2001). A husband's externally oriented description of his wife's cancer, hospitalization and treatment, for example, might concentrate on those features of story that are most troubling, and might further implicitly assign the narrator a preferred identity in the story, perhaps as a stalwart protector of the family, a caring companion, and so on. For this reason it is important to understand even external narratives not merely as literal accounts of observable events, but also as social texts that position the self and others in a moral discourse (Burr, 1995; Neimeyer, 1998).

Internal narratives

Unlike external accounts, internal narratives of loss focus on the author or speaker's emotional and experiential responses to observable events, more than on the events themselves. In the context of bereavement, they often refer directly to the keen pain, sadness, longing and despair that accompany the death of a loved one, and especially to those emotional reactions that are most in need of recognition and understanding by self and others. Often, self-narratives will point suggestively to important affective themes woven throughout the narration, through recapitulating similar responses in slightly different words (for example, anger, frustration, losing control) (Neimeyer, 1993). Research on self-narratives in the context of therapy suggests that client stories that are rich in internality are associated with greater therapeutic movement and more favourable outcomes, relative to those that are more exclusively external in orientation (Angus and Hardke, 1994).

Reflexive narratives

Finally, reflexive narrative processes include our efforts to analyse, interpret and make meaning of an event or our reaction to it. They thus constitute a form of reflection upon the content of the other two narrative processes in a way that facilitates our further contemplating, evaluating and planning our responses to them. Bereaved persons engage in reflexive processing of their stories of loss when they struggle with 'what it all means', as described in terms of our discussion of sense-making, benefit-finding and identity reconstruction above. For instance, the young adult who relates the death of a friend in a motor vehicle accident might review the events leading up to the tragedy and identify a sharp pang of guilt as he talks about leaving his friend at the bar that fateful evening. He might go on to recognize that, at some level, he blamed himself for his friend's subsequent decision to drive home under the influence of alcohol, a decision that led to his death. Ultimately, he might work toward finding deeper significance in the event, interpreting it as a 'wake-up call' to begin leading a life of greater responsibility for self and others. In this illustration, both the self-blame and the larger existential 'message' that the young man carried away from the story would be seen as products of a reflexive process. In a still larger sense, our very appraisal of ourselves as 'survivors' who cope successfully with adversity is itself a narrative achievement, as it represents a distilled construction of self derived from a reflexive review of one or more specific stories of our resilience in the face of life challenges (Neimeyer and Levitt, 2001).

Healing stories

How do people who are struggling with loss work toward finding significance in their suffering, making sense of the event itself, teasing out the life lessons it contains, and growing into a new and larger self in its wake? And how do the various narrative processes described above facilitate this reconstruction of meaning, in such a way that the grief associated with the loss can be experienced as less oppressive? Our own attempts to address these questions have led us to study closely the way in which people frame and reframe their loss experiences over time, when simply given an opportunity and encouragement to do so. In particular, we have been impressed by the power of narratives, whether spoken or written, to assist in the transcendence of tragedy, and are currently completing a large, longitudinal research project on this very process. In this final section, we will describe how we are investigating the ebb and flow of meaning-making across time and offer a detailed exploration of the narrative of one young man, Kevin, grappling with the difficult death of his beloved godfather six months before. Our hope is that this case study will help bring to life the various contexts and processes involved in meaning reconstruction, and suggest to readers some useful concepts and strategies for healing the wounds of profound loss.

The Pennebaker paradigm

In its typical form, narrative is an inherently social process. We spontaneously relate the events of our day to our loved ones when we return home from work or school, tell stories that we hope will impress or entertain our friends, and seek the compassion and counsel of others – including professionals – through sharing accounts of adversity. Although relating stories of loss in such a social milieu serves vital functions by recruiting a supportive audience for our account (Neimeyer, 2000a), it also makes it difficult to disentangle what processes contribute to our benefiting from the experience. For example, how much of the new insight or optimism that results from telling stories of our losses is a function of the narrative process itself, and how much arises from the responses or contributions of others to it? This question is important if we want to identify the 'active ingredients' of meaning-making, in such a way that we can engage in more supportive caregiving practices with those we serve.

To help sort out these questions, Pennebaker (1997a) studied narrative self-expression in an unusual context, in which the only audience to the account is the author. Typically, Pennebaker invites people to write about the most traumatic experiences of their lives – betrayal, illness, injury, loss of face, assault, bereavement – and to do so in a way that expresses their 'deepest thoughts and feelings' about the event, without getting caught up in concerns about grammar, spelling, or sentence structure. Accordingly, they write for approximately 20 minutes a day, for a series of three or four closely-spaced days. The results of this sort of narrative 'journaling' are surprisingly robust, with participants reporting improved mood, fewer health complaints and fewer restrictions in their daily activities in the weeks and months following the writing than before. In fact, replications and extensions of this work by other investigators have even confirmed positive physiological responses to such journaling about loss, such as increased antibody response to Epstein–Barr virus and Hepatitis B (Petrie et al., 1995). Importantly, such changes are observed equally in cases when the written accounts of loss are shared with the experimenter or erased following the writing experience, ensuring that the writing will never be read by another human being (Pennebaker, 1997b). This suggests the healing power of narration itself, even when undertaken in an entirely private context.

Our own goal has been to further identify the active ingredients of this procedure. Prompted by reports that this form of narration is particularly effective when authors express signs of 'insight' during their writing (Esterling et al., 1999), we are especially interested in studying the distinctive processes that are associated with the reconstruction of meaning. Thus we have invited nearly 140 recently bereaved persons to come into our lab and write private accounts of their losses, under conditions of either high narrative structure (telling a story with a clear beginning, middle and end) or low narrative structure (simply listing separate thoughts about the loss in whatever form they come to mind). Likewise, we request that they do so in either an external, or internal/reflexive narrative process, by attending to either the objective 'facts' of the loss, or its subjective meaning, respectively. We then assess their level of problematic or 'traumatic' grief and 'normal' grief about the loss, along with standard measures of depression, health behaviour and so on, prior to, immediately following and several weeks after three sessions of such writing. Our hope is that this will yield useful insights into what type of 'processing' of loss is helpful to bereaved people, whether undertaken alone (perhaps as therapeutic 'homework') or in the presence of others.

Although it is too soon to tell what overall conclusions this study will suggest, one thing is clear: some participants are using the opportunity for narrative reflection to work toward profound trans-formation of the tragedies about which they are writing. Kevin was one such participant. At age 23, Kevin had lost Terry, his 51-year-old godfather, to a widely metastasized cancer just six months before. His resulting grief was profound, as he scored well above the clinical cutoff for standardized measures of traumatic grief, normal grief and depressive symptomatology. More descriptive, perhaps, were his responses to selected individual items on the grief inventories, as he endorsed statements such as, 'Ever since Terry died I feel like I have lost the ability to care about other people', 'I think about Terry so much that it can be hard for me to do the things I normally do', and 'The death of Terry feels overwhelming or devastating'. Clearly, Kevin was grappling with a grief reaction of some severity, one that research has indicated placed him at risk for a range of dangerous health and mental health outcomes in the months and years to come (Prigerson and Jacobs, 2001).

Having been invited to take part in the study on the basis of a screening of bereaved college students, Kevin eagerly volunteered, and was assigned to the internal/reflexive journaling condition. Accordingly, he was requested to report three times over a period of one week to a private space in our research laboratory, and write for 20 minutes, allowing himself to remember the most difficult parts of the death of this person, telling the story of what he felt, and the manner in which the death affected him in the past and continues to affect him today. Sections of his three journal entries follow,[4] interspersed with our observations about the content of his writing, and the narrative processes by which he began to reconstruct the meaning of his loss.

Session 1: Death notification
When I learned that my godfather had died, I was in complete shock. His daughter, one of my close friends, just left me a message on the answering machine. I wasn't expecting it at all. ... Terry had just passed away in his sleep. He had only been diagnosed with cancer for two months, and had left the hospital like two days before he died. Everyone thought he was getting better. Me and Susan talked for a long time about her dad. It kind of upset me, though, because she wasn't crying, and I was. She was Terry's real daughter, not me. That really bothered me.

At the funeral, his family seemed at peace, and I believe I took his death harder than anyone. ... The familys [sic] that were there were all smiling and talking about [how] they were going to go party, 'cause that is what Terry would have wanted. I didn't think that would be what he wanted, though. When the funeral was over, everyone went to the house. My parents gave their little speech about 'we're so sorry, blah, blah, blah,' and left. I wanted to stay with Susan, so we talked. I don't think she has even cried about her dad dying to this day. It really bothers me, 'cause I still get teary-eyed about it. ...

I just wish I could accept his death like everyone else. I mean, I accept he is dead, but I just want people to grieve like I have grieved. I just felt so out of place with everyone else, like I did not belong. All my life I was told that we were this huge, great big, strict Catholic family, and it just wasn't true. I just felt I didn't belong. ...

In this opening narration, Kevin establishes a schematic plot structure for his account, concentrating on the death notification and funeral, providing just enough factual information about the death of his godfather to provide a framework of intelligibility for his central concern – namely, his feelings about the loss and his family's reaction. Thus, Kevin develops a suggestive external narrative that supports a predominantly internal narrative process. The overall tone of the account is one of shock, incredulity and alienation, suggesting his initial inability to make sense of the death and a germinal, but regressive reconstruction of his family identity as founded on a certain level of callousness and hypocrisy. Perhaps the most striking theme in the narrative is the 'disenfranchisement' of Kevin's grief (Doka, 2001), in a family system that seems to meet his unique anguish with a sense of empathic failure (Neimeyer and Jordan, 2001). Any hint of hidden benefits or constructive life lessons in the loss is entirely absent.

Session 2: Last encounter
When I found out that Terry had cancer, I was in complete shock. I couldn't believe that someone so strong and so close to me had been eaten up by this horrible disease. I figured they would find the cancer, fix the problem, and then he would be back to the same person that I have always known. But that didn't happen and I accept that. But I just wish he was still here.

The last time I saw him was about four or five days before he died. When I walked in the house, I remember it smelling clean. There was no cigarettes lying around, and the smoke didn't just close in on you as you walked in the door. He had always looked like a football player, but he had lost so much weight he reminded me of some wormy accountant. He just sat in the chair and watched TV. I don't even think he knew what he was watching, [or] whether or not he was asleep or awake. I don't want my last days before I die to be sitting in front of a television.

The mood in the house was so quiet. Usually everyone's talking or one person's cooking. But on this day everyone was just staring at one another. No one knew what to say or what was going to happen next. It never crossed my mind that he would die. I assumed he would get better in a few months and everything would be back to normal. No one wanted him to die in the hospital, so that was the real reason I think he was home. I knew he didn't lead a very healthy life. But he was so good to everyone around him. He was like my dad. He was everybody's dad. He smoked way too much, and he knew that, but every time someone would ask him to quit he could never do it.

He has cancer all over. In his liver, bones, lungs (of course), he might have even had something wrong in his brain. I felt so stupid not to realize that what he did in life and how he treated his body had such a big impact on my life. I remember the way he always wore black T-shirts and jeans. No matter the occasion. He wore that to everything. But should he have been buried in it? I thought we should at least get him into a normal shirt. Then when he decided to die, I was just shocked. I thought somebody like him would live forever with beer/cigs wearing a black T-shirt and jeans. Now I guess he got what he wanted. He will always be wearing his black shirt and jeans. But I will never see him wearing it again.

In this segment of his narrative, Kevin opens with – and occasionally revisits – the sense of shock that pervaded his earlier writing. But the primary structure of the passage is provided by an imagistically rich external narrative of the last scenes in Terry's home: the jarringly clean smell of the usually smoke-filled atmosphere, Terry's 'wormy' thinness, his mesmerized somnolence in front of the TV, the uncanny quiet of the family. As suggested by Gonçalves et al. (2000), this 'objectifying attitude' seems to support Kevin's 'exploring the multiplicity of the sensorial world as a tool to expand the limits of one's experience' (p. 275). Re-entering this visual stream of his final encounter with his godfather, Kevin begins to articulate an ambivalent acceptance of the loss, and acknowledges his present-tense yearning for Terry. He also begins to grasp the deeper motivation of the family to bring their dying member home, not for cure, but for care and comfort at the end of life. This glimmer of new sense-making regarding the death is then expanded into a detailed exploration of the medical facts of Terry's metastasized cancer, with its implicit life-lesson linking the way we treat our bodies with the outcomes we obtain. This hint of reflexivity again yields to a concrete visualization of his godfather, dressed in his characteristic black T-shirt and jeans, 'deciding to die' and 'getting what he wanted'. As he closes on a note of sad reminiscence, Kevin seems to entertain a new interpretation of the death as a 'subintentioned' (Schneidman, 2000) choice on Terry's part, one that was tragically appropriate to the way he had chosen to live. Thus, Kevin appears to be embellishing his explanation of the loss, tacking between re-experiencing critical scenes and achieving new insights into the intentionality of the actors in a manner that contributes to progressive narrative reconstruction (Guidano, 1995).

Session 3: Continuing bonds
When Terry Williams passed away, everyone who cared about him wished he was here, but knew that he was in a better place. I can always think about the good times we all shared, and they will never go away. It took me by surprise, his death, [but] I have to learn to accept it though. Finding out someone close to me [died] was hard for me to accept, but I am sure it was even harder for him to know he was going to die. I wish he was here, though. We had some really good times together.

But, I still have other good times in my future. I don't think he would have wanted me to be as upset and depressed as I am. He would have wanted me to celebrate his life, not his death. I just came to realize that what he wanted was for everything to be OK. He didn't want people crying over him, he *would* have wanted a party. ... It's funny because everyone besides me weren't really that upset. I just thought that once someone dies you are suppose to mourn. But everyone is different. I accept that. I just don't think I understood why he had to die. Everyone grieves in their own way. In a way, I [am] glad I realized this, so maybe I will not take life for granted all the time. It's pretty bad someone has to die to make me realize that, but I think Terry would understand. He had cancer, and he couldn't change that. The doctors couldn't, he didn't want to do it. It was his time and if he accepts it, why shouldn't I?

I sometimes thought towards the last couple weeks he was alive, he really didn't know who I was. But at the same time, I didn't really know who *he* really was. He had changed, [but] it didn't make me love him any less. I think he knew who I was too, he was just exhausted, and his usual response didn't show. I'll always miss him physically. He was a great person and I was fortunate to have him in my life as long as I did. He could never leave my mind. I even catch myself doing some everyday things that he would do, and I just smile. It proves, I think, how big of an influence he had on me. The purpose of his life was to change others.

In this closing entry, Kevin abandons altogether an external narrative voice and delves deeply into internal and especially reflexive processes as he forges new meaning in his loss. He opens with consoling reflections on Terry's passing, and then begins to develop the predominant theme of this segment: his continuing bond with his godfather (Klass *et al.*, 1996). Strikingly, Kevin seems now capable of re-accessing cherished memories of their time together, with less pain and greater acceptance. This shift – elaborated in the paragraphs to follow – recalls Fleming and Belanger's (2001) definition of grieving as the process of 'moving from losing what we have, to having what we lost' (p. 314). Although he will always miss his godfather in a physical sense, Kevin finds new comfort in a sustaining symbolic connection that need not be relinquished.

Importantly, this same bond seems to sustain him in his movement toward a hopeful future, one that accords with Terry's wish for him, as well as with his godfather's celebratory attitude that gives posthumous permission for his mourners to affirm his life, rather than grieve his death. This realization seems to pave the way for Kevin to recognize the individuality of grief, and in so doing release some of the bitterness about the discrepancy between his family's grieving style and his own that preoccupied him in his first session entry. In passages like these, Kevin seems to be beginning to renegotiate not only the meaning of the loss for him, but also its shared significance with others.

Kevin's final entry closes with a cascade of moving insights, life lessons and hidden benefits harvested from the loss. Prompted by the inevitability of his godfather's death, Kevin now realizes that life cannot be taken for granted. He also grapples with the existential theme that we are ultimately mysteries to one another, but are nonetheless connected by bonds of (partial) understanding. Kevin closes with the affirmation of this life-shaping bond with his beloved godfather, which is reflected not only in his mind, but also in his everyday actions (Attig, 2001), configuring a progressive reconstruction of his sense of self. With a bittersweet smile, Kevin concludes his entry, grasping that the overarching purpose of his godfather's life was to change others, as it surely changed him.

It is sometimes clarifying to reflect in quantitative terms the qualitative shifts in meaning-making captured in a loss narrative like Kevin's. Prior to his writing, Kevin's score on the Inventory of Traumatic Grief (ITG) was 72, in the top 15 per cent of the bereaved persons in our study. Similarly, his scores of 26 on the Core Bereavement Items (CBI) and 20 on the Beck Depression Inventory (BDI) suggested cause for clinical concern on both measures. After his three sessions of journaling – completed across a single week – his ITG score had dropped to 56, his CBI score to 15, and his BDI to 10, suggesting a marked improvement in all three indices of distress. Even more importantly, this shift continued in the month that followed the writing, resulting in scores of 45, 11 and 4 on the three measures, respectively, placing him in a non-clinical range on each. Thus, Kevin's subjective trauma associated with his godfather's death half a year before was substantially transcended in a week of narrative exploration, permitting him to find a new significance in his loss and a gentler way of grieving the ending of a life that had so deeply touched his own.

Grief and the search for meaning: A clinical coda

In this chapter we have sketched the outline of a meaning reconstruction approach to grief, an emerging paradigm in our understanding of loss that is currently being written with many hands (Neimeyer, 2001c). In particular, we have drawn upon this new body of theory to listen in a fresh way to the stories of loss told by those with whom we have worked clinically, and those we have studied systematically. In doing so, we have worked to tease out some of the contexts and processes by which people struggle to wrest meaning from adversity, and find new orientation in a changed world. We hope that the illustrations of these contexts and processes offered in this brief chapter suggest the clinical fertility of this approach, although their implication for meaning-based strategies of bereavement interventions must be reserved for fuller explication elsewhere (Neimeyer, 2001b).

By way of closing, we extract a few general guidelines that emerge from this approach, which we hope will be helpful to professional helpers concerned with issues of loss. Each is offered in terms of a straightforward 'point to remember':

- *Bereavement is, among other things, a crisis in meaning.* The more profound the loss, the more deep-going a reconstruction of the griever's assumptive world is required.
- *The reconstruction of meaning in the wake of loss entails two complementary movements: to conserve what was viable in one's pre-loss sense of self and life, and to construct a new way of being-in-the world when this attempt at assimilating the loss into old meanings fails.* Both movements are to be respected, and both can be consciously supported by professional caregivers.
- *Contexts of meaning reconstruction include making sense of the loss itself, finding a silver lining of existential benefit in the dark cloud of bereavement, and establishing a changed sense of identity as a conse-*

quence of the transition.   The ability of the griever to forge new and progressive meaning in each of these domains constitutes a central process in integrating loss into our self-narrative.

- *Sense-making is often the most urgent need in the aftermath of loss, and its achievement promotes early adaptation.*   Listening for and gently asking for how the bereaved person makes sense of the loss can facilitate this adaptation, as can helping members of a family or caring community jointly negotiate the meaning of the loss for their collective survivorship. However, it is important to remember that any sense made of the loss – in practical/medical, existential and spiritual terms – soon after its occurrence is likely to be modified repeatedly as survivors 'mature' in their grief, representing a provisional placeholder for meaning-making, rather than a fixed foundation for rebuilding a life in the months and years that follow.

- *Benefit-finding is elusive in the immediate wake of loss, and typically emerges gradually months or years later.*   This implies that sensitive queries about life lessons, changed priorities, and so on are best reserved for later points in adaptation, as new meanings begin to come into focus. As with all meaning-making contexts discussed in this chapter, it is also critical that the professionals respectfully follow, rather than authoritatively lead, in this process. The most sustaining benefits are constructed from the raw materials of one's own grief; they cannot be simply prefabricated by a well-intentioned caregiver.

- *Identity reconstruction similarly unfolds over time, as one rediscovers latent resources in the self and social world, and experiments with new roles in the changed world one inhabits.*   Inquiring about such changes, and anchoring them in the responses of relevant others to this emerging sense of self helps consolidate new self-narratives that accommodate the loss without being constrained by it (Neimeyer, 2001a).

- *Various narrative processes promote this critical process of meaning reconstruction, including telling the story of loss in an external voice rich in sensory detail, and a more internal or reflexive voice that explores associated feelings and meanings.*   Tacking back and forth between these modes of 'storying' the loss helps make it more intelligible to the bereaved themselves, and more communicable to others. In general, we suspect that unconstrained grief narratives tend to shift from an early engagement with factual descriptions and associated emotions to personal, philosophical and spiritual significance over time, suggesting a helpful pattern of questioning for the practitioner.

In closing, meaning-making is a core dimension of grieving, one that has relevance for most, though not all, people whose lives are touched by loss.[5] We hope that some of the concepts described and illustrated in this chapter offer encouragement to professional caregivers who want to refine their sensitivity to the struggles encountered by the people they serve, by attending to the shifting contexts and processes through which the bereaved seek new significance in a world transformed by loss.

Notes

1. This, and all case material appearing in the chapter, is true, and unedited except to preserve the anonymity of those persons who consented to the inclusion of their stories.

2. This is not to say that we dismiss the wisdom of models that recognize core features of grief and its expression (Parkes, 2001). However, these common behavioural responses to the disruption of attachment (pining, searching, suppression of appetite and activity) are shaped by not only our biological evolution as a species, but also our cultural and personal evolution.

3. We share the scepticism of Thompson (Introduction to this volume) and others regarding the adequacy of Kübler-Ross's stage theory of adaptation to loss, which has served as a prototype for many others. For a detailed critique of stagic models of bereavement, see Neimeyer (2001c).

4. Evocative writing of this kind often deviates from academic conventions, sometimes sacrificing niceties of grammar and punctuation to follow the requirements of a more personal muse. As we have conducted this study, we discovered that tears were not uncommon among our participants, suggesting something of the emotional press felt by many of the writers of these loss narratives. For this reason, we have tried to stay close to the actual words and punctuation Kevin used in his journal, providing only those copyedits necessary to protect his confidentiality and ensure understanding of the written text by the reader. We appreciate the generosity of all participants in the study who consented, like Kevin, to our anonymous sharing of their experience in contexts such as the present chapter.

5. Nothing in what we have said is intended to imply that all bereaved persons undertake an agonizing search for philosophic meaning in their loss, or that professionals should instigate such

a search when the bereaved themselves do not do so. Indeed, a minority of even traumatically bereaved persons – about 15 per cent according to the best available data – seem to cope practically, straightforwardly and successfully without such an explicit search (Davis *et al.*, 2000, Neimeyer, 2000b). For most, however, a search for significance is compelling, and the central question for caregivers is how to accompany those they serve on the journey that such a quest entails.

4 Race and Culture

Suki Desai and Denise Bevan

Introduction

This chapter focuses on the use of Thompson's PCS analysis (Thompson, 2001a) as a framework for understanding the complexities of how racism impacts upon losses experienced by black and ethnic minority people. The usefulness of an analysis within such a Personal, Cultural and Structural understanding is twofold. First, it allows us to examine the impact of racism in a much more interrelated way, thus ensuring that racism is not brought down to some very simplistic analysis (for example, that racism is the sole result of 'prejudice and power' – see Sibeon, 1991, for a critique of this) or that understanding people's cultures is the sole way for better race relations. Second, examining racism from a personal, cultural and structural analysis allows us to move away from seeing a 'commonsense' understanding and pathologizing of other people's cultures and lifestyles as being the 'truth' about how such people and communities live. A classic example that continues to be offered as an explanation by many social care agencies for not providing services to many Asian communities, is that such communities prefer to 'look after their own' (Patel, 1990). This is a theme picked up within this chapter, which not only shows how Asian communities have been marginalized within many health and social care services because of this 'fact', but also how such communities themselves have been pushed into a position where they have to care for their own.

PCS analysis therefore not only highlights the issues of race, culture and loss in relation to the views of human services workers (the *P* or 'personal' level of individual attitudes and actions), but also identifies how such views impact on their practice and are maintained through a common understanding (the *C* or 'cultural' level of shared meanings) that develops about black and ethnic minority communities, together with a set of institutionalized power relations (the *S* or 'structural' level of the sociopolitical context). Such views on their own may not necessarily be racist or negative – for example, the concept of 'looking after their own' is not necessarily derogatory. However, when it becomes a common shared view about all black and ethnic minority communities, it becomes a racist view because it then brings with it the power to be discriminatory and, when such views become entrenched within organizations as part of their organizational culture, they form the basis of institutionalized racism (Penketh, 2000). This process of systematically excluding or discriminating against black and ethnic minority communities is often based on the assumption that such communities either integrate and conform to what is on offer or go away and 'look after their own'.

To begin with, we explore in more detail a theme that appears as an aspect of later discussions in this chapter, namely the tendency to concentrate on issues of ethnic sensitivity at the expense of developing anti-racist practice. Our next major theme is that of migration and diaspora and the significance of these factors in relation to the experience of loss. From this we move on to look at palliative care and consider how factors related to ethnicity and race are not generally given the attention they deserve.

The impact of racism

The literature base relating to multicultural aspects of loss and grief is a large and growing one (see, for example, Doka and Davidson, 1998; Parkes *et al.*, 1997). However, as we shall note below, it is only relatively recently that it has been recognized that there is a need for an anti-racist (rather than simply ethnically-sensitive) approach to be established in order to do justice to the complexities of the experience of loss on the part of people who have to contend with the pressures of racism in addition to the pain of their particular loss or losses.

An early but rare example of the drawing of links between racism and loss is to be found in the work of Burke (1984). He found that loss was the major dynamic force when persons were relentlessly attacked by word of mouth or by mass media or by physical violence in everyday life. This loss, according to Burke, reactivates the despair of earlier losses and leads to the anger and sadness associated with grief. Burke identifies three phases of reaction to racism. Summarized briefly, these are adjustment, resistance, and finally, reassessment and realignment. He associates adjustment with settlement and argues the case that the impact of racism can be vastly overwhelming, so much so that black groups are more likely to experience despair at this stage than, for example, Irish or Jewish people. Resistance on the other hand, is associated with anger; but anger which results from racism can become revenge by the victimized group, crossing the fine line between resistance and revenge. The final stage, that of reassessment and realignment, according to Burke, cannot take place until there is a fundamental shift away from institutional racism.

However, Thompson's (2001a) PCS analysis takes this further in arguing that a shift is not only necessary in relation to racism at an institutional or structural level but also in relation to racism and racist attitudes that exist at the personal and cultural levels. Such shifts are very important, especially in the messages that many black and ethnic minority people receive about themselves as a result of stereotyping and discriminatory assumptions being made. Robinson (1995) examines this aspect in relation to self-esteem and self-concept in the identity development of black and ethnic minority young people:

> The mainstream view of black identity has a number of variants; but the basic model is that living in a racist white society, where blacks are viewed and treated as inferior, and where they are in poverty in a powerless community, leads blacks early in life to internalize negative beliefs and negative feelings about themselves and other blacks. (p. 91)

Young black people are influenced by racism and the losses associated with it in several different ways. For example, a loss of self-esteem results in feelings of worthlessness and self-hatred through the idealization of white people and the devaluing of their own group (Baldwin, 1995). This is not to say that the majority of black children and young people have a crisis of identity. The problems occur, as Maxime (1986, p. 107) states, when there are those: 'who experience difficulty in maintaining a positive sense of racial identity'.

Racism, as we shall explore in more detail below, involves a range of losses by the individuals and communities so affected (a degree of loss of social standing, for example). When dealing with black people who are experiencing other losses (for example, as a result of one or more of the various loss arenas discussed in Part Two of this volume), we therefore need to be conscious that there is a very real likelihood that we are dealing with a situation of compound or cumulative losses. Traditional approaches to loss can be criticized for being 'colour-blind', for ignoring the reality of black people's experiences of racism. This chapter is therefore part of a process of raising awareness of the need to go beyond ethnic sensitivity to a position of anti-racism. We attempt to do so by exploring first the significance of migration and diaspora for members of ethnic minorities and second the need for palliative care services to take account of the role of racial discrimination at personal, cultural and structural levels.

Migration and diaspora

Migration has been a feature of the history of many of the peoples who now form the UK's diversity of ethnic minorities. Such migration has led to what is often referred to as 'diaspora', which Cashmore (1996) describes in the following terms:

> Drawn from the ancient Greek terms *dia* (through) *speiro* meaning 'dispersal, to sow or scatter', diaspora and its adjectives have been utilized in recent years in a variety of ways. ... A key dynamic to bear in mind, according to Stuart Hall, is that cultural identities 'come from somewhere, have histories' and are subject to constant transformation through the 'play of history, culture and power' ... For Hall, diaspora comprises ever-changing representations which provide an 'imaginary coherence' for a set of malleable identities. (pp. 99–100)

The processes of migration and diaspora can be seen to be very important in understanding loss. This is because, for many black and ethnic minority communities, the process of migration itself can create a feeling of a deep sense of loss, in so far as it involves breaking bonds with important aspects of our background, heritage and roots. The migration of such communities is particularly pertinent as it has an historical context linked closely (though not exclusively) to slavery and colonialism. The ways in which some South Asian communities have migrated to Africa, through colonization and the ways in which Africans have been displaced through slavery to the Caribbean can be seen to have had a specific impact on how those communities have endeavoured to maintain their own identities as well as taking on various aspects of the host communities. How such communities survive over time is, of course, a main feature of diaspora. The definition of diaspora therefore incorporates a variety of different facets of cultural identity, which many black and ethnic minority communities strive to maintain. The importance of maintaining cultures and heritage can form a crucial part of individual and group identity, and indeed serve a purpose as a refuge from racism. The relevance of cultures and heritage can also be an integral part of the identity of subsequent generations and helps to form links with the past. The maintaining of such links can be seen as an important part of dealing with the sense of grief that losses can so often generate (Klass *et al.*, 1996).

Brah (1996) suggests that diasporas are 'composite formations' made up of journeys to different parts of the world and that each one of these journeys has both its own history and particularity that forms its own narrative. Examining these narratives in terms of a personal, cultural and structural analysis enables us to recognize the complexities of loss, especially loss of culture and common shared experiences through generations resulting in redefining the meaning of culture. For example, many older ethnic minority people may still harbour a longing to return 'home', even where this is an unrealistic expectation, whereas those of second, third and subsequent generations are more likely to see Britain as their home, but challenge the traditional notions of identities and of being British. Hence, some young black and ethnic minority people will articulate their ethnicity as being English, Welsh or Scottish, not necessarily within the restrictive notions of such identities, but within a much broader sense (see Stuart Hall's work on new ethnicities – Hall, 1992).

The losses experienced by many black and ethnic minority communities are often articulated through personal loss associated with the loss of a particular lifestyle. The loss experienced by migration can be linked to isolation and alienation experienced by coming into a new community and the apprehension that is linked to this. Westwood *et al.* (1989) focus on the narratives of those children who migrated from Africa and the Caribbean to join their parents. These narratives are pertinent in that such children have had to live with the notion of feeling that they had been rejected by their parents as well as dealing with the apprehension of adjusting to a new lifestyle.

Aziz describes his experience of leaving Uganda in the following terms: 'When I came to England I missed Uganda so much and I didn't like it here' (Westwood *et al.*, 1989, p. 13). Elroy, who was convinced that his parents did not want him and upset at leaving his grandmother, reflects on his experience as:

My parents didn't want me, and when I was coming I didn't want to come. I remember on the boat being scared and not wanting to come here. I liked life in Barbados. I knew life there. They brought me here and then my dad went back to Barbados anyway. (ibid., p. 13)

The belief that home is somewhere else can create an intense feeling of loss and a lack of sense of belonging, perhaps leading to feelings of estrangement and alienation. This, coupled with negative aspects of racism experienced in a new community, can, for some people, raise grief-like reactions. Indeed, the interrelationships between racism and loss constitute a neglected area in the literature and so we return to this topic below.

In examining the composite formations of diaspora, Chailand and Rageau (1995) highlight another aspect of diaspora, which is relevant to the understanding of loss. They state:

A diaspora is also defined by the role played by *collective memory, which transmits both the historical facts that precipitated the dispersion and a cultural heritage.* (p. xv, emphasis in original)

Cultural heritage is often linked to religion for many black and ethnic minority communities, and aspects of grief and loss are often explained within such narratives. This is evidenced especially in coming to terms with the 'loss' of a member of family through mental health problems and in dealing with distress. In this regard, Beliappa (1991) highlights the use of prayer as a common method of dealing with distress. In her study both the use of prayer and the seeking out of faith healers (spiritual people such as gurus, mataji and hakims) were identified as one of the key ways of helping restore 'strength and balance' so that families could cope with the situation of the loss of their family member. Webb-Johnson (1991) also draws on the healing aspect of prayer for Asian communities. She describes how one woman coped with her son's mental health problems:

(with) no real source of help available she was able to overcome her depression and cope with her son's problem by turning to God and praying. She saw this as her 'main anchor'. (p. 46)

Also, in the case of another woman:

Once Mataji started helping me I started feeling much better. She gave me special prayers. My sister-in-law had a curse on me. With these prayers I found renewed strength to face the situation. (p. 46)

Although the Government has allowed since 1985 the prescribing of spiritual healing on the NHS by general practitioners, the actual referrals made are limited. Spiritual healing is considered inferior to scientific explanations of mental health problems and hence, at best spiritual healing is acknowledged as complementary medicine. This results in a general dissatisfaction with the NHS and the seeking out of other support. This reinforces the myth and stereotype that Asian communities 'look after their own'. In addition to this, it puts those communities accessing such services in a vulnerable position, as there is no way to monitor the quality and effectiveness of such services or indeed publicize when abuse occurs. There are not many spiritual healers in Britain and their reputation is founded upon word-of-mouth. However, as in many aspects of living, there are those people who cross professional boundaries. Where such services are dependent upon word-of-mouth, the reporting of abuse is not likely to take place due to fear of recrimination from the community due to lack of anonymity offered to the victim. The increase in evidence-based health and social care practice (see, for example, Sheldon and Chilvers, 2000) means that alternative forms of help such as spiritual healing will be further marginalized, resulting in poor surveillance of such practices.

It is important to remember that, whilst aspects of religion may be important to some people from black and ethnic minority communities, this is not the case for all, and hence they should not be seen purely as a homogeneous group. It is also the case that there is always likely to be a part of a diaspora which assimilates and largely disappears. Therefore, for some people, recourse to religion and spiritual healing is not experienced as helpful. For example, Manjit had been taken to a hakim and was encouraged to pray, but as he commented: 'I am not religious and it did not mean anything to do that. Now my brother tells me I should turn to God but I don't believe in any of that' (Westwood et al., 1989, p. 36).

Where such aspects occur there can be a creation of another form of loss – that is, the loss of a way of life, lost through time and generations:

> The loss of our children is the price we have paid on coming here. We spent all our early years tending over them. But now they have grown apart and are often disrespectful. They question us on everything and for some of these questions we have no answers. (Beliappa, 1991, p. 18)

At the C level, a change in cultural values creates changes within power relations between parents and their children and within generations and thus interrelates with the S level of social structure.

Migration and diasporas enable us to understand some of the losses experienced by black and ethnic minority communities. The existence and influence of racism at a structural level can be seen to compound these experiences. This is particularly evident in the support and care of dying people and their carers where the personal values of human services workers, coupled with little or no understanding about black and ethnic minority communities and their cultures and lifestyles, have often resulted in the systematic exclusion of such communities from receiving palliative care. It is therefore to this important topic that we now turn.

Palliative care

Palliative care issues also need to be thought of and approached in structural, cultural and personal terms in order to support dying people and their carers in ethnically-sensitive and anti-racist ways. An approach based on PCS analysis should address individual needs within the cultural and structural context of individual life experiences. To provide this support, cultural and religious differences, as part of the broader concept of ethnicity, need to be acknowledged and addressed through the provision of services that are sensitive to the importance of both ethnicity and racism. This section will therefore examine the current state of the provision of palliative care services to people from minority ethnic groups, relating this to the available evidence of racial inequalities in health. This will be viewed within a framework of acknowledging that problems of ethnocentrism and racism so often affect the characteristics, attitudes and practices of palliative care services.

The complexity of this task is reflected in Smaje and Field's (1997) arguments that these broader issues must be considered and analysed in relation to cultural and material contexts, and that it is important not to simplify the issues by discussing ethnicity in terms of homogeneity. They argue that those from minority groups may collectively share the experience of prejudice and discrimination; this can be seen, for example, within inequalities in health (Acheson, 1998). Within this contextual framework we must, however, not lose sight of the person as an individual, as experiences of racial disadvantage are as unique and diverse as are death and dying themselves. It is therefore important to acknowledge that individual life histories will differ, even within a group sharing a culture. Smaje and Field argue that what we may understand to be true generally of a particular culture may actually differ for the individual at the time of their death or loved one's death. They argue that:

> Far from finding distinctive orientations to dying and caring for the dying which are peculiar to a given culture or ethnic group as a naïve culturalism would suggest, we are likely to find a multiplicity which is structured in particular ways across the lines of class, gender, age and so on. (p. 155)

Thompson (2001a), whilst acknowledging these important factors, also points out the dangers of too narrow a focus on ethnicity without considering the implications of race. He argues that race as a distinct factor is often submerged within the notion of ethnicity; this tends to present ethnic minority groups as biologically different from, and thus inferior to, the ethnic majority. This sort of narrow culturalist framework can fail to grasp that race is not a biological entity but a social and political process that significantly affects life chances (we return to this point below).

Failing to understand how race and ethnicity operate at a sociopolitical level makes it more difficult to challenge racism and provide ethnically-sensitive social work. For example, as noted earlier, a simplistic view of the provision of care to Asian people may assume the position of 'they look after their own' and therefore neglect to address community care needs. Patel (1990) argues that the myth of 'they look after their own' allows local authorities to overlook their responsibilities to provide appropriate and acceptable services to minority groups. This omission in practice amounts to racial discrimination; indeed evidence of the low take-up of community services can be seen as significant in highlighting racism at the organizational level. The assertion that services are 'open to all' means in real terms that, if Asian clients are not assimilated adequately enough to fit into available services, the state does not see it as a responsibility to provide specifically for the needs of all its citizens. This fits with what Macpherson, in his influential report, described as 'institutional racism', which he defined in the following terms:

> the collective failure of an organisation to provide an appropriate and professional service to people because of their colour, culture or ethnic origin. It can be seen or detected in processes, attitudes and behaviours which amount to unwitting prejudice, ignorance, thoughtlessness and racist stereotyping which disadvantage minority ethnic people. (1999, cited in Singh, 2000, p. 33)

The racial dimension of working with social problems must be acknowledged as a significant influence, in order for interventions not to go on to reproduce and reinforce institutional or other forms of racism. For example, Ahmed (1987) stresses that assessment needs to take account of racism:

> I am not against better cultural understanding but I am against an *over-reliance* on cultural explanations that distract attention both from significant emotional factors as well as structural factors such as class and race. The important point is that, for Black clients, the centrality of racism needs to be more explicitly acknowledged in the assessment process and cultural explanations need to be considered in the context of racism. (Cited in Thompson, 2001a, p. 74)

Reviewing the literature relating to cultural aspects of death and dying, there does seem to be a considerable amount of discussion and research available on what the issues are and the implications for practice (Doka and Morgan, 1993; Parkes *et al.*, 1997). The issue of how racial inequality and discrimination impact upon the experience of death and dying and how anti-racist practice can intervene, has begun to feature in more recent literature (Clark and Seymour, 1999; Corr *et al.*, 1997; Jones, 1994; Field *et al.*, 1997). This literature seems to draw quite heavily on palliative care services as a way of securing some evidence of the inequalities in the provision of hospice and palliative care services to members of black and ethnic minority communities.

A report published by the National Council for Hospice and Specialist Palliative Care Services (1995) highlighted the low take-up of specialist palliative care services by ethnic minority groups. The report recommended equal opportunities anti-discriminatory policies along with a more culturally specific approach to service provision. The potential role of black and other minority ethnic volunteers in developing services to meet these needs has been acknowledged with the recommendation that volunteers from these communities should be actively recruited and trained to support the work of specialist palliative care services.

The acknowledgement of the need for greater multicultural awareness is undoubtedly welcome. However, what must be guarded against are the pitfalls of a descriptive and categorical working framework. Factfiles have been developed to give professionals working with black and ethnic minority people basic information about different cultural and religious practices around death and dying. This provides reassuring guidance on cultural practices but, taken in prescriptive isolation, can act to exclude dying people and their families from services – assuming that patients will ascribe to a set of practices gives little opportunity to explore and express the individual's existential needs (Gunaratnam, 1997). An example of this can be found in Haworth *et al.*'s (1997) work. They studied interpreting services in palliative care in an NHS trust and found that the interpreters were inadequately trained to deal with the range of knowledge and skills needed in dealing with palliative care issues.

It has been argued that professionals' fears of getting it wrong and not being knowledgeable about someone's cultural and religious needs can inhibit professionals from offering services (Green, 1989). Hospice staff related such fears within a focus group to researchers:

> There is the fear of dealing with people from different cultures – that you don't want to 'get it wrong'. It is harder to take the risks that you might do with people from your own culture ... It is also about dealing with people who are dying – death conjures up an atmosphere of danger. (Cited in Gunaratnam, 1997, p. 172)

Gunaratnam argues that, whilst factfiles address the tasks that may be involved in death practices they do not explore black and ethnic minority people's subjective and emotional experience of death and dying:

> The relationships between individual identity, meaning frameworks and cultural contexts are thus constructed deterministically, without 'space' being accorded to the gaps which exist between self-identifications and culturally related behaviours. (p. 174)

Further to this, it could be argued that the lack of knowledge and awareness given to religious and cultural values would spiritually disenfranchise people who are dying and bereaved (see Moss, Chapter 2 in this volume). To be spiritually disenfranchised is to be oppressed at a number of levels, as the spiritual touches every aspect of what it means to be human. The spirit integrates the political, historical, social, racial, cultural, familial and personal self, creating wholeness of spiritual being. The collective and individual sense of bereft isolation and loss of expression arising from their spiritual needs being disenfranchised through racism will compound the dying experience of those already disadvantaged through race.

In a similar vein, Irish (1995) highlights the importance of seeking fully to understand the meaning attached to loss. His conclusion from working with children across a variety of cultures and linguistic groups was that communication differences can create more difficulties in trying to grasp their meaning of death. He stresses the significance of asking questions in order to gain insight – through a translator, if necessary. Irish points to the diversity within ethnic categories and high-lights that there may be differences in the customs observed by the gen-erations of a family. For example, for the child of the family, there may be belief systems attributed to assimilation into the dominant culture. The viewpoints of more recent theories of loss recognize the potential for traditional approaches to be unwittingly racist because they have not accounted for cultural differences in grieving patterns. Rosenblatt (1993) comments:

> Western cultural concepts such as 'dying' and 'grief' originated in the context of its culture. It now seems that realities differ so greatly from culture to culture that it is misleading and ethnocentric to assume that Western concepts apply generally. (p. 13)

Similarly, Smaje and Field (1997) highlight and voice their concerns over this tendency to reify culture – to treat it as a fixed entity. They refer to Neuberger's (1987) argument that, if a health worker dis-plays some knowledge about a person's cultural needs, this can enrich the contact and indicate thoughtfulness and respect. Smaje and Field also argue that, despite these issues being on the health care agenda, the advancement in actually providing appropriate and adequate palliative care has not been successfully engaged with.

It does seem that, despite the focus on providing ethnically and culturally sensitive palliative care, little progress has been made in providing an equitable service. A culturalist framework which, from a consensus point of view, continues to deal with the C level of cul-tural barriers without attending to the S level of structural inequali-ties, will inevitably fail to address health inequalities. This is because focusing on cultural adjustment neglects how the powerful influences of structural inequalities, such as poor housing, racial harassment, disadvantage in employment and lower income have a significant impact on health chances.

Similarly, in striving for equitable provision of palliative care, Doka and Morgan (1993) believe that death and dying should be seen as crises that affect many levels: 'medical, physical, logical, familial ... social ... and spiritual' (p. 131). They argue that the needs of the individual should be met holistically – that is, psychologically, spiritually, socially, physically and culturally:

> Because of the different backgrounds, experiences, spiritual needs and con-cerns of persons with life-threatening illness, one cannot assume common language, definitions, beliefs, experiences, or needs. Caregivers then should explore each individual's spiritual perspective separately. (p. 131)

The need to respond sensitively to diverse cultural and religious customs and the need for solutions enabling a range of death practices to be honoured is a matter of urgency (Laungani, 1997; Patel *et al.*, 1998). Further to this Patel *et al.* (1998) advocate that anti-racist practice needs to:

- consider the religious/faith aspects of minorities;
- ensure that appropriate care is available to ethnic minority service users; and
- adopt a structural approach to microlevel work that advocates sociopolitical change in order to maximize support and choice.

There is also a need for white practitioners to open themselves up to the learning that is needed to develop ethnically sensitive and anti-racist practice. We feel that Barrett's (1998) comments are a useful start in that direction:

> I am often asked by those who are culturally different if they can be an effective caregiver for a Black individual who is experiencing loss and grief. Whilst race, culture, and ethnicity should not be taken lightly, they should not be perceived as insurmountable barriers. Be yourself, be honest, be real and be open to and teachable about those aspects of the Black experience that may be a bit different from your own. Have faith in our common humanity to connect and support one another in our experiences of loss, grief, and pain in spite of our separateness and apparent differences. (pp. 95–6)

Conclusion

Traditional approaches to loss and grief have tended to focus primarily on the individual level. Some work, particularly in recent years, has placed greater emphasis on the cultural level. Culture has been found to have major influences on grieving processes and mourning practices (Stroebe and Stroebe, 1987). Cultural perspectives on loss are increasingly being examined and there is evidence from research indicating firstly the need for continued attentiveness against ethnocentric stereotyping; and secondly highlighting the benefits of working together internationally to develop crosscultural insights and sensitivity towards the diversity of death systems (Parkes, 1997; Spruyt, 1999).

However, what is also required is an extra awareness of how racial dimensions at a structural level impact upon the experience of loss. We have examined how narrow assumptions of what may be helpful from a practitioner's viewpoint may fall short of actually understanding racial and cultural variability, with the results of delivering services which are inequitable and unacceptable to many individuals within black and ethnic minority communities.

We believe that the argument for a fair and just holistic perspective towards individuals' and communities' experiences of loss, which takes account of sociopolitical, racial, cultural and personal contexts, is the way forward towards being able openly to understand and share the uniqueness and diversity of loss.

5 Gender and Sexism

Gordon Riches

Introduction

Across a range of activities, gender often appears to be a significant predictor of attitudes and social behaviour. Male traits of risk-taking, competitiveness, reluctance to reveal feelings and abdication of primary care tasks to women show up in patterns of loss and reactions to bereavement. According to Field *et al.* (1997) men are more likely to die from cardiovascular illness, suicide, murder, accident and warfare. In 1999 in the UK, one in five males aged 16–24 was a victim of violence compared with one in ten females of the equivalent age. Men are three times more likely to die through taking their own lives than women. Men die younger than women. In 1997, nearly two out of every three people aged 75 and over in the UK were women. A quarter of all families are headed by a single parent, practically all of whom are women (Gibson, 2001). Women appear to be at greater risk from domestic violence, though, typically, figures reflecting the 'true' picture of the victimization of men by female partners are notoriously difficult to obtain. With all victimization, as with mental health problems, men are less likely than women to admit a problem, to seek help or to visit a doctor. Women's lives are more open to surveillance by the medical profession. They are two and a half times more likely to be treated for depression than men (Gibson, 2001).

Hockey (1997) argues that men's social roles are more likely to expose them to accident and danger, as well as putting them in the principal roles associated with 'managing' death – as clergy, doctors and funeral directors. In contrast, the roles women occupy generally present less physical risk. Few women escape responsibility for caring for other family members. This experience is likely to explain their greater responsiveness to illness, their willingness to ask for help and their familiarity with medical services. Help-seeking and help-giving are associated more with female roles. However, women are more likely to gain direct experience of loss, with substantial numbers of pregnancies ending in miscarriage, stillbirth and perinatal death. Women still vastly outnumber men in occupations dealing with the care of sick, dying and elderly people; 1.2 million women in the UK care for an elderly relative (Gibson, 2001).

This chapter explores why, in accounts of loss and grief, men and women appear often to cope with loss and bereavement in different ways. It draws on examples from fieldwork with bereaved parents undertaken between 1994 and 1999 (Riches and Dawson, 2000). I use the word appear because it is important to note that masculine patterns of grief may be shared by many women, just as more men may occupy roles that enable feminine skills and attitudes to be practised. However, evidence still points to sufficient patterning of these differences to make gender a useful explanatory factor (Doka and Martin, 2001).

The division of emotional labour

Studies show some notable gender differences in reaction to the loss of a child. Men tend to grieve for shorter periods of time; to deny the extent of their feelings; to deal with their loss through activity such as work, fund-raising or through challenging the cause of their child's death. They take on (though sometimes resentfully) the role of emotional supporter for their partner (McGreal *et al.*, 1997; Puddifoot and Johnson, 1997; Schwab, 1992).

Mothers, on the other hand, appear to be far more preoccupied with the emotional impact of their loss, suffering severe physical reactions and experiencing longer-term emotional distress. This gendered division of 'grief work' has been explained through the different role positions men and women tend to occupy both in the family and in the outside world. A number of studies distinguish between instrumental and expressive tasks within families. Early work of Parsons and Bales (1956) recognized two distinctive roles in family leadership: one that managed the family's 'public face'; the other that supported the internal family dynamic. They recognized that these tasks often divided along gendered lines in typical 'modern' families.

There have been massive changes in the nature of family life and in the roles of men and women since the 1950s. Nevertheless, more recent research tends to confirm that gender still plays a significant role in the division of emotional labour, even though there have been radical shifts in patterns of marriage and employment (Altschuler, 1993; Duncombe and Marsden, 1999). Women still appear to carry most emotional responsibility for children and empirical evidence of the 'new man' taking a more equal share is difficult to find (Finch and Morgan, 1991). Silverman and Worden (1992) note that children are less likely to be able to talk about their feelings, suffer more disruption in their daily routines, and experience greater difficulty adapting to change if they lose a mother rather than a father. Given that a quarter of all families with children are now headed by a lone parent (overwhelmingly the mother) the separate tasks of emotional support and practical management may increasingly have to be accommodated within the role of single parent (Gibson, 2001).

Research by Masters et al. (1994) confirms the myth that 'women express, men repress' (p. 18). Duncombe and Marsden (1999) similarly note newly married women's disappointment with their partners' inability to share feelings or a satisfactory degree of intimacy. Most women they interviewed felt their male partners lacked 'emotional participation' either with them or their children. Official statistics confirm that twice as many wives divorce their husbands as husbands file for divorce against their wives. The grounds on which they claim irretrievable breakdown are also distinctive: men tend to cite infidelity, women cite incompatibility or mental cruelty (CSO, 1994).

Doka and Martin (2001) argue that men deal with grief more cognitively, suffer a greater loss of dignity if they lose emotional control, and learn, through their cultural role of protector, to suppress all strong feelings except for anger. Thompson (2001b) takes this argument further, suggesting that loss creates such a profound threat to men's assumptions about the nature of the world and their place within it that they may avoid facing its full implications. Male anger features in many explanations of domestic violence. In cases where family murder is followed by suicide of the perpetrator, the majority of victims are women and children. Where women do kill their partners, children are rarely involved. Deeply ingrained beliefs about possession, male dominance and protection appear to drive some men to extreme measures in avoiding the threatened loss of their families (Barnes, 2000).

In our own study (Riches and Dawson, 2000) this masculine trait of 'abdication' from painful emotional demands was exemplified by one father who, according to his wife, adopted the attitude that 'life had to go on' when he discovered his adult son had brain cancer. Alf's son and wife were both employed in the family building company and their visits for hospital treatment increasingly disrupted his business routines. Alf responded by putting in longer hours and immersing himself in the practical problems resulting from their absence. He appeared to deeply resent the time Betty spent nursing their son and avoided hospital visiting whenever he could. On the day the consultant gave the results of the tests confirming their worst fears, Alf had arranged to visit an important client so could not attend. Betty felt that, emotionally, Alf had cut himself off entirely. Their marriage collapsed immediately after their son died.

Another father expressed discomfort and embarrassment at his wife's insistence that they bury their stillborn twins in the local cemetery. Because their small community knew them as childless and because his wife had miscarried at twenty weeks, Keith felt keenly conscious of appearing to be 'abnormally' grief-stricken and of occupying a 'status' (of bereaved parent) that he felt unjustified in claiming. This contrasted with his wife's intense sense of personal loss. To Margaret, other people's perceptions were irrelevant. By being able to regularly visit their grave she gained enormous comfort. Keith, however, continued to be very reluctant to accompany her. A year later she was particularly hurt by his attempt to conceal the flowers and the reason for their journey when they met a neighbour on the way to the cemetery. Disagreements between family members over how the bereaved family should be represented to the 'outside world' are not uncommon (Brabant, 1994).

Patriarchy, mindset and suffering

Feminist theories of patriarchy challenge conventional beliefs that men's and women's behaviour is based on 'natural' biological differences. Feminist writers have identified links between masculinity, scientific thinking and the 'modern' mindset (Smith, 1987). The supremacy of rational over intuitive thought is seen as a source of women's disadvantage in the public sphere of work and politics. Women's 'natural' skills in caring are associated with domesticity and the private sphere. The philosophies, abstract systems and bureaucratic procedures of male thinkers permeate the history of western 'civilization'.

The dominance of this detached 'objective' position in social knowledge helps explain gender differences in perceptions of loss in modern societies. Das's (1993) study of suffering following the Bhopal disaster found that men were more likely to rely on rational explanations of their loss. Using the term 'theologies of suffering' to investigate bereavement reactions, she described how fathers and husbands used 'broad brush' explanations to make sense of the deaths of their loved ones (histories of conflict, myths of heroism, theories of economic or political exploitation). In so doing they subordinated and controlled the more socially threatening responses of their womenfolk. Bereaved mothers and wives gave strong emotional voice to the view that life and death and, by implication the social order, were arbitrary, chaotic and meaningless.

Seale's examination of professional models of dying in late modern society similarly reveals tidy 'clinical' rationalizations of 'heroic death' that contrast starkly with the messy reality of terminal cancer wards (Lawton, 2000). Meaning is offered to terminally ill people and to their relatives through reference to an established 'trajectory' of dying with predictable phases, turning points and 'tasks to be accomplished'. Purpose, objectivity, order and 'heroism' can be achieved if they embrace the opportunities offered by this 'last inner journey' (Seale, 1995a). The findings of Klass (1996) and Walter (1996) similarly question the 'clinical lore' that often underpins bereavement counselling. As with Das's argument, these writers suggest that abstract cognitive explanations function to integrate (and subordinate) the emotional work of carers and mourners within a rational, ordered and medically controllable world.

For women, therefore, grieving provides an example of an emotional activity in which consciousness becomes 'bifurcated'(Smith, 1987). Women's mental worlds are grounded in the everyday 'realities' of painful, messy, often sudden, and generally very distressing loss. Yet the only legitimate concepts through which they can interpret their experiences are 'masculine', giving rise to an even greater sense of frustration and isolation. Men's mental worlds, on the other hand, may need to be free to deal with the more objective, external challenges that the loss creates for the family's survival.

We came across examples of very different responses in bereaved mothers and fathers that illustrate this. Whilst Gillian became more isolated and more depressed following their baby daughter's death from Leukaemia, Anthony invested enormous energy in raising funds for Leukaemia research, travelling the country and achieving national recognition for his charitable work. This 'active' project provided a purpose and release for his grief and an alternative role to that of father that continued to offer him a purpose and social status. Two years after their daughter died, Gillian and Anthony separated.

In another case, after their adult son's death in an air disaster, Robert invested more time as lay minister in his church, interpreting his bereavement in terms of God's mystery. Meanwhile his wife quietly rejected the faith they used to share. During her interview, she noted that she kept these feelings from her husband and Robert seemed unaware of her changed beliefs. These responses reflect ways in which masculine and feminine meaning structures can produce greater emotional distance between marital partners.

Loss and the construction of gendered identity

These differences can be explained, at least in part, through analyses of identity formation and the portrayal of gender in popular culture (Hart, 1996; Chodorow, 1989; Seidler, 1991; Thompson, 1997). Young children are exposed to the concepts of 'male' and 'female' as contrasting cultural stereotypes. The general category of men and women is created (increasingly by the media) from immediately recognizable clusters of 'idealized' traits and characteristics. These myths exert a powerful influence on the role models and behaviours young people use to construct their own personal identities. Men and women build a positive sense of self around only those traits and experiences that match the labels they want to be known by, ignoring or suppressing those traits that appear to fit alternative labels. Hart argues that this process leads men to dissociate themselves from behaviour and emotions that might be described as feminine. Chodorow argues that men's emotional behaviour is characterized by 'detachment' – reflecting their suppression of feelings as they struggle for an identity independent of their mothers. Seidler argues that it is 'normal' for men to have a low sense of personal worth, believing that esteem is dependent upon 'right' public action.

Paradoxically, Hart argues, this makes men more dependent upon women to play out their own denied 'feminine' traits by proxy. There is also a tendency for men to idealize their relationships, interacting with mental constructs of their loved ones rather than with the 'real' person. This gives rise to problems of emotional expression, especially in their ability to achieve a sense of intimacy.

When faced with the loss of those hidden aspects of themselves previously held in their partners, or when faced with events that threaten to re-engage them with their suppressed emotions, men may experience hostility and an inability to communicate. Men will not reveal pain if to do so will discredit their masculine self. Loss of emotional control, as demonstrated in irrational behaviour, emotional expression, weakness or dependency on others is highly discreditable to masculine identity (Kotara, 1977; Seidler, 1991).

The following example from our data illustrates that, where this emotional division of labour is well-balanced in traditional partnerships, mutual benefits can be identified. Following their daughter's death in a foreign accident, Jessica stated that she could not have got through it without the 'rock' of her husband. She clearly valued his constancy, dependability, stoicism and ability to 'hold things together'. Paul, similarly, believed that, in helping Jessica, he had done the right thing by his daughter's memory. Unlike his wife who felt they would one day meet again in heaven, he confided that he had no faith in the afterlife and had privately faced the total irrevocability of his loss. Paul's life was characterized by his dedication to his professional work, sharing only indirectly in the intimate mourning that Jessica was able to accomplish with her daughter's close friends and acquaintances.

In our interviews generally, fathers tended to talk more about their wife's grief than about their own. Their attitudes varied from impatience (frustration with wife's continuing mourning) to sympathy (appreciation of wife's inability to get back to normal and appreciation of what their lost child meant to her). A number of bereaved fathers accompanied their partners to support groups, to bereavement counsellors and even to clairvoyants, but none we spoke to had sought help directly for themselves. Most claimed that any support they received was secondary to its benefits for their wives.

In contrast, where partners fail to see this uneven division of labour as mutually beneficial, marital tension is almost inevitable, particularly in cases of male anger and emotional withdrawal. Alf's response to his son's terminal illness was to control himself, and attempt to impose his definition of what was happening onto his wife. As this control broke down, he resorted to verbal and finally physical violence to impose his view of how events should be managed. Though nowhere as extreme as this example, our data contain a minority of women (usually in full-time professional employment, or who are the chief or only breadwinners of the family) who respond in ways that reflect similar masculine traits of rationalization, self-control and diversion from painful feelings through immersion in work.

Changing society, changing expectations

A number of writers help explain the dilemmas faced by both 'new' men and 'liberated' women as traditional roles, expectations and family patterns shift in a rapidly changing society. Women are increasingly expected to maintain a career whilst still assuming a principal responsibility for childcare and childrearing (Duncombe and Marsden, 1999; Finch and Morgan, 1991). Many men appear to be caught between the 'rock' of masculinity and the 'hard place' of postfeminist expectations. Cook (1988) and Puddifoot and Johnson (1997) describe the 'double-bind' in which many men feel caught. On the one hand, they experience cultural demands for competence, assertiveness, rationality and the ability to perform, yet on the other, they are criticized for being unable to get in touch with their personal feelings and openly express their emotions.

Against this backdrop of changing roles, Cook describes four strategies that bereaved men used in dealing with these contradictory expectations. First, some men worked at blocking out images of the loss, actively 'filling' their minds with other less painful thoughts. Second, some men intellectualized their loss, thinking it through until they could devise a broader framework of meaning into which it would fit. Third, some worked hard at activities that diverted their attention from the loss. Work, drinking, affairs, organizing pressure groups and writing books are all examples within the published literature. Lastly, and significantly, many grieved in ways that were just as emotionally expressive as their female partners, but in private places where no one could observe this breakdown of control.

Most crucially, Cook found men claimed to use these strategies because they felt an 'internal pressure' to hide their feelings. In one of our joint interviews, one bereaved mother said 'I don't think you (looking at husband) have felt it the same as me. I cried for months, but I don't think I have ever seen you cry.' Her husband, obviously for the first time, told his wife directly: 'That's what you think ... We've got this shed at work ... There's many a time I have locked myself in there and just howled.'

Contemporary culture still, on the whole, associates masculinity with the control of self and others. Those who take this responsibility may have to hide their personal distress from others, and their vulnerability from themselves. Each of the four strategies recognized by Cook can be explained partly through Chodorow's argument that masculine identity is formed on the basis of disassociation from the 'mother' and all things feminine. This negative identification is reinforced through subsequent experiences of male and female role models in junior and secondary schools, in the media, in commerce and industry, and in professional occupations (Hearn, 1987). Seidler (1991) argues that men work hard at suppressing, or hiding or avoiding their grief, not out of wilful insensitivity or a sense of personal preservation, but out of a sometimes debilitating sense of moral duty.

Ironically, amongst the women we interviewed between 1994 and 2000, a number appeared to adopt very similar coping strategies to those outlined by Cook in 1988. These examples cannot be explained using Chodorow's analysis but do suggest that 'vocational' demands of professional employment and the increasing importance of work-based roles may be competing with the family for women's identity commitment in the same way it has done for men for generations.

Obstacles in gaining support

Because of the emotional paradox of men appearing to cope, while women appear to need help, many men face numerous but often unseen obstacles in seeking or finding support.

Men may lack the ability to recognize what they have lost. They may literally not know what their child or partner meant to them either in an emotional or a practical sense. In embracing the role of protector, and in dealing actively with the practical problems presented by death, they may fail to understand the enormity of the emotional change confronting them or to signal to others that they need support. They may well resist any support that is offered. Campbell and Silverman (1996) in their study of widowers highlight the fact that these men have maybe lost the one person who could have helped them through their bereavement. They note that wives were often the only source of social contact outside of the husband's workplace and were frequently their only 'confidant'. Amongst older men, wives also were generally the primary channels of emotional communication between their husbands and their children. Weiss (1990) argues that most men 'delegate' responsibility for managing their social lives to their wives. Consequently, newly bereaved husbands may lose the one person who kept them in contact with friends and wider family.

The tendency for men to respond cognitively rather than affectively to loss leads in some cases to a strategy of 'replacing' a deceased partner. Stroebe *et al.* (1996) argue that, even though social networks often appear to be highly supportive, they cannot 'buffer' bereaved people from the loss of social, emotional or domestic functions previously undertaken by the deceased person. Again drawing on the work of Weiss (1975), they distinguish between social loneliness and emotional loneliness, arguing that whilst close friendships can help overcome the former, intense feelings of isolation cannot be compensated for. This problem is particularly acute where deceased partners were relied upon to maintain both the social and the emotional context of their lives. This partly explains Campbell and Silverman's finding that 52 per cent of all widowers in the US remarry within eighteen months of bereavement. They also demonstrate that these remarriages are exceptionally fragile (50 per cent break down) because husbands may, without realizing it, expect exactly the same emotional tasks to be fulfilled by their new wife.

One example from our own data illustrates how a widower's remarriage, though apparently meeting some of the needs of the bereaved males in the family, can create significant problems for the adaptation of a surviving daughter. Jane bitterly resented her father's 'dating' six months after her mother's accidental death. Following his remarriage a year later, she found it impossible to stay in the family home when she returned from college. Her mother's ornaments, cooking utensils and furniture had been rearranged and mixed in with the belongings of the 'new' wife. In a very literal sense, her mother had helped shape both Jane's father and the home that she took for granted before her mother's death. A new wife meant a new home, new siblings and, to a certain extent, a reshaped father. His apparent contentment with his 'replacement' wife, and her own brother's apparent lack of concern at the changed circumstances added to Jane's sense of anger, isolation and unreality.

In similar ways, bereaved mothers who mourn deeply and for long periods may also cease to provide the social and emotional services they undertook prior to the death of their child. A number of researchers identify husbands' frustration with their wives' inability to return to any semblance of 'normal' living, and Helmrath and Steinitz (1978) describe the ways in which this can lead to marital conflict and eventual divorce. Schwab (1992) also quotes bereaved fathers who felt that their wives were 'so wrapped up' with grief that they failed to engage with the needs of daily living. Many bereaved fathers we spoke to consequently felt very lonely, not only isolated by their own often unrecognized grief, but also by the responsibility they felt for having to hold together an apparently collapsing family.

Challenging sexist thinking

Cook's (1988) argument that men work as hard and suffer as much pain as women in dealing with bereavement challenges patterns of existing support services. Sexist assumptions (their own particularly) constrain many bereaved men to grieve in a more isolated, less conscious and invisible way, thus being easily overlooked or misunderstood by family, friends and professional support networks. Nowhere is this inability to share profound despair more painfully demonstrated than in the rise of young male suicide across Western society (Donaghy, 1997).

Many analyses point to the painful dilemmas faced by men who are caught between mourning their own personal loss while at the same time bearing the responsibility for maintaining the family's survival as a complete unit (Peddicord, 1990; Bryant, 1989; Cordell and Thomas, 1990; Cook, 1984, 1988). In contrast, we must also question conventional assumptions that bereaved people (though in practice overwhelmingly women) need to work through their emotions in order to 'move on'. The gendered divisions of labour in society are changing. As more women commit emotionally to vocational roles, as more members of the population live without partners, as more men occupy caring and nurturing roles, then gender stereotypes may be recognized as a very unreliable indicator of personal needs and responses to loss (Lupton and Barclay, 1997).

Our data offer a number of examples where social and employment factors appear more significant than gender roles in influencing grief responses. Women's professional employment, men's role as primary carer of the deceased person, and men's isolation from work or from other support networks, can each be identified as contributing to cases where women maintain self-control and men become severely distressed. One father we talked to had been made redundant just before his only adult son's death. They had shared a love of cycle racing and spent years together in this pursuit. He had hardly left the house in twelve months, and appeared to be more despairing than his wife, who had continued with her own part-time job.

Another father, whose agricultural work gave plenty of time for isolated personal reflection but very little opportunity for social distraction, expressed deep loneliness and a continuing sense of grief, three years after his son's death. His wife, in contrast, though deeply upset herself in the twelve months following bereavement, had 'managed' her grief through taking on a new career soon after the death. This effort to 'make a new life' for herself had, in her own words 'moved her on'. She acknowledged that her husband was

getting worse, reflecting the same mixture of objectivity and exasper-
ation we found in many men's views of their wives.

Traditional patriarchal expectations that until recently limited both
men's and women's emotional responses appear to be changing.
Popular culture increasingly offers examples of emotionally open men
and strong, independent women. There is more public debate about the
problems of men's aggression. In both fictional and documentary forms,
the media portray men who can weep and women who can be emotionally detached. These changes are reflected in a growing minority of
men who become involved in grief support groups or present themselves for bereavement counselling. We have evidence from bereavement conferences of The Compassionate Friends both in the UK and the
USA of men sharing intimate experiences and of being prepared to let
go of emotions in semi-public settings. They remain, however, a small
proportion when compared with women, and evidence suggests that
any man who occupies a caring or emotional function is still not generally perceived as 'normal' or masculine (Smith, 1998).

Loss and restoration: an alternative to gender categorization

Stroebe and Schut (1995; 1999) offer a 'dual process' model of grieving showing how both direct working through of personal grief and
'taking time off' from painful emotions play a part in successful long-
term adjustment to bereavement. They note the tendency for women
to concentrate on the former and men on the latter in dealing with
bereavement, but argue that, in combination, both are beneficial and
that, sooner or later, men and women will engage in both.
Momentary forgetfulness, brief distraction and involvement in new
activities, rather than being signs of denial, may provide temporary
relief and enable the 'restoration' of daily routines and a chance to
rebuild a more stable sense of self. Ruminating and feeling the distress of a loved one's absence, rather than being signs of a failure to
'let go', may provide the opportunity to work through unfinished
relationships and stock-take the contribution that a loved one made
to the bereaved person's life. Klass (1996) argues that such emotion
work, especially if conducted in conversation with others, helps
bereaved people create new ways of holding on to lost relationships.

It is the exclusive use of either of these orientations, they suggest,
that produces complicated or unresolved grief. Either continually
avoiding or continually embracing the pain of loss may lead to even-

tual problems. However, Stroebe and Schut argue that most bereaved people will oscillate between these two strategies for managing their grief, at times adopting a loss orientation while at other times 'taking time off' from the sheer physical pain of grief work. They argue that social context and the nature of the loss will play a major role in determining whether the bereaved person primarily swings initially towards the loss or towards the restoration orientation. Stroebe and Schut suggest that many widows need little help in facing their grief, but may benefit from support in overcoming problems of finance and the practical management of house and garden. Conversely, many widowers need little support in practical or domestic issues, but they do appear to benefit from support in exploring and expressing their emotional responses to their wives' deaths.

This simple model offers an alternative approach to gender stereotypes without losing sight of the continuing nature of patriarchy in modern societies. In cultural settings where individuals are encouraged to control their emotions, to think rationally and objectively and where work role is a central part of identity, it is likely that a 'restoration' approach to grief will be more accessible and supported by existing social networks. Bereaved individuals are more likely to remain within a 'loss' orientation if they were the primary caregiver of the deceased, if their identity was created largely around this role, if there are no valued alternative roles available and if there are few supportive social relationships outside of this lost relationship. These tendencies would be irrespective of the gender of the bereaved individual, yet, at the same time, cultural messages regarding appropriate masculine and feminine responses would inevitably have some influence on how these individuals make sense of their loss.

Conclusion

Work with trauma victims indicates the value of talking about stressful events and the feelings arising from them (Tehrani and Westlake, 1994). Evidence suggests that suppressing painful emotions following 'awful' deaths such as murder also complicates the longer term process of grieving (Rynearson and McCreery, 1993). News reports frequently describe men's reluctance to acknowledge that such 'debriefing' is necessary, confirming the male stereotype identified by Hart (1996) and Seidler (1991).

The uneasy relationship between women's emancipation and traditional patriarchy can be seen in the survival of 'canteen cultures' – such as in emergency and public services. Yet, as work and household patterns change, more men may feel 'liberated' to explore and express emotions previously identified as feminine. At the same time, the need for social order and its implications for emotional control in public, may influence more women to adopt masculine attitudes as they occupy more positions of power and gain equal entry to masculine occupations.

More positively, taken in conjunction with Stroebe and Schut's analysis, there may be increasing opportunities to combine the most useful traits of both genders. In grief work especially, men and women may be gaining the capacity to move between the need to express and feel, and to move on and reconstruct the rest of their lives. Practical ways need to be found for supporting bereaved men and boys in ways that they can understand and that do not challenge their self-identity. There is adequate evidence that they need such support. Conversely, maybe women and girls may also benefit from roles that enable them to 'take time off' from grief and from the assumption that they have to carry the major responsibility for society's 'emotion work'.

6 Poverty and Deprivation

Denise Bevan

Introduction

This chapter explores the implications of class and poverty in relation to loss, with a particular focus on death-related losses. Western cultural traditions present death as the 'great leveller'. Underpinning this belief is the view that biologically we share the same inevitable encounter with death and leave this life as we came, with just what we were born with. However, this commonly held assumption is challenged with the depth of growing evidence that people's experiences of dying, death and grieving are unique and diverse. The experience of death will be affected by differences such as gender, culture, race, sexual orientation, age and class (see Desai and Bevan, Chapter 4 in this volume). Although the major focus here is on death and dying, the analysis also has implications for a wider range of losses.

The central theme of this chapter is the argument that, not only do those disadvantaged through poverty and deprivation continue to experience inequality in their time of loss, but also these factors compound and complicate the sadness, loneliness and powerlessness of death and dying. This theme will involve exploring the relationships between class, power, citizenship and death to argue that those socially excluded through poverty have less authority to lend to their way of life and death, and thus, even in death, discrimination and disadvantage persist.

The discussion will consider various dimensions of poverty and deprivation – that is, how the personal, cultural and sociopolitical integrate and interrelate to affect this experience. The discussion will have a particular focus on how discrimination and oppression feature within the lives of those living in poverty, and how socioeconomic inequalities create and compound the difficulties not only of living but also of dying.

The analysis addresses the dynamic interconnectedness of social structures in terms of the personal, cultural and structural dimensions of inequality (see the discussion of PCS analysis in Chapter 4 of this volume). This contrasts with much of the historical literature on loss, which has tended to focus on individualistic accounts of how people adapt to loss (Walter, 1999). A basic premiss of the discussion, therefore, is the need to draw upon sociological explanations of inequalities in order to add to, and counterbalance, the evidence from medical and psychological perspectives.

Beyond the individual level

Critical understanding reached by exploring death from a wide variety of perspectives can unify and connect theories of loss to create consistency and common ground in which practice knowledge can respond collectively to death with authenticity and respect for individuality. Field *et al.* (1997) highlight this point, drawing attention to the difficulties of reductionism inherent in the biomedical model. They argue that an overreliance on such a focus would not address fundamental socioeconomic inequalities and the range of multifaceted social divisions. They illustrate this argument by pointing out that, while, for example, gender and ethnicity are important social divisions, they are 'not homogeneous but heterogeneous categories' (p. 22).

Similarly Clark and Seymour's (1999) literature review demonstrates a demand for a move away from the individualistic psychosocial and physically biased research to an acknowledgement of the importance of structural aspects of inequality and loss. Taken from this structural view, poverty and deprivation can be understood to complicate and compound all other disadvantages and inequalities (Jordan, 2000).

An important point to recognize is that the hardship associated with poverty and deprivation creates a range of external and internal pressures for those who are so affected. That is, in terms of external pressures, a person's experience of living with, or dying of, a life-limiting illness will be affected by their social location. Within this location, there will already be influential and established features of the individual's life. These features go on, despite having an illness and facing one's own, or a loved one's, mortality. Therefore, to understand the full extent of loss, the subjective and objective interface of internal and external pressures, which exist alongside the phenomena of illness, death and bereavement must be taken into account. This interplay of the personal and the social must be considered in relation to the overall experience and outcome of the situation if interventions are to be effective.

Thus, it may be that an expected and accepted part of family life with teenagers, for example, is to have difficulties managing the changes and demands characteristic of this period. These experiences, although difficult, are generally shared ones and considered to be a part of life. However, the individual's experience of dying, and the untimely death of a parent and the subsequent bereavement for this family, would undoubtedly bring with it what may seem unfair and insurmountable challenges. For an adolescent, this period of life is characterized by transitions, change and loss. Therefore, the tasks of adolescence – for example, becoming independent from their families and forming their own separate identity – will ultimately be more difficult to navigate along with the loss of a parent during this time (Rando, 1984). Similarly, the losses the dying parent feels may be all the more acute because they are dying before their children reach adulthood.

These losses must be seen not only in relation to psychological responses, but also within the cultural and structural contexts in which the death and bereavement occur. For example, there may be socioeconomic constraints adding to the sense of strain and loss of control. This strain may be the dying parent worrying about funeral costs and related expenses (Corden *et al.*, 2001). These worries may affect those who are bereaved – wanting to have a funeral that meets the needs of their grief but far exceeds the amount paid by state benefit funeral payments. It is within these challenges that each individual member and the family as a whole would draw on their internal resources and external supports to cope with this crisis in order to restore homeostasis and a sense of equilibrium (Thompson, 1991).

Factors such as poverty, class, gender, race, age and sexual identity can all be seen to have an impact on the life-chances and opportunities of those families facing death. The Black Report of 1980 (Townsend and Davidson, 1988) identified that health inequalities are related to class: higher incidences of infant mortality and chronic sickness rates, a higher rate of accidents, and: 'working-class people make more use of GP services for themselves (though not for their children) than do middle-class people, but they receive less good care' (cited in Thompson, 1998b, p. 118).

Thompson briefly points out some of the associated causes and factors within inequalities in health:

- poor quality housing, overcrowding and so on;
- poor diet linked to low income;
- higher rates of smoking in working-class groups;
- industrial injuries and diseases more prevalent within working-class groups;
- the stress associated with discrimination and oppression. (p. 119)

Inequalities in health are inextricably linked to sociopolitical inequalities (Jones, 1994). The constraints associated with poverty and class divisions have a profound effect on the conditions of daily living and the experience of coping with loss (Field et al, 1997).

It can be argued that many of the difficulties people living in poverty have are compounded by the fact that their socioeconomic position deprives them of opportunity to exercise the power and influence they need to deal with the problems they face. For example, in the UK, financial resources are available to those deemed as having a terminal illness with a short prognosis. This benefit is to ameliorate the extra costs generally incurred when living and dying of a life-limiting illness, such as needing better or special foods, extra heating or clothes. However, this small weekly allowance does not enable any significant buying power or control over their social circumstances.

Control of many practical elements can be lost, particularly for those who are socially and economically disadvantaged, just at a time when crisis threatens the basic needs of maintaining some security. For example, in order to meet the needs of the dying person, a family living in a property rented from the local authority may have to move to an already adapted property rather than be allowed to have specific adaptations to their existing home. This can have implications for retaining existing social support for the family and may also remove the family from the comfort of their familiar home and perhaps schools. Therefore, although this move may seem the obvious answer, it is also important that consideration of other factors is included in the decision-making process. In order that human services practitioners may be in a position to assist people in their attempts to access appropriate services, they need to be aware of how social structures relate to inequality. If these factors are not acknowledged and accounted for, there is a danger of reinforcing discrimination. By understanding how and why inequality exists, we can avoid colluding with it and thus make a contribution to challenging the status quo.

How these inequalities have developed and now present themselves needs to be understood in order to know where to start in working with the person within this structure. Understanding the roots and nature of inequality is important if professionals are to be able to maximize the potential of the current situation with their client, whilst also recognizing and challenging any discrimination. Answers to these important issues begin to form by understanding the sociopolitical and historical context in which people from all manner of backgrounds struggle to make sense of, and rely upon, a health and welfare system to meet their needs.

Poverty and deprivation

Given the contested nature of poverty, any discussion which draws on this concept must begin with a working definition of what poverty is, as a basis for ensuing argument and analysis. Although poverty is a highly debated concept, with different interpretations, the arguments put forward here are based on a conception of poverty as a form of multiple deprivation which excludes people from social participation (Roll, 1986). This view of poverty sees it as a form of multiple deprivation, in that it is not only about income, but also about equality and the rights of citizenship. Measurements of poverty from this viewpoint must therefore relate to the standards of a particular society, at a particular time. This view refutes the notion of 'absolute poverty' as too narrow in so far as it does not take account of Townsend's (1979) argument that people not only have physical needs, but are also complex social beings with obligations at the workplace, in the home, the family and the community. Roll suggests that this view recognizes that: 'It is not just that physical needs have a social aspect but that social needs should be recognised in their own right' (p. 9).

Evidence of class-based inequalities – for example, in accessing health services – highlights that poorer people do not have the same quality or quantity of care afforded to them as those of higher social classes (Benzeval, 1995; Morgan, 1995). An illustration of this inequality can be seen in the capacity and limitations of being able to choose where to be cared for, and where to die. This choice of where to die is often limited for those who are socially and economically disadvantaged. This is generally because of lack of social support; lack of financial resources; poor environment, such as inadequate housing (many new houses built today have just one living room compared to the older designs of having a separate dining room). This lack of space and ability to provide adequate facilities and privacy causes a lot of restrictions and distress for those families who wish to care for a person, especially when, earlier in their illness, they have expressed a wish to die at home.

This choice therefore depends on: having the support of informal carers who are able to provide adequate care within a suitable environment; the proactive support of a primary care team; effective communication within the primary health care team; and access for this team to specialist palliative care professionals if or when they are needed (Clark and Seymour, 1999). It is therefore apparent that there are many variables, which can be seen to affect the opportunity of choosing to die at home. The constraints of an individual's socioeconomic status underpin and influence all the above variables of choice and opportunity. As Bailey (1988) points out, it is unlikely that a poor household will have the additional resources to cope with a crisis.

Inequity is increasingly evident – for example, being able to be cared for at home relies on an individual's ability to resource their own care, despite compelling evidence that most people would prefer to die at home (Clark and Seymour, 1999). Thus, the dilemma is that, unless people have a suitable environment and informal carers to support them, or can afford private nursing care, they face the considerable risks of remaining at home without adequate support or entering reluctantly into twenty-four-hour care within an institution. These factors have also been identified as reasons for people having to be admitted into hospital, thus reducing the dying person's choice of place of death, resulting in succumbing to an institutionalized death (Hunt, 1997).

It seems that increasing numbers of people with palliative care needs are admitted into hospital immediately preceding death. A study by Townsend et al. (1990) of randomly selected patients with cancer who were expected to die within a year, reported that: '67 per cent (41) of patients stated a preference to remain at home if their illness became worse', and if 'circumstances were instituted to allow the choice'. This compared to 16 per cent (10) of patients who said they preferred to die in hospital, and 15 per cent (9) who said they preferred hospice care. Significantly, Townsend et al. report that of the 55 per cent (32) of patients who eventually died in hospital,

82 per cent would 'ideally have preferred to die elsewhere' (cited in Clark and Seymour, 1999, p. 158).

In order to understand why poverty limits choice and control, and how oppression features in the lives of those marginalized and alienated because of social class and poverty, it is necessary to explore the cultural and sociopolitical context. This alienation may be understood contextually by examining western cultural values. If, because of illness, disability, death or bereavement, people are judged as redundant and not able to participate in 'citizenship' as ascribed by western capitalist ideology – an ideology in which youth, productivity and success are valued – there will be elements of rejection and discrimination towards them, particularly where one or more of these values are threatened, or are not manifested.

This ideology is a powerful determinant of state provision for those in need – for example, the lack of statutory rights for leave from work because of bereavement. This relies upon each employer making a decision, and therefore leaves considerable scope for variation – depending on how compassionate and understanding the individual employer is towards the needs of bereaved people. As Abbot and Sapsford (1987) clearly identify, social consciousness is characterized by a set of values and beliefs. They argue that: 'there is a clear relationship between prevailing social structures, dominant ideology and the way society handles its deviants' (cited in Oliver, 1990, p. 43).

This illustrates very clearly how important it is that cultural norms are not accepted without first questioning how these norms may have the effect of disadvantaging certain people. For service users, the problems they are experiencing may well not be perceived in terms of structural inequality and oppression, but rather individualized and thus reduced to terms of individual pathology. Becker (1988) comments that social workers (and, by implication, other human service workers) are, in effect, part of this problem, as they tend to view poor people as victims, in fact contributors to their own difficulties. This view is accentuated by their clients' apparent inability to cope: 'As a group [social workers] appear supportive ... But as individuals their poverty awareness has tendencies towards hostility and prejudice' (cited in Bevan, 1998, p. 31).

This tendency to overlook poverty and deprivation is, of course, dangerous and neglectful. This is because, as already discussed, poverty is a cause of social exclusion, with those living in poverty being at risk of poorer health, homelessness and earlier death. As Jones and Novak (1999) argue:

The poorer people are, the less long they will live, the more disease they will suffer and the more stunted will be their lives than those of the rich. Currently this is reflected in the fact that in Britain infant mortality is almost four times higher amongst the poorest than it is amongst the richest of the population, while once beyond childhood, life expectancy is cut short by some seven or eight years. Although these consequences have only been reliably measured for the past 100 years, it has always been thus. That this is well known – and there are volumes of research, both official and unofficial, that document the consequences of poverty – does not make any difference. (p. 108)

These factors of poverty need to be acknowledged and taken into account within assessment, in order for planning to be effective. Walker and Walker (1998) argue that, because the majority of clients are poor, social workers come to see this as commonplace and therefore do not recognize it as a particular disadvantage or as an issue of discrimination. Further to this, they argue that, although social workers will often work with the person to help them to manage their poverty, they neglect to challenge and tackle the underlying structural causes.

Structural inequalities affect and reinforce attitudes, perceptions of self and others. Social and cultural customs and norms will affect the individuals concerned, their families and the professionals involved. These attitudes to self and others somehow disabled or suffering affect the quality and quantity of the service they receive. The reasons for this rest partly on what underpins the policies, which inform and provide a legislative base for social and health care – the ideological foundations. Thus dominant medical discourse which emphasizes an individualistic approach, tends to pathologize, rather than enable people to participate actively in determining how their needs could be met (Oliver, 1990, discusses how medical discourse affects the way disabled people are treated – see also Sapey, Chapter 9 in this volume). Being in need is something that is often viewed as a concern for charitable and sympathetic attitudes – a paternalistic approach, rather than one that addresses the issues from a more holistic social model.

This latter approach identifies the sociopolitical causes of personal situations and circumstances. Such a model encourages social change and widens the issue of individual need to one in which the question of how society can provide for the rights of its citizens is addressed. The social model would advocate for the rights of individuals – for example, welfare rights, thereby acknowledging poverty as a disadvantage to be dealt with. Dominant paternalistic views permeate throughout society on different levels, bringing a historical legacy of victim-blaming and non-deserving poor into both the macro and micro systems of contemporary society. Costain Schou and Hewison (1999) argue that, all too often, the research chosen by governments to inform policy is used to defend political decisions. They give the example of how one small section of Whitehead's *The Health Divide* was abstracted from its broader context of unequal access to conditions that promote health, to support the Conservative Government's policies promoting health as an individual responsibility. This approach of individualism and 'consumer rights' to health matters does not result in greater choice for people but increases the likelihood of inequalities in relation to health care services (Mohan, 1991).

These ideologies limit the opportunities available to a person managing loss – whether this is coping with an illness or bereavement. Thus, if the resources are available, and the person is well placed to avail him- or herself of what is needed, then the notion of individual responsibility may well produce a satisfactory outcome. However, this ideological framework does not account for a social and cultural difference in the way ill-health is managed. Anderson *et al.* (1991) comment on the interrelationship between these variables and the experience of illness:

> Dominant ideologies are interwoven into, and are reproduced in ongoing social interactions; they are used to assess how well one is doing. For example, tacit knowledge about the value of 'inner strength' and 'taking responsibility for self', provide the background for interactions in the patient–practitioner encounter. (p. 111)

Living within this sociopolitical context, people may understandably internalize these cultural norms, and may therefore come to feel that they have failed to manage their situation. They may view themselves as undeserving and may therefore not demand an equitable service. Recent decades have seen much discussion about when and how health and social care should be delivered, and in effect rationed. Personal details such as diet, whether someone smokes or drinks, whether they exercise, and whether they are obese have been analysed, debated and finally judged.

These debates should not focus solely on the behaviours of individuals to the exclusion of understanding the social context of health matters. For example, research indicates that smoking-related deaths have halved in this country in the last twenty-five years. However, the evidence highlights the fact that it is now poorer people who are more likely to smoke and are thus most likely to contract lung cancer: 'the difference in tobacco deaths between rich and poor people accounts for most of the inequalities in health' (Peto, 1998, p. 13). Such research could easily be interpreted as evidence of personal inadequacies leading to ill-health, with no account being taken of the wider issues of health promotion. Consequently, opportunities to reduce the chances of pathologizing continue to be missed.

These victim-blaming tendencies present difficulties when an individual also feels that they should accept their predicament. Radley (1989) explores how the meaning and significance of illness are culturally defined and constructed. This research linked heart disease patients' attitudes towards their illness with their socioeconomic situation. Radley argued that working-class people were more likely to be fatalistic about their illness compared to middle-class patients. Working-class patients were found to cope with the illness by denying its effect on their lives, whereas middle-class patients saw their illness as something that was to be managed. This is clearly an indication of how having the means to manage a situation is empowering and can affect the experience of the illness; the working-class person has less opportunity and power to control these life events, and is therefore going to have to accept his or her 'fate'. Perceiving a life event in this way may well be the best way of coping with this powerlessness.

Similarly, there are clearly very real class divisions in terms of expectations and the actual service that people of a poorer socioeconomic status receive. By examining access to GP services, we can see this very clearly and simply. Studies have identified that time allowed by GPs for this group of people falls short of the consultation time given to those patients from a more affluent socioeconomic group (Costain Schou and Hewison, 1999). This would mean less time to discuss the significance of the illness – for example, the psychosocial aspects. There would be less information given, yet it has been argued that those patients given more specific advice from their doctors may choose different treatment options from those medically advised (Simiroff and Fetting, 1991).

Referrals to specialists, including specialist palliative care services, can also be seen to be inequitable for poorer people (Clark and Seymour, 1999). To understand why, we need to examine what is important in accessing services.

Communication is a key aspect of determining how our needs will be assessed and respected. Codes of language are no doubt an influence on how we express ourselves and how these needs are understood and met by those around us (Bernstein, 1973). Language in relation to class can be either an advantage or a disadvantage, depending on one's social location. Bernstein's arguments of how the restrictive language used by working-class people disadvantages them have been sometimes misrepresented as a reason for educating people to speak standard English in order to be accepted by those in positions of power. This argument does not address issues of discrimination and oppression. Instead, it promotes assimilation rather too easily as an answer to a problem, which identifies and reflects a class system full of fundamental discriminatory attitudes. These attitudes exclude and disadvantage elements of society, rather than address the underlying structural and cultural problems of class division.

This discrimination is not limited to health and social care, as inequalities can be seen to exist in relation to access to areas such as: education; legal services; adequate housing; and financial services – the greater one's financial difficulties, the less flexible are the possible solutions (for example, consider how so many people whose income is above a certain level can expect to have relatively little difficulty in obtaining a moderate loan, while those whose income falls below that level are excluded from this facility). It is from this position that those that have been excluded have low expectations of their needs being met adequately, and subsequently experience multiple losses at many levels.

Assessment

We need to recognize the propensity to internalize oppression, thereby accepting a less than just existence. Assessment must acknowledge that identity is bound to sociopolitical location. It is not purely a psychological matter wherein people need to be helped to adjust to their circumstances. Professional assessments must take into account wider factors such as social location in order to understand how they impact on the delivery of anti-discriminatory practice (Thompson, 1998b). Berger (1966) comments on the way society influences and shapes the cultural norms we internalize:

> Only an understanding of the internalisation makes sense of the incredible fact that most external controls work most of the time for most of the people in a society. Society not only controls our movements, but also shapes our identity, our thoughts and our emotions. The structures of society become the structure of our own consciousness. Society does not stop at the surface of our skins. Society penetrates us as much as it envelops us. (p. 140)

It also needs to be recognized that one's sense of identity is often challenged with the onset of disease, major changes and transitions in life (Billington *et al.*, 1998). Challenges can be perceived as a threat and a crisis. Chronic and acute illnesses may result in the known phenomenon of 'broken identity' (Sutton, 1994). A person's sense of self and meaning-making systems are questioned, their ontological security and homeostasis threatened. Forms of oppression such as racism, ageism and sexism may already play a part in threatening this security, so these factors must be considered in relation to the presenting problem.

An important aspect of coping with loss is how a person perceives they are valued and cared for as a human being. A person who perceives that they are valued will find it easier to maintain a sense of hope and attach meaning to their life and death. Hope is a coping strategy often present in the lives of those confronted by an acute or chronic illness. Poverty, because of the stress and practical difficulties it causes, reduces the chances of these aspects being achieved, and it can therefore be argued that poor people are more likely to have a sense of hopelessness and helplessness.

It can be seen historically that the themes underpinning the studies of death, dying and bereavement have been mainly limited to the physical and psychological responses of an individual's experience, insofar as accounts of the experiences of living with, or dying of, a life-limiting illness are mainly from psychodynamic models, as are the intervention responses. For example, Kübler-Ross's (1969) concepts of the phases a person may experience whilst dying have been put forward as a process which people who are dying move through, and in which professionals can facilitate the experience in order to achieve a 'good death'. Similarly, other theories of bereavement describe stages and tasks which the bereaved work through, to reach a point where their loss is accommodated (Parkes, 1993; Worden, 1991). Other theorists, for example those from an interactionist perspective, emphasize the meanings we attach to death and dying, how people make sense of their experience and how this affects their social roles and identities (Field *et al.* 1997 – see also Chapter 3 in this volume).

Thus, by examining the historical nature of underpinning theory, it becomes evident that little account of the socioeconomic and structural elements of palliative care has been taken (Costain Schou and Hewison, 1999). Historically, explanations of the differences in health status and access to services focus on the fact that inequalities do exist and the reasons why this might be the case. However, these arguments and analyses do not expand to develop a framework in which political and structural changes can be addressed. If one considers the concept of 'need' as an example of this, it can be seen that the definition of need has also been traditionally narrowed to biomedical accounts and dimensions, rather than drawing on a wider definition which encompasses the structural and political components of the provision of palliative care.

Practice implications

The implications for practice include the dilemma of having a seriously ill person being asked to take part in a comprehensive needs and financial assessment. This obviously inconsiderate situation has been partly overcome by good practice referring to the guidelines of the National Council for Hospice and Specialist Palliative Care Services (NCHSPCS, 1993). The document emphasizes that the 'responsibility for financing the social and health elements of home care should be clearly established and agreed' (p. 2). The document cites the NHS Management Executive Circular, EL (92) 16, which defines terminally ill people as:

> those with an active and progressive disease for which curative treatment is not possible or not appropriate and death can reasonably be expected within twelve months. Such care and support may be provided in an inpatient, day or home setting, and should, wherever practicable, be available without regard to the individual's diagnosis. (p. 1)

It is known, however, that despite some improvements in palliative care services, there is still a shortage of funds and specialists in this area to realize the goals set by Calman–Hine and NCHSPCS (Costain Schou and Hewison, 1999). Recommendations from the Calman–Hine Report (Chief Medical Officers' Expert Advisory Group on Cancer, 1995) have focused on working in partnership with patients and their families. The importance of clear information, continuity of care, choice and guidance, with care being patient-centred are emphasized as crucial to providing a good equitable service. These recommendations have found themselves to be central to UK governmental NHS reforms identifying cancer services as a high priority to benefit from plans for investment. Strategies rising from this cancer plan aim to reduce inequities in service provision and tackle inequalities in health (NHS Cancer Plan, 2000).

Despite these recommendations, the developing arena of providing palliative care has been planned for on the basis of epidemiological studies (Clark and Seymour, 1999). It is therefore apparent that, from this basis, assessment of need would not account for psychosocial problems and the range of personal difficulties people with palliative care needs may encounter. An illustration of this common problem is the issue of transport to far off specialist cancer units for treatment appointments. The journeys themselves are often exhausting and weakening for patients – a strain for the carer, who may have to take unpaid leave to accompany their loved one, with the financial worries only partly met by a small inadequate reimbursement to those on Income Support.

Clark and Malson (1995) discuss the notion of need in relation to palliative care. They warn that it is too convenient to use a functionalist concept of need: 'that needs only exist where there is a service available to meet them' (cited in Clark and Seymour, 1999, p. 144). They argue that needs that are difficult to define or respond to may not be identified. They point out that this difficulty, of course, includes not identifying, acknowledging or providing for the rights and needs of those who are underprivileged, socially marginalized, excluded and generally unheard.

It would seem that determining need for individuals on the basis of epidemiological studies and biomedical models does not adequately inform policy or provide explanations in relation to the socioeconomic consequences of death, dying or bereavement. Such an approach does not address issues of inequalities at a structural level. The underpinning power that marginalized and underprivileged groups are denied and the way they are excluded from the means by which they could effect change will not alter until inclusive participation in policy development is developed (Field et al., 1997).

Conclusion

What we have explored here are the concepts and theories relating to, and underpinning, inequality, social deprivation and loss; relating how poverty equates with disadvantage and discrimination. This discrimination can be seen in the context of the personal, cultural and structural dimensions of living with, and dying of, a terminal illness and bereavement. I have argued that sociopolitical aspects of this situation are often not identified and explored, particularly from an historical perspective. I have further argued that, without taking account of these aspects, we cannot fully address the needs and concerns of people with palliative care needs. Predominantly functionalist accounts of the provision of

health and social services have produced narrow, service-led assessments of what is needed. The experience of loss may first be intensified
and compounded by existing inequality and, second, loss may be a
product of oppression and discrimination. Adopting a multidimensional
approach to loss and the needs of those with palliative care needs
allows us to build models of loss which acknowledge and respond to the
complexities different people may experience. Theoretical views of loss
have come to recognize a more critical approach that appreciates the
socially constructed nature of loss, rather than as purely a biological
and psychological phenomenon. Fundamental to this approach is the
view that there is diversity in the ways people respond to loss, that patterns of grief and mourning are culturally and structurally constructed.

Poverty and class-based discrimination can be seen as major sources
of inequality and injustice throughout the life course. Jones and Novak
(1999) point out the price we pay for allowing poverty to persist:

> Poverty and inequality are amongst the most fundamental human-rights
> abuses in the world today. They distort, corrode and destroy people's lives.
> They condemn vast numbers to intolerable conditions which are neither
> acceptable nor necessary in a world which has the capacity to provide
> every single person with the means of a decent, human existence. That this
> potential is not realised is not some inevitable mystery of nature, but rather
> a consequence of human agency. It need not be. (p. xi)

It is therefore essential that, in dealing with people who are dying or
bereaved, or indeed experiencing grief for any other reason, we
should be aware of the impact of poverty and deprivation and take
the necessary steps to address them as fully and effectively as we
possibly can.

Part Two

Arenas of Loss

7 Children and Divorce

Brynna Kroll

I wish I had a magic wand to wave it (life) all back to the way it was. It's a pity it isn't like a video that you can put back into the machine and wind back to the place when it was last good. (Naomi, aged 8, in Kroll, 1994, p. 155)

In this chapter, I explore issues of loss for children in the context of separation and divorce. This will be linked to attachment theory, mourning processes in children, the way in which children manage pain and the possible protective factors that may support a child through the experience of family transitions. I conclude by looking at the implications for practice raised by this particular form of family breakdown.

Although I focus primarily on the child's experience, because this is so interlinked with what happens for the adults concerned, some issues for parents are also discussed. This is particularly relevant when looking at mourning processes and the ways in which children and parents can be in very different places. They may coincide – in which case, mutual empathy and support are possible, although despair and stuckness are a danger. However, they may not connect in any way; an angry parent may be faced with a despairing child and the space between them may not be bridgeable. This is where professional intervention can be crucial, based on a clear understanding of the theoretical roots of this lack of connectedness.

My starting point is simple. Assumptions are made about children on the basis of their size, age and understanding; many people still believe that children below a certain age see nothing, understand nothing and know nothing (Kroll, 1994). This causes many separating parents to deny their children's feelings, either because they cannot believe they know what is going on or they do not want to do so (Hemmings, 1995; Mallon, 1998; Dowling and Gorell Barnes, 2000). This is in no way malevolent but a reflection of the fact that society often fails to respect the child's capacity for thought and feeling. Children are also relatively powerless, despite their power to evoke strong feelings in others; things happen around them and to them, many of which are beyond their control. Parental separation is an obvious example of this, often decided upon and enacted with no reference to the children and, in some cases, without warning, preparation or any kind of discussion (Mitchell, 1985; Wallerstein and Kelly, 1980; Curtis and Ellis, 1996; Swan-Jackson, 1996). Within this context, children often become 'invisible' to workers, in the same way that they can become invisible to parents, in the midst of their own pain and grief. Children's grief is therefore often not acknowledged, addressed or worked with and their behaviour can be either not understood or misinterpreted (Jewett, 1989).

Children also get used as pawns and weapons during the process of divorce. They can be primed, prompted, brainwashed, bribed, overindulged, castigated and rejected, depending on the requirements of the adults. Children, one of the largest oppressed groups at the best of times, can, in this context, be exposed to domination, manipulation and emotional abuse on a grand scale. To witness this as a professional can engender feelings of powerlessness and rage that are hard to manage.

A significant number of children now grow up within family units that do not conform to the traditional idea of the 'nuclear' family (Dowling and Gorell Barnes, 2000). Two in five marriages now end in divorce, with the majority of children remaining with their mothers. It is estimated that one in five children have experienced separation or divorce and, if current trends continue, 19 per cent of children within a marriage will experience divorce by the age of ten and 28 per cent by the age of sixteen (Rodgers and Pryor, 1998). These figures, however, do not reflect the true picture, as they do not account for the children of parents who do not marry but separate after living together (Dowling and Gorell Barnes, 2000; Rodgers and Pryor, 1998). Many children will also experience parental separation more than once.

Many families manage changes that parental separation brings and parents and children adapt to their new family construction. However, 100,000 children a year lose contact with a departed parent, usually the father (Walker, 1996; Kroll, 2000a) and this, as a variety of studies show, often compounds and intensifies the original loss and any feelings of rejection, and has significant implications for general child well-being (Wallerstein and Blakeslee, 1989; Holroyd and Sheppard, 1997). This has bearings on the consequences for what has been termed 'socio-genealogical connectedness' (Owusu-Bempah and Howitt, 1997) – the idea that a sufficient amount of knowledge about a departed person, combined with a favourable picture of them, has a significant impact on children's behaviour, attainment and self-esteem and that contact is an important vehicle for this. In addition, it is argued that:

> the severance of contact between a child and his/her natural parents encourages idealisation of the parent and fantasies of reunion, thus depriving the child of the opportunity to address the reality of the loss and its causes. (Owusu-Bempah and Howitt, 1997, p. 203)

Because separation and divorce are now so common, at least in white, western culture, there is a tendency to assume that this makes it easier to manage. I would argue that this can prevent professionals from responding to each situation as unique in its own way. This has particular implications when working with families from different races and cultures for whom the experience of separation or divorce and the stigma, embarrassment and shame that might go with it may lend a very different flavour to emotions and reactions (Jones and Kroll, 1998).

Throughout this chapter, 'divorce' will be used to mean either divorce or parental separation.

Divorce as a process

> Divorce is deceptive. Legally it is a single event but psychologically it is a chain – a sometimes never ending chain – of events, relocations and radically shifting relationships strung through time, a process. (Wallerstein and Blakeslee, 1989, p. 18)

Divorce is now generally seen as a type of bereavement. The fundamental difference between death and divorce, however, is, of course, the lack of a body to mourn; somewhere there is the continued existence of the 'lost' person, who may be deeply mourned, intensely hated or a cause of sorrow, resentment or bitterness, for whatever reason. This makes a difference to the process for all concerned.

Separation is rarely experienced with indifference; the loss, whether one initiated the separation or not, leaves one lost, too – at least for a while. Continued contact with the lost partner for the sake of the children can, as a consequence, be fraught with pain and littered with emotional land mines. Divorce and separation, of course, rarely happen out of the blue. Prior to the actual separation, there is inevitably a period where it is apparent that things are problematic. There may be acrimony, arguments, violence, distress, all or some of which may be witnessed or simply sensed by the children. The process leading up to the separation becomes increasingly significant since prolonged conflict and uncertainty can be particularly damaging to everyone, particularly children (Kroll, 1994). To ignore this is to oversimplify the whole phenomenon.

Equally important is the fact that the process takes different forms, and moves at different speeds depending on the people concerned. Our capacities to deal with painful situations vary depending on all the factors that make us different from one another. The timescale for recovery cannot be dictated by anyone – courts, lawyers, social workers, parents or children.

It is in this emotional climate, then, that the worker must operate, engaging with, managing and containing rage, despair, depression, distress, feelings of loss and grief, revenge, bitterness – in short, working with people expressing very primitive reactions to pain, disappointment and fear (Jones and Kroll, 1998). There is competition for attention, since the adults are often as needy as the children and it is sometimes difficult to resist concentrating on the former – who are usually more able to articulate their needs – to the detriment of the latter. Working with divorce and separation, then, calls upon a complex knowledge base. It is not only essential to know something about how individuals might behave under such circumstances but also to have a grasp of family dynamics, attachment and loss theory and child development.

The impact of divorce on parents and children

Separation rarely brings out the best in anyone, however much of a relief it may be. The range of emotions, so similar to those associated with other losses – denial, anger and depression – often undermine the coping, adult, parent part of the self. What the worker is then faced with is an adult in a bereaved and very childlike state, who is unable to see, or respond to the needs of the real children in the family (Hemmings, 1995). 'What about me?', one mother was heard to cry, 'all I hear is "what about the children?".' Well, I'm a thirty-five-year-old child. When is anybody going to listen to *me*?'

One of the consequences that flows from the abdication of the parent/adult role is that this becomes available to be taken up by the children in the family. The worker may find him- or herself in a roomful of adult children and childlike parents, all muddled up in one another's worlds. Even very small children may adopt an adult persona, and it is not uncommon to hear a four-year-old express concerns about maintenance, unpaid gas bills and unhoovered carpets. Adults, meanwhile, often retreat to earlier stages of development, resulting in unusual behaviour that puzzles and disconcerts their offspring. This may be characterized by mood swings, emotions very close to the surface and other changes – a series of new relationships, or a sudden, sartorial transformation from business suit to lycra. Everyone is finding their way, wondering what has hit them, puzzled about where and who they are.

In such a context, it is easy to absorb the pain, confusion and rage that is flying through the air. Feelings of depression, desolation, hopelessness, and despair can seem contagious. Yet, for the worker to understand what is happening in the life of the parent and to gain some insight into what life might be like for the child, he or she must be accessible to these feelings although not so overwhelmed that the professional self ceases to function. Denial of this dimension, although a tempting means of avoiding additional stress, is likely to detract from the quality of any assessment being made.

The child's experience

Research makes it clear that most children want their parents to stay together, however awful things may be (Walczak and Burns, 1984; Mitchell, 1985; Tugendhat, 1990), with the exception of those who live with abuse or domestic violence (Mitchell, 1985; Hester et al., 2000). Children are rarely told what is happening, or helped to talk about their feelings and often feel they have nobody to turn to, at what is invariably a difficult time (Cockett and Tripp, 1994; Curtis and Ellis, 1996). The worker therefore occupies a unique position in being able to provide a safe and neutral space in which children's voices can be heard and where loss and change can be explored, at a number of levels.

On a practical level, divorce can have significant implications for housing, lifestyle and general material circumstances. Indeed, economic and social disadvantage as a result of family breakdown has been acknowledged as a key factor in children's adjustment (see, for example, Rodgers and Pryor, 1998). Children may have to become accustomed to a parent who used to be at home having to go out to work, relocation may mean changes in environment, schools, friends, familiar landmarks – all important things that children cling to, in the face of loss. Routines may change, as may caring responsibilities; depending on how the parents cope, children may find themselves acting as confidante, partner, and co-parent. The practicalities of contact also have to be managed.

On an emotional level, children have to cope with the loss of a loved parent whose presence could be taken for granted, and who is now somewhere else. Grief is managed differently in all families and in different cultures and ethnic groups and this will affect the extent to which children will feel they have permission to grieve, to be sad or angry. Part of the loss may be the fact that the departed parent represents an important part of the child's cultural identity, and this aspect may become hard to hold onto without him or her there on a daily basis. Loss also occurs when the wider family is divided by the separation and links with the extended family may be stretched, undermined or lost completely, as members take sides in the partners' battle. Fears and anxieties about the future are also common. What will happen to me/us? Will mum/dad be OK on their own? If one parent can leave, does this mean the other might go too? The world becomes a wobbly place.

Emotions are also generated by changes in parents' behaviour in response to their situation. Children may feel angry, powerless, anxious, distressed and desperate to blame someone for what has happened. Feelings of guilt are also common – was it something I did? was it the way I behaved? if only I hadn't ... and the message that children are not responsible for what has happened sometimes fails to get across. Such feelings can lead to behaviour that it is often easy to misinterpret. Many parents see changes in their children as, at some level, a way of punishing them for what has happened or a child's desire to exploit a parent in a vulnerable state. What is more often the case is that the child is trying to manage a range of strong, complicated and often conflicting feelings – sometimes for the same person – and that the behaviour is simply a manifestation of that.

Attachment, separation and loss

Attachment between child and caregiver has long been recognized as the cornerstone of healthy psychological and emotional development, both during childhood and in later life (see, for example, Bowlby, 1988; Parkes, 1996; Howe et al., 1999). It is not just about physical proximity, but extends to include a child's sense of emotional closeness to a caregiver – the belief that they are there for them psychologically as well (Howe et al., 1999). As a consequence, 'attachment figures who are emotionally unavailable and unresponsive are just as likely to cause anxiety and distress as those who are physically absent' (Howe et al., 1999, p. 14). Parents' grief, anger or denial may often cut them off emotionally from their children's experiences (Hemmings, 1995); the child then not only loses the departed parent on a physical level, but may also lose both parents on an emotional one, at least for a time.

Within the attachment relationship, the child will develop what has been called 'an internal working model'. This has been defined as 'mental representations ... of ... worthiness based on other people's availability and their ability and willingness to provide care and protection' (Howe et al., 1999, p. 21). Different attachment experiences will generate or create different internal working models, and through these the child will gain a sense of him- or herself, other people and the link between self and others.

Loss will inevitably affect a child's internal working model (Brandon et al., 1998) and this may generate changes in attachment behaviour – the child's way of obtaining reassurance and protection at times of anxiety. As a result, children may begin to exhibit acute separation anxiety which may place additional strain on parents who may be managing separation anxiety of their own. These feelings can leave children in a very vulnerable state and reactivate behaviour from earlier stages of development. Children may become clingy, unusually interrogative – Where are you going? When will you be back? You won't forget to pick me up from school will you? – and skills attained may suddenly be lost: wet beds, tantrums, return to the bottle, inability to accomplish tasks that have always been confidently achieved, may all feature in this context.

Children and the grieving process

For most children the experience of loss following divorce will have all the hallmarks associated with bereavement (Brandon et al., 1998). For children this will often mean what Hemmings (1995) describes as: 'intermittent pockets of intense and profound involvement in the thoughts and emotions related to and generated by the loss' (p. 114).

In other words, children can be griefstricken one minute and appear to be playing happily the next; they move in and out of pain, according to what they can manage or, indeed, what others around them can manage. If the message from adults is 'being sad is not OK', this will clearly have an impact and other behaviours may come into play instead. Although the child may appear to be carrying on as usual, for some of the time, this is unlikely to be the way he or she feels inside; this oscillation between appearing to be coping and entering pockets of emotional turbulence is very much a feature of the 'dual process' of bereavement identified by Stroebe and Schut (1999). Although, when the child appears to be fine it is tempting to assume that they have 'got over' the loss, it may simply mean that there is a need for a break from the pain. It is also worth considering that it may only be in the neutral space created by the worker that the pain can be expressed and that, as a result, the parents may blame you for its emergence. It is not uncommon to spend time with an angry or distressed child who is then returned to their parent in good spirits because some of the pain had been expressed and contained (Kroll, 1994).

Of course, some children make it easy. They can and will talk about their pain and rage. Some will just show it, by moving anxiously from one parent to the other or trying to drag reluctant parents across the room to sit beside one another. Ben, aged four, was very angry and sad when his father left and showed it in various ways, both verbal and physical. In contrast, Tanya, also aged four, spent sessions rocking and keening, unable to play or to speak.

Children's grief in the face of loss has traditionally been described in terms of having distinct stages with interplay and fluctuations between them (Bowlby, 1988; Aldgate, 1988; Jewett, 1989) and some contemporary writers still adopt this 'stages' model (Brandon et al., 1998; Mallon, 1998; Daniel et al., 1999; Howe et al., 1999). These phases are essentially seen as states of being rather than rigid stages, which, rather than having a linear progression, take the form of a fluid, often vacillating process with no set pattern. Each 'state of being' is accompanied by a constellation of behaviours that need to be understood in the context of the grieving process, rather than being misunderstood as deliberately wilful, bad or provocative behaviour.

The value of these phases is to provide a framework by which such behaviour can be understood, contained and worked through. These states of being are described in broad terms as early grief, acute grief and integration, resolution and acceptance, incorporating various specific reactions within each one. In addition, Goldman (1994) identifies four psychological tasks to be undertaken in order for the child to adjust to the loss – understanding, grieving, commemorating and going on.

The first phase – early grief – tends to feature shock, numbness, denial, disbelief and alarm. Often children are anxious, cut off, and may harm themselves; denial can include literally covering ears so as not to hear, denial that the person has really gone, or rejection of the lost person as being of any importance. Denial of feelings as a way of denying the value of the relationship is also not uncommon – ('if I had really loved him/her I would be feeling sad, but as I'm feeling OK, I probably didn't love him/her anyway'). Busyness, hyperactivity, and the need for constant noise could all be indications of denial – examples of behaviour that is not only easy to mis-interpret, but likely to receive an unsympathetic reaction, particularly from an equally bereaved adult.

In this state of mind, what children need is some grasp of what has happened. Answers to some common questions – 'Why has she left?' 'Will he ever come back?' 'Will he/she still be my dad/mum?' 'Why has this happened to me?' – become more urgently required. For children of divorce another often unspoken question, reflecting a deep fear, is 'Was it my fault?' The potential for grasping what is happening is influenced by a number of factors: lack of coherent information; the power of 'magical thinking' (the belief the child can make or unmake things happen and is therefore responsible for the breakup – Jewett, 1989; Daniel *et al.*, 1999) and the use of euphemism (Goldman, 1994). Children need to be provided with a coherent narrative to enable them to grasp the story behind the event (Dowling and Gorell Barnes, 2000) and it is important that the parents are part of that construction. The assumption is that this needs to be the full facts in all their (possibly gory) details; this is not what is required. Rather, what is needed is a simple, age-appropriate account that leaves the child free of blame and guilt and secure in the love of both parents, who still have intact repu-tations. Parents may need support in constructing a 'story' in this way and the worker can play an important role here. Part of the story may also have to be the jettisoning of euphemism. Many children of divorce are told that absent parents are 'away working', 'will be back soon' or 'have gone on holiday' (Kroll, 1998). Young children in particular are concrete thinkers and will take such euphemisms quite literally.

The second phase, often described as 'acute grief', very closely reflects the stage identified by Bowlby (1988) as 'yearning and protest' and that described by Brandon *et al.* (1998) as 'searching'. In children this phase is often accompanied by periods of regression, preoccupation with happy endings, and is a constellation of emotions often reactivated by contact with the 'lost' parent. In this period, too, strong and power-ful emotions tend to come into play – sadness, anger, guilt – as well as a sense of disorganization, inability to concentrate, weariness and despair, often accompanied by a helpless, dependent bleakness. Anger may lead to the rejection of the parent who is still there and of the parent who has left. The latter case will have significant implications for the management of contact.

It is during this part of the process that there is a tendency both to feel lost and to get lost or fear getting lost or being forgotten, and this is linked to the searching, disoriented behaviour identified in other studies (Parkes, 1996). This can be reflected in children's play and research with children of divorce suggests that enacting scenarios where babies got lost or forgotten, getting 'lost' somewhere in the office and having to be found, or worrying about other people getting lost/disappearing were common ways of expressing anxiety about loss (Kroll, 1994).

The strong feelings associated with this phase are hard to cope with, particularly if, as a parent, you are struggling with strong feelings of your own which may be the same or may be very different. Many parents have felt that some of these behaviours, particularly those associated with regression, are designed specifically as attention-seeking or irritating gestures (Kroll, 1998). Anger is particularly hard to deal with and is less acceptable to those around you (Daniel *et al.*, 1999). Two of Goldman's psychological tasks are relevant here. The first is simply that of grieving – to deal with the anger and the grief so that the child feels that these emotions are contained, are seen as normal, as healthy reactions to something overwhelmingly sad, and are respected. The second is 'commemorating' – remembering the lost person and feeling free to talk about him or her. Contact is an obvious way of undertaking this commemorative task and will, in time, help the child to manage the pain of loss. Being able to talk positively but realistically about the lost person to a sympathetic adult will also help with this process, since this may not be possible with the resident parent. Of course, if contact, for whatever reason, does not take place, a further set of 'griefs' will need to be managed.

Ultimately the child can be helped to integrate the loss and grief, reorganize internal resources, come to terms with what has happened and derive reassurance from the capacity to have survived the ordeal. A crucial step in this process is a sense that feelings of anxiety, loss, anger, despair and sorrow have been validated. There is a sense of resolution and acceptance, although this can take a long time and it has been argued that for some, this point is never reached (see, for example, Wallerstein and Blakeslee, 1989). Much depends on the relationship between both the separated parents and the child and parents. Parental conflict, for example, makes the process much more difficult and sometimes impossible (Neale and Wade, 2000). If the lost relationship was good, the good bits can be held onto and taken into the future through contact. If the relationship was fraught or abusive, resolution is harder. If it falls somewhere in between, then the child may vacillate between a number of states of being for some time (Hemmings, 1995).

Because second marriages have a higher breakdown rate than first marriages (Rodgers and Pryor, 1998) many children will experience the equivalent of parental separation more than once. This may affect internal working models, capacity for trust and attaching anew, and a fresh loss may activate previous losses that are still unresolved.

Contact and the return of grief

Feelings associated with the early and acute phases of the mourning process can be resurrected by contact with the departed parent and many parents and professionals alike use this as a rationale for either stopping contact or reducing it (Kroll, 2000a,b). Sophie, aged eight, really looked forward to seeing her father. When it came to saying goodbye, though, it was unbearable; she tried every way she could to get him to come into the house, stay for dinner – anything to put off the moment when he walked out of the door, again. Her mother assumed that seeing him upset her and saw post-contact distress as a strong argument for limiting or stopping it. In fact, it was losing him every week that was causing the problem. What children like Sophie are telling us is that distress is a normal response to a traumatic separation which triggers all the feelings associated with the original loss.

Vulnerability and resilience

Children will vary in their ability to manage the strain of divorce, depending on their age, level of understanding, temperament, personal resources and levels of support from both inside and outside the family (Rodgers and Pryor, 1998), as well as their attachment histories and past experiences of loss (Brandon et al., 1998).

Familial and social factors contributing to children's resilience to the impact of divorce are varied. They include a positive sense of the departed parent, lack of conflict between the adults concerned, good relationships with brothers and sisters and a supportive family network (Cockett and Tripp, 1994). An understanding school environment is also important. Children, as I have suggested, need a coherent story about what has happened; this is even more critical where a departed parent ceases to be part of the child's life (Dowling and Gorell Barnes, 2000). This may be particularly difficult if the resident parent still has strong feelings about a partner and support and help to enable this story to be constructed may be a valuable intervention. It is also important to enable children to form a positive view about the new shape or form their family has taken.

Issues for practice

Working with family breakdown can be challenging for a number of reasons, many of which I have suggested above. Various sets of feelings have to be managed, not least the worker's own.

Children and parents may be at very different places in response to what has happened; the father may be spitting nails at the departed mother while the child keeps asking to see her every day. Bridging the gap between these two emotional states, so that the issues can be worked with, is a task well worth doing. This may mean giving everyone the space to talk about their feelings and may also involve interpreting each person's set of feelings to the other. Acting as a conduit in this way will help both communication and understanding. It is important to avoid taking sides, and to interpret children's behaviour to parents in a way that promotes empathy and understanding rather than self-blame and guilt. Equally important is supporting separated parents to find new ways of being parents so that something positive, albeit different, can evolve. This may include encouraging and promoting creative arrangements to enable children to maintain links with parents via, for example, shared parenting (Smart and Wade, 2000).

Supporting parents who have, for a time, lost their adult, coping self is a crucial task both in its own right and in relation to child welfare. Although the parental child can gain satisfaction from the new role, in the long term it is not helpful and will prove harder to change later when the parent part of the adult is ready to return (Kroll, 1994). Working with role reversal, and role confusion is part of working with mourning; in supporting the 'child' parent the child's right to a childhood is also protected. In addition, a range of assumptions may be made about grief-related behaviour based on culture or ethnicity. Such assumptions may spring from a host of places and could lead to fundamental misunderstandings about what is happening to the family in general and to the child in particular (Jones and Kroll, 1998).

In the course of working with family breakdown, it is important to avoid what has been called the 'cascade' model of intervention (Hemmings, 1995). This is the belief that pouring resources and support into the adults in the family system will automatically have a positive, knock-on effect for the children. Of course, it may help the adults to deal with their issues and establish a better co-parenting relationship. However, children are people in their own right and deserve a service too; investing time to enable grieving children to explore their feelings and their fears can help them to move towards coping with their loss and adapting to their new circumstances (Kroll, 1994).

Being exposed to the realities of children's lives, their feelings and their sorrow can be very harrowing. The temptation to rescue and reassure is strong. The dangers of becoming the ideal parent, the only one who understands, are real. The child who asks if they can come back the following day or go home with the worker is saying something powerful and important about their plight. While essential for assessment purposes, this type of communication can feel unbearable. This, then, is about understanding and managing children's pain and coping with your feelings – the resurrection of your losses, your own attachment issues, your own divorce. Children's pain can reach the parts that adult sorrow may leave intact – support and supervision are therefore crucial.

Many children do not need hours of therapy – simply moments of real understanding. Children's levels of grief will fluctuate and there is a limit to how long any of us can stay with pain. While it is important not to deny feelings or to minimize them, it is also important to help children to identify things that can help, people that can support them and things they can do to manage how they are feeling (Kroll, 1998).

Conclusion

Divorce and parental separation are facts of life which no amount of Government rhetoric is likely to alter. Everyone in the family will be affected, but the most vulnerable and powerless are the children. Understanding their experiences of loss and grief, managing their powerful feelings and enabling them to achieve either resolution or a way of being that enables them to cope are important tasks; at a time of significant need, they deserve an equal service.

8 Adoption and Foster Care

Mary Romaine

This chapter is an examination of the emotional journeys of children, birth parents, foster carers and adopters in family transition. It highlights the importance of supporting them in grieving for unrealized expectations of past relationships so they can bring an enhanced sense of self understanding and confidence to their futures and their future relationships. It is argued that children and adults are more able to manage their transitions and trust in their new relationships if they are supported in grieving for earlier losses. Moreover, new family relationships will be better aspected if practitioners are able to help adults and growing children recognize how their identity, security and ways of relating to people are necessarily bound up with their earlier relationships. It is the job of practitioners to help growing children and their parents or carers to come to a peace with their pasts so they can also come to a trust in their joint and separate futures.

Foster care and adoption services facilitate the building of new family relationships. Foster carers look after children who are unable for a time to live with their families: adopters become the lifelong parents of children who cannot be raised by their birth parents. Successful outcomes for children and families are more probable if we recognize that the positive aspects of building new families take place in more negative contexts of separations from or losses of existing relationships.

Children who prosper in supportive foster families are nevertheless still separated from their parents and siblings, and need support and clarity in the plans for their reunions. Confoundingly these reunions will thereby disconnect children from their foster carers, ending these supportive and sometimes close relationships.

Children secure in adoptive families have none the less been disconnected from their original families, with all that this implies in terms of certainty of identity, certainty in relationships and positive self-esteem. Their birth relatives who have permanently lost a child or sibling to a new, usually unknown, family may also have to deal with such negative emotions and personal uncertainties. Adoptive parents may have had to deal with distressing and uncertain experiences connected with not having had a child by birth, and from birth.

> Separation, whether temporary or permanent, from meaningful relationships precipitates an acute sense of loss. 'Grief' is the process through which one passes in order to recover from a loss. (Fahlberg, 1994, p. 133)

Moving away from our parents, our brothers and sisters, our friends, familiar environments at home and school, family pets, daily routines, and accepted ways of relating to others can profoundly affect our sense of identity, security and self-esteem, our readiness to trust others and the optimism with which we view our futures. We usually gear ourselves to making this move soon after our transition into adulthood. In some families, however, children and young people find they have to do so earlier. Some will have no memories of the move, some will remember every sound and scent of the event. Children in family transition will need helping adults around them to help with their uncertainties, their fantasies, anxieties and expectations.

Lowe *et al.* (1999) highlight the key role of those who support children and adults through the adoption process, as 'passage agents' – working to achieve a successful navigation from their previous social and family statuses to their new ones. They identify primary passage agents as adoption agency staff, with complementary roles being undertaken by those from the medical, legal and educational domains.

Triseliotis *et al.* (1995, p. 22) consider the partnerships supporting children and families temporarily separated in foster care:

> The social worker, as the agency representative, is the key and unifying figure in [the] dynamic relationship, holding the situation together ... but others ... are also of crucial importance ... psychologists, doctors, teachers and ... foster carers themselves.

Separations for fostered children

> Nobody understands how much I miss my family, however bad living at home was. People can't understand that a foster family are nothing like a

real family and that I feel so alone. (16-year-old-girl: Who Cares? Trust, 1993, p. 80)

All moves into and between placements at some level negatively affect children and young people, despite there being allied benefits for them. Schaffer (1996) comments:

> Children within an age range of approximately six months and five years are particularly vulnerable: any break in the bond whereby the parent is no longer readily available constitutes a considerable trauma for such children and especially so if it involves the child being looked after by unfamiliar people in an unfamiliar environment ... repeated separations have an effect which tends to be cumulative ... the more risk factors a child encounters the greater is the likelihood of long-term psychopathology. (p. 367)

Fahlberg (1994) advises that two factors positively influence moves into, through and out of the foster care system. These are pre-placement preparation for the child (and others) and post-placement contact with important people.

Preparation for placement will require that all participants give consistent, age-appropriate information to children, listening to them as they explore their uncertainties and feelings, perhaps arranging for them to meet prospective carers beforehand or at least describing them for the child. Children should know who will accompany them in the move and when they will see or hear from their family members afterwards. When they move, children should be able to say proper goodbyes with those they are separating from and to take familiar comfort objects with them.

Some children will spend only a short time in placement before returning home. Others will spend longer in care in a single placement. Other children will move several times. It is widely recognized that multiple placements significantly damage children's development. Fahlberg (1994) highlights that:

> Children with multiple moves during the first three years of life are particularly vulnerable to severe problems in the development of social emotions, carrying with it long-term implications for interpersonal relationships, conscience development and self-esteem. (p. 138)

Government requires authorities significantly to reduce the number of children who experience multiple placement moves (Quality Protects Programme in England, Children First Programme in Wales). These programmes include an allied objective of ensuring that 'children are securely attached to carers'. This may be easier said than done, even

where children and young people remain in long-term stable placements. Jackson and Thomas (1999) caution us that:

> We do not know how many children who remain in long-term care are
> likely to have experienced secure attachment in infancy, but it is almost
> certainly a minority. This makes it more difficult for them to become
> attached to substitute carers ... but paradoxically it also reduces their
> capacity to deal with loss and separation ... it is remarkable that so many
> children do, nevertheless, form warm, loving relationships with new
> carers. (p. 27)

Separation for parents

The majority of children being looked after in foster care will return
home, with the family receiving continuing social work support.
Bullock *et al.* (1993) studied the factors contributing to successful
returns, and included as a factor the nature of the separations that
had taken place at the start of placement:

> At the moment of separation, parents are highly likely to be preoccupied
> with their own problems and changes at home ... they may find the
> trauma of separating from their child overwhelming or may use the
> stress of separation as an excuse to avoid facing the problems that neces-
> sitated the child's removal. (p. 145)

The study highlights the importance of keeping the two worlds of separated children and their parents within reach of each other, avoiding a
mutual sense of loss that will be reinforcing for children and parents.
They recommend helping relatives and children anticipate and prepare
for their reunion – parents giving children information about changes
at home and both having shared timescales for reunification.

Separations for foster carers

The role of foster carers is changing from that of being solely a
temporary substitute parent to being additionally a member of a professional team providing services for a child being looked after by a
local authority. Ambiguously, of course, carers still look after
fostered children in their own homes alongside their own children.
Foster carers support the newly placed child who has just been
separated from his or her family or from the previous carer. They
contribute to managing those moves into placement that are well-

planned and prepared for: they also deal with emotional fallout when moves are made in emergencies and without warning. Sometimes a child's response to a move can trigger for foster carers memories of their own separations in the past.

At the other end of the placement, when a child or young person leaves, foster carers will almost always have an emotional response. Their major emotions may be positive – happiness for a child going home, satisfaction for a young person making a successful move into independence, relief at having completed a challenging placement. Often, however, these positive emotions can be accompanied by distress at their parting. Moreover, some children will have become particularly special for carers and when these children move on their grief can be quite intense. Edelstein *et al.* (2000) comment:

> Theirs is a 'disenfranchised grief': the assumption is that a foster parent–child relationship is not strong enough to warrant grief upon its dissolution, or that, since the foster parent knew all along that the relationship was temporary, giving the child up should not elicit grief. (p. 12)

Foster carers need the permission and time to grieve. It will be important both for themselves and for the next child being placed, that they are not still dealing with grief for the child just gone. It is also important that the local authority or foster agency provides its carers with training in issues of attachment, separation and loss. Carers should be encouraged within their training to develop awareness of their own attachment styles and the ways in which they cope with grief. The wider fostering family and the agency are partners in supporting primary carers when children move away.

Losses for adopted children and young people

> I was surprised actually (that I was going to be adopted). Any child would be surprised if they knew their parents were going to give you to someone else. Any child would be surprised. (Chantell, nine years: Thomas *et al.*, 1999, p. 33)

Many adopted children grow into adulthood entirely at ease with the fact of their adoption, with no apparent need to grieve for the loss of their first family. It is difficult to estimate the number of adopted people who search for information or who seek contact with their birth families but all indications are that they are a minority. Of course, of those who search and of those who do not, there is a range of psychological adaptation to their adoptive status. Howe and Feast (2000) found that non-searchers were more likely to describe their feelings and experiences positively (74 and 53 per cent). Both for those who were adopted as infants and for those who were adopted when older, there will be a psychological adjustment to the loss of their first family at some level as they grow up. For some children, losing their first family can create a profound wariness that it will happen again, and they will find difficulty in trusting and getting emotionally close. Some children will simply retain an awareness of the loss of biological continuity. Some, at times, when growing up will miss having the same 'status' or social histories as their peers.) Others will have experienced such emotional pain at and beyond separation from their birth families that they will need ongoing therapeutic support from carers and professionals, and in turn by adopters if their experiences are not to prevent their willingness or ability to make and sustain close relationships.

Many adopted people, irrespective of whether they can remember the move into their new family, grow up with distinct perceptions of the nature of the separation. Fahlberg (1994) suggests that the transition may be perceived either at the time or in retrospect as having been taken away from the birth parent, as having been given away by the birth parent or as if the adopted person him- or herself had in some way caused the move.

> Children who perceive the separation as being taken away, especially if there has been no preparation, are prone to chronic fears and anxiety (with) a diminished trust of adults and self. Children who perceive a move as being given away ... may have concomitant sadness and depression. If the child worked hard to 'measure up' but still faces a move, he or she will probably be angry as well. The child who believes they did something that caused the move may come to believe they are responsible for all subsequent events and should be in charge of all future decisions. (p. 145)

Adopted children can be helped in adjusting into their new families with age-appropriate information about why they could not grow up with their birth family, together with affirming messages about being securely a part of their adoptive family. Most children will be happy in their younger years with understanding that they are 'special' to and 'chosen' by their adoptive parents. At around the ages of seven or eight however, children will come to realize that the other aspect of having been chosen by their adoptive parents is that they had not been 'chosen' by their birth parents. Adoptive parents may need to help their children in these pre-adolescent years with a new ambivalence about being adopted. In adolescence many young people will reappraise their ideas of 'self', incorporating new roles and relationships with those of the past. Adopted young people will have additional dimensions to this process. They may need to make sense of information about their adoption in new and different ways – reassessing what the loss of their first family means for them and dealing with fantasies of how they may have been parented differently.

An adopted child's relationship with his or her birth siblings deserves special mention. Relationships between siblings can be the longest of family relationships. A shared history nearly the length of one's life can make the sibling relationship a uniquely important one. Brothers and sisters often hold insights, understandings and knowledge about each other that no one else does. For separated siblings a sense of loss can be accompanied by a profound sense of injustice. A survey of registered birth relatives (Harper, 1993) reported siblings of all ages expressing both sadness and anger at having been denied this important relationship.

Grandparents can also hold special importance for children and young people, at times being the one safe, trusted adult – close enough to confide in but distant enough to be unthreatening. For many children, in the period before a move into care, a grandparent can have been an important confidante or safe haven in a situation of dispute, abuse or neglect. In both temporary and permanent moves, continuing contact with grandparents can ease transitions and provide a continuum of security throughout children's growing years.

The concept of 'open adoption' was developed in recognition that information and understanding about our origins – the families we were born into – contribute to a holistic, integrated sense of identity. While almost universally endorsed, open adoption in practice has not been without its problems. How do we give affirming messages about origins in circumstances where children have been conceived in violent attack, or of incest or where there is no available information about paternity? Less dramatically, but potentially no less important for children's positive sense of self, is the need to help children deal with the knowledge that they could not remain with their birth families and be safe or be well cared for by them.

Children and young people affected by adoption should always be offered 'direct work' on issues of identity. Direct work aims to facilitate communication with children and young people, to allow them to explore with a helping adult their emotional connections with changes in their lives, past, present and forthcoming. 'Life story work' is a specific area of direct work in which the child or young person and the adult helper engage co-operatively in chronicling the child's past life, perhaps giving more attention to specific periods. The aim is to help the child come to a better understanding of events, of other people connected with these events and of themselves.

Many black or mixed heritage adopted young people who are adopted by white parents describe their sense of loss of their black identity or of 'belonging' to their white parents. Howe and Feast (2000) found that more transracially placed people reported feeling 'different' than did white same-race placed people (71 and 48 per cent). Children adopted not only transracially but also from other countries will have additional needs in terms of integrating their identity. Samwell-Smith (2000) comments:

> Adoptees can feel isolated because of their concern about being 'special' and being different from their peers. This is especially apparent in intercountry adoptions because they are usually of a transracial nature ... isolation ... often occurs as a result of racism. Post-adoption services should be prepared for an adoptee to feel this way, and therefore have appropriate support services ready in anticipation of any problems. (p. 494)

Adopted children grow to understand that, although the loss of their first family is permanent, it is in a sense retrievable. Usually the individuals they are separated from are not dead. Brodzinsky and Marshall (1990) point out that, in terms of the grieving process, the adoptee does not consciously accept the permanence of the loss.

Jewett (1982) offers constructive guidance that has relevance for supporting children and young people through and beyond separations and losses:

> Because every major loss disrupts the development of self esteem [and] the smooth progression of life ... recovery from such a loss requires that damaged self esteem be repaired ... First the child must understand that he [sic] was born to a mother and father; he must know who they were, why he was separated from one or both of them ... he must experience and share any strong feelings of anger, sadness, guilt, or shame that he has been holding back. Second the child must know what persons or families have cared for him if he has lived away from his birth parents ... why did he go to those places and why did he leave. Third the child must say goodbye, directly or symbolically, to past caretakers. Fifth the child must get ready to face the future with increasingly diminishing concern about the past. (pp. 129–30)

Losses for birth parents

There is comparatively little researched information about how birth fathers experience the loss of their children through adoption.

Research suggests that both relinquishing birth mothers and those whose children were removed, experience similar emotions connected with the loss of their children – principally sadness, guilt and anger (Hughes and Logan, 1993; Mason and Selman, 1998).

In most cases the resolution that professionals seek is for birth parents to become accepting of their loss. This 'becoming accepting' may have dual meaning. If a birth mother relinquishes her baby in adverse circumstances, she will be helped to accept that she did her best for her child, that her child will have a good – a better – life and her child's new parents will have been given a most wanted and precious gift. If, on the other hand, her child was removed because the child was being abused or neglected, a birth mother may be expected to accept that she has forfeited her right and privilege to be a parent, that the child had a right to be cared for and safeguarded and adoption was the appropriate way of ensuring this for them.

Adoption agencies are required (Adoption Agencies Regulations 1983. reg7) to provide a counselling service for birth parents to ensure they are aware of their rights and responsibilities, that the nature and implications of adoption are fully discussed and alternatives to adoption are realistically explored. For many, the offer from social workers of 'counselling' is difficult to accept, especially if offered by the same workers or agency that have been instrumental in removing their children, when it can be viewed as 'adding insult to injury'.

Information about how their child is progressing can help some birth parents. Some will simply want to know that their child is alive. Some will want more information about their welfare and progress. Birth parents have no legal rights to information about their adopted children, but an increasing number of adoption agencies are prepared to give non-identifying information in some circumstances; some will pass on a letter from the birth parent to the adoptive family or will place one on the child's file.

It is important for professionals to work in the context that counselling for birth parents is not a one-off event during the process of adoption. Many birth parents report their ongoing or intermittent need for sensitive, empathetic support, perhaps at particular times. Macmillan (2001) describes Susan relating the overwhelming emotional impact of her reunion with her adult birth son:

> I came to realise that I'd managed to survive the previous 24 years by believing I'd done the best thing for him – not that I'd ever really believed it but I'd persuaded myself so I could live with myself.

Self-esteem can be a distant prospect for many birth parents. The reality of loss and failure can be overwhelming. Fratter (1996) describes Beverley's decision to place her daughter Claire for adoption: '(I felt) totally worthless ... I felt desperately sad. I was made to feel as if I was "mentally defective"' (p. 150).

Being supported to be involved in planning for their children's futures can be positive for many birth parents. Beverley was determined she would have a say in who would adopt Claire: 'I felt I was able to be a responsible parent in choosing what I still regard as an ideal family for Claire. This lessened the pain' (p. 151).

Birth parents can find it affirming if they are able to give 'parting gifts' to their children. These may be mementoes of their time together, or cards or letters expressing their feelings about the life-long parting, or wishes for the children's futures. Many birth parents provide information about the family and the children's early lives for the adopters to share with the children as they grow up. Sawbridge (1991) comments:

> Many birth parents could be helped to do something like this, and to express some of the love and sorrow they feel, instead of being left thinking that all they had to show the child had been anger or abuse. ... Birth parents ... have made or have had made for them the hardest decision any human being has to make. (p. 125)

Losses for adopters

Many people come to adoption having learned at some time in their relationship that they are not able to have children through birth. It will be important for them and their future adopted children that they can be supported in recognizing what this loss means for them as individuals and as a couple. They will need to explore the impact of any fertility treatment. They should additionally explore what it will mean for them to be no longer childless, but still infertile. The emotional journey from wanting a child by birth, to wanting a child by adoption, to wanting *this* child by adoption, can be long and complicated.

Some prospective adopters are single men or women. Many children are successfully raised by single adopters and, indeed, for some children this will be the placement of choice. Owen (1999) highlights that some single female adopters who were infertile had had additionally to come to terms with the 'desertion by the partners who had hoped for natural children by them. ... Sometimes it had been the very act of considering adoption that had caused a male partner to leave' (p. 34).

Agencies are becoming more open to considering applications from same-sex couples. There is evidence to suggest that, although lesbian women and gay men may have had to deal with homophobia in their families or elsewhere, they may not have had to deal with the same experiences of loss as other adopters. Hicks and McDermott (1999) reported that:

> for more than half of the contributors [to their study] fostering or adoption was their first choice in considering ways of having children, which had nothing to do with issues of 'childlessness' and the failure to conceive a child biologically. (p. 149)

Adopters frequently report having thought about adopting for a long time, sometimes for years, before they contact the agency. Owen (1999, p. 32) identifies 'in many cases' personal changes involving loss in the time immediately preceding enquiry about adoption. These changes include a partner ending a relationship, the death of a family member, grown up children having moved away or 'simply, of spent (lost) youth'. Sometimes adopters had recently lost touch with family friends and they had come to realize that they specifically missed having children or young people around.

An assessment of applicants' suitability to adopt will always explore their motivations. It will specifically explore how applicants have experienced losses of important people in their lives and how they responded emotionally and behaviourally at the time and over time. Assessment will involve seeking to come to a view with applicants about how their experiences and coping responses might affect their parenting of an adopted child.

As adopted children are likely at some time to have questions and emotions around their own separations and losses, adoptive parents who can reference their own experiences may feel more able to help. On the other hand, assurance will be needed that applicants are not coming to adoption in active grief – that the feelings of loss that are current for them will not impede their ability to understand and respond to their children's separate and unique emotions.

After what can be a long period of waiting before they have children, adopters will understandably seek to establish, fairly soon after placement, a close, loving relationship with their children. Some children settle naturally and quickly into their new families. Other children take longer. They may have come to adoption after having been unsettled for some time. Perhaps they have had numbers of moves between home and foster care, or between placements, and had limited opportunities to sustain relationships. Children with these experiences may have developed skills in sequential, superficial relationships at the expense of close, enduring relationships. It may be some time before they are able or willing to integrate fully into the adoptive family. Watson and McGee (1995) report adoptive parents' descriptions of the emotional distance still taken by their children after some years: 'I think his view of himself is partly as a member of this family and partly as a free agent outside the family. He is ... like a lodger' (p. 12).

For most adopters and children, the 'visiting child' period is a short stage to feeling like a 'forever family', but for some it is a longer stage, and adopters can find themselves reconciling to parental relationships that are qualitatively different from those they had envisaged. Adopters can be helped to remember that it usually takes a time for people to develop love for one another: for children who have been serially separated from those they were close to in the past, it can take much longer.

A real difference for adoptive parents is a loss of privacy in having children. Not many people will have anticipated they would start a family with a phone call to someone they do not know. During the assessment period, very personal issues are shared with a social worker and described in a report submitted to an independent panel and the adoption agency. Assessment *is* intrusive in that applicants are facilitated to intrude their own psyche, getting close to issues they may have previously dealt with by creating distance. Continuing post-adoption support is becoming the norm, and it is not easy to parent in the context of attending professional meetings to monitor how you are getting on. Professionals need to manage the relationships and interactions sensitively, while applying objective professional judgement in the process.

Many adopters find to their surprise that they grieve for the weeks, months or years of their children's lives before they were placed with them. These feelings can be compounded if their children had experienced neglect or abuse in their birth families. Preparation courses and post-placement support will assist adopters in accepting their children's separate early lives – both birthdays and adoption days are happily celebrated and adopters integrate received stories of their children's early lives with their own shared memories.

Separations of children and professionals

Jewett (1982) reminds us that those who work with children will need to be aware that, when the work is concluded, they and the child will themselves be separating:

> If you help a child who is not your own ... you will probably become a trusted friend and source of support. Because the child has only recently resolved one loss, [you] must be sensitive to the child's vulnerability when terminating the relationship. Like any loss, separation from the helper should be expected and gradual. It should not leave the child ... feeling helpless but should be planned with the child's participation, should allow the child to express any sadness or anger that he feels at the parting, should enhance the child's self esteem, and should leave the child feeling strong and confident about his ability to cope. (p. 138)

Adults who work with children and young people who are in family transition should take care to be sensitive to the pace needed by the individual child. Children may need to approach some emotional issues with caution, tentatively exploring their understanding and feelings; they may need to revisit some issues many times; they may need simply to confirm for themselves the circumstances of separations; they may seek to understand how others feel about being separated from themselves.

Children and young people need to be able to believe that, over time, they can come to terms with difficult separations and should be helped to feel they have a right to their emotions connected with them. If we can help them in their explorations and understandings of family partings in their childhoods they will gain confidence in experiencing and weathering both the expected and the exceptional separations and losses they will inevitably meet in their adult lives:

> I feel a bit more confident in myself ... it's just really knowing more you're able to make a better judgement of what their lives were like and why I was adopted. (Leanne: Howe and Feast, 2000, p. 49)

Practitioners need to help children, their original parents, their new carers and adoptive parents integrate their complex heritage of relationships with the positive aspects of creating their futures. Birth parents of children in temporary foster care need to be able to manage the inherent emotional distance and yet to strengthen their parental roles. Birth parents of children being adopted need conversely to be supported in being able to grieve and mourn in relinquishing their children and their role as their parents. Support for foster carers crucially must address their mixed emotions when children move on and their anxieties for the children's futures. Many growing adopted children will need support in understanding the nature and reasons why they could not be raised in their original family: some adopted people will not seek such understanding until they are older – many others will be content with minimal information about their origins. Adopted children and young people may need focused support in integrating their dual family identities or in dealing with the permanent loss of family members associated with their sense of well-being, security or self-esteem. Practitioners working with prospective adoptive parents will need to support their journey in resolving previous expectations of becoming parents by birth. They will specifically need to support them in being parents of, but genetically unrelated to, their adopted children with all that this entails both emotionally and practically. Finally, supportive practitioners need themselves to be able to move appropriately out of the lives of the children and adults they support. This separation should itself model positive transition, and further add to the abilities of those involved to manage their future life transitions in benign and positive ways.

9 Disability

Bob Sapey

In 1988, Raymond Berger, Professor of Social Work at the California State University, published a paper in the magazine *Social Work Today*, which dealt with the issue of working with people who had experienced some form of traumatic loss. Whilst primarily addressing a social work audience, this paper dealt with the ways in which a wide variety of health and welfare professions work with disabled people. The paper was significant for two reasons. First, it was quite extensively researched in comparison to most articles that appeared in that or other weekly professional magazines. Indeed, the following week one reader cited this paper as partly responsible for him finding that edition to be accurate, practical and analytical. However, the second reason for the paper's significance was the strength of response it received from Mike Oliver, now Professor of Disability Studies at the University of Greenwich. He bemoaned the disablism within Berger's paper and in the magazine's decision to publish it, and compared it to having:

> topless social workers on page three as a means of combating sexism in social work, or a pictorial history of the black and white minstrel show as a guide to anti-racist practice (Oliver, 1988, p. 12)

Why should a paper on loss, considered by one person to be accurate, practical and analytical, lead to such a response?

I should say, before moving on to look at the content of this argument, that at the time of its publication I was chair of the editorial board of *Social Work Today*. Whilst that did not involve me in the decision to publish the paper, for this was entirely an executive task, it nevertheless gave me some insight into the intentions and motivations of the editorial staff. This was a period of time in which *Social Work Today* was attempting to publish positive stories about

139

oppressed groups of people. We felt that a focus on the ways in which racism, sexism and other forms of oppression operated within the welfare arena was certainly necessary, but that without stories that placed people within mainstream activities, the overall tone would always be negative and would reinforce the view of certain people as solely victims. Resources had been invested in this, and everyone involved took the policy seriously. So certainly, at the very least the decision to publish Berger's paper would have been taken by someone who had some awareness of the nature of overt disablism, and therefore it was not an intentionally oppressive act. The issue was more subtle and concerned with the ways in which theories of loss had been felt to add a degree of professionalism to the caring task but, in the process, were also partly responsible for some of the ways in which health and welfare workers were disabling people with impairments.

Berger started by defining traumatic loss as including injury, illness, being a victim of crime, having a close relative die or being disabled. However, he then went on to use the phrase 'traumatic loss and disability' in a way that combined the two, and which made the assumption that to be disabled necessarily meant to have suffered a loss. He also argued that it was a major role of professionals to facilitate coping in such circumstances. His review of the literature on loss suggested that initial denial is common, as people's ability to perceive the reality of their situation is impaired. People were also said to report an inability to feel, and that they experienced emotional detachment. These were said to be normal and to constitute a first step toward integration and acceptance.

The psychological analysis was continued as Berger explained how those who appear to cope well may break down in the future following relatively minor events. The social worker, and by implication other human services professionals, is encouraged to identify this possibility in both the 'survivors' and their 'caretakers'. He suggested that the professionals involved might even undertake preventative work through educating groups of people thought to be most at risk of experiencing loss. He went on to describe those who experience loss as victims, and seemed to suggest that this was often the result of an irrational self-blaming process. While social workers are expected to deal with some of this, he also recommended counselling from clergy when such blaming has a religious basis. He argued that social workers and related professionals need to help people to 'bear witness' as a form of therapy. Berger also suggested that it is often professional workers who restrict disabled people by encouraging them to have lower expectations, but that he could cite examples of individuals who had overcome such tragedies and achieved great things.

For those with an understanding of the social model of disability, the reasons for Oliver's objections will be clear. The social model of disability had been developed as a response to the dominant understanding of disability as a deviation from the norm. It argued that disabled people experience oppression, rather than loss, and that solutions lay in political change, not in the acceptance of limitations through the psychological adjustment of individuals. Some five years earlier Oliver had argued that the application of psychological theories of loss to the understanding of disability was prominent in upholding the individual model of disability within welfare, despite the considerable evidence from disabled people themselves, which showed that they did not necessarily experience their impairment in this way (revised in Oliver and Sapey, 1999).

Furthermore, the ideas being presented by Berger constituted a sort of Catch 22 situation. If a disabled person were to deny that they had experienced impairment as a loss, they were in denial, rather than not having experienced their impairment in this way. The following extract from a textbook of the era, which took a Kleinian approach, illustrates how these concepts of loss and of denial were to be combined in work with disabled people:

> Illness and accidents at any age may confront us with slow or sudden loss of abilities. Denial of the limitations imposed can only lead to a superficial adjustment, which hides underlying persecution and depression. It is only when the work of mourning has been done and the anger, despair, and depression are eventually mitigated by love and courage, that the individual can go forward. If anger and despair predominate permanently, the individual regresses to an earlier stage of development, becoming self-centred, self-pitying, with a chip on his shoulder and begrudging others their freedom, or infinitely demanding of their time and attention. If the loss can be admitted, mourned and accepted with courageous resignation, a heightened appreciation of the remaining gifts and opportunities can lead to development in a different direction. (Salzberger-Wittenberg, 1970, p. 106)

The dismissal of the possibility that a disabled person might not experience loss, and the assertion that they need to adjust in this way, indicates an ideology of superiority on the part of non-disabled people. As Finkelstein (1980) has argued, the assumption that a disabled person had suffered a loss was: 'a value judgement based on an unspoken acceptance of the standard being able-bodied normalcy' (p. 12).

This theory, which argues that the individual who has experienced loss should progress through a series of stages in order to reach the point where they can begin to lead some new form of fulfilling life, fails to take account of the actions of non-disabled people who may not have made the same progress, and who make up the bulk of the social environment within which disabled people have to live. Slack (1999) describes this dilemma in the following terms:

> Communication with new people can never be fresh and barrier free, because they draw on their visual sense first and take the cue from there. They have made some judgements already because they are privy to visual information about me which they then feel at liberty to comment on. The opening to a conversation will mostly be, 'how long have you been in that wheelchair?', or 'what happened to you?' Some people feel they have a natural right to hear my life story, whether I wish to tell it or not. This poses serious difficulties in new acquaintances because the agenda for the conversation has been pre-written by someone else. The effect is to block the possibility of opening the conversation with equal information sharing about each other. (p. 33)

In this sense, the aim of adjustment, the development of life in a different direction, is in fact a fallacy, because the social environment within which disabled people live is dominated by non-disabled people's failure to accept impairment as anything other than a tragedy. The primary cue for many non-disabled people in their interactions with disabled people will be the latter's impairment and, in this sense, what disabled people are being asked to adjust to, is the failure of non-disabled people to accept them in ways that they would accept other non-disabled people. It is the impairment that continues to dominate the individual's characteristics in the minds of non-disabled people. Thus, placing the responsibility to adjust on the person with an impairment might itself be viewed, from a Kleinian perspective, as the transference of anxiety from non-disabled people to the disabled person.

Abberley (1991) accounts for the dominance of theories of loss in the psychology of disablement, by the fear of non-disabled people and their perception of impairment as a form of death. He argues that this fear runs so deep that it is almost impossible for disabled people to convince non-disabled people that this is not the case and, as such, the scientific credentials of traditional loss theories must be questioned. He concludes that:

> If disabled people display psychological abnormalities it is because they have been socialised into such traits ... Disabled people do not need to deny the individual psychological costs they pay, rather we need to iden-

tify them as a most directly experienced aspect of oppression, and dispute not the existence of psychological distress in disabled people but the kinds of causal account that are produced. (p. 4)

From a political perspective, we should also bear in mind Finkelstein's (1980) argument concerning stigma, in which he points out that the signs borne by slaves were in fact placed there by the slave-owners for economic reasons, to make it harder for them to escape. Thus it is wrong to reverse this, as he argues Goffman did, so as to suggest that there is something inherent in the person with the stigma that lies at the cause of the problem:

> it is a distortion to view the person who has been forcibly branded so that he or she permanently carries a stigma as the 'signifier' of a bad moral status. This is to invert the real social relationships whereby the one who assigns the stigma is the 'signifier' and the one who is chained and forced to bear the oppressor's views of himself is the bearer. To say the bearer of suffering is the 'signifier' of attributes assigned to him is to take the standpoint of the oppressor in the slave/master relationship. (p. 19)

Rather, we need to regard those theories of loss and bereavement, which require disabled people to follow a particular pathway in order to achieve some form of specified recovery as the imposition of the views of the slave-owner, in this case non-disabled theorists. The other major criticism Oliver made of Berger's paper was that he had failed to review any of the literature that was critical of the ideas he was seeking to promote. Others had come to different conclusions:

> Our review of the available literature suggests that a great deal of variability exists in individual reactions to negative life events, both within a particular life crisis and across different crises. We have found little reliable evidence to indicate that people go through stages of emotional responses following an undesirable life event. We have also reviewed a substantial body of evidence suggesting that a large minority of victims of aversive life events experience distress or disorganization long after recovery might be expected. Current theoretical models of reactions to aversive outcomes cannot account for the variety of responses that appear. (Silver and Wortman, cited in Creek et al., 1987, pp. 20–1)

The central role of theories of loss in informing the individual model of disability has meant that few writers within the disability studies field have considered them to have any merit. Instead, academics have looked to sociology, and perhaps social psychology, for an understanding of how people might experience the onset of impairment. Oliver and his colleagues (Creek et al., 1987) had already argued that a more appropriate means of understanding the reactions of people to such change was through viewing the onset of impairments as significant life events. This approach does not deny the impact of impairments, but it questions the implications that traditional loss theories have for those who do not conform to the phases of grief:

> Clearly, breaking one's back or neck may have tragic consequences for some individuals but as most people appear to cope with such a happening, such coping can thus only be explained by reference to such unscientific notions as the indomitable nature of human spirit. This gives rise to the 'super cripple' phenomenon where those who cope are ascribed with heroic characteristics and flies in the face of the everyday realities of people with spinal cord injury who see themselves as ordinary people coping with extra-ordinary circumstances. (Creek et al., 1987, p. 19)

The argument for viewing the onset of disability in terms of significant life events is that it is possible to include the impact of impairment, the social responses towards people with impairments and the meanings that individuals attach to what is happening to them. It is this social interactionist aspect of meaning which allows for the development of the notion that events may be significant, and therefore to expect responses to be different according to the circumstances of each individual (see Chapter 3 in this volume). Indeed, one of the conclusions of this study was that: 'There was a considerable variety of differing personal responses to spinal injury which could not have been predicted using the generally accepted indicators' (p. 418).

Creek et al. argued that a wide range of personal, social and economic issues need to be considered when attempting to understand people's responses to traumatic events and that the onset of impairment should not be considered in entirely different ways to other significant life events. These could include divorce, moving house, the birth of a child or the death of a relative. In some instances these events may be stressful, but nevertheless positive, while for others they may not. The point is that a person's response to such events will depend upon their individual circumstances, both in terms of how they may have constructed the possibility of impairment, preceding its onset, and in terms of their personal, social and economic resources which will affect what happens next. The following message from the *Disability-Research* email discussion group illustrates two of these points: first, that it can be the organization of resources which affects the future most, in this case institutionalized accommodation, and second, that disability does not necessarily imply a negative future:

Adjusting to that loss – for many of us, it's NOT easy. It takes time. And opportunities to build a GOOD life as a disabled person. (If you're stuck in a nursing home, with no hope – it's hard to feel good about your life, and your future!)

It's possible for disabled people to live full, meaningful lives – despite the barriers the community still puts in our way. Highly possible! (Strong, 2001)

While it is clear that theories of loss, which construct the onset of impairment as some form of tragedy or death, have been rejected by disabled people, this does not extend to a denial that impairment, or the experience of oppression following its onset, may not result in distress for some individuals. Indeed, what is actually being argued is that the nature of the causal relationships within such processes has been misunderstood and that non-disabled theorizing has resulted in models of practice that are oppressive. While few writers in disability studies have considered such theories to have any relevance to the social model of disability, the notion of loss and its causes is not entirely absent.

Morris (1997) has pointed to the fact that many disabled children spend a significant proportion of their lives away from home, either formally or informally in 'care'. The majority of these children are in residential special schools and for some, the prospect of leaving institutional provision is very limited. As with other children in the care system (Masson *et al.*, 1997), the issue of losing contact with parents and siblings can result in disabled children growing up with little or no family life. In terms of the approach of Berger or Salzberger-Wittenberg, certain questions arise: Is the loss of contact with family something that needs to be accepted as simply a consequence of impairment and therefore something that the person must come to terms with? At what point do the consequences of impairment cease to be seen as the result of a causal relationship and acknowledged as disablement in the social model sense – that is, as having their cause within the social systems? These are important questions, as they will affect the ways in which we respond, whether we seek adjustment within the individual or whether we assist them to situate their position within a politically and socially constructed world.

Clearly, there is no doubt that losing contact with their families will have an impact on children, though quite what that is may vary considerably from one person to another. However, the actions, which lead to this situation, begin not with the children, but possibly with their parents or maybe the education policies of the local authority where they live. It could be that they are rejected because they are impaired, or that the difficulties in maintaining contact when they were taken away from their homes lead to an effective loss of family. The psychological impact of this loss therefore does not arise because of their impairment, but because of the disablism that they have experienced. Responses from professionals need to situate the cause of this loss in the social relations that have dominated the child's life, not as an inevitable consequence of impairment.

However, Morris (1991) has raised some important questions about whether the social model of disability might also lead to the promotion of a false dichotomy:

> Such a perspective [the social model] is a crucial part of our demand to be treated as a civil rights issue. However, there is a tendency within the social model of disability to deny the experience of our own bodies, insisting that our physical differences and restrictions are *entirely* socially created. While environmental barriers and social attitudes are a crucial part of our experience of disability – and do indeed disable us – to suggest that this is all there is to it is to deny the personal experience of physical and intellectual restrictions, of illness, of the fear of dying. (p. 10, emphasis in original)

This feminist position in which 'the personal is the political' has been extensively accepted within disability studies, but resistance continues because of the dangers that are envisaged if it were to result in giving welfare professionals some form of permission to justify the use of more oppressive theories of intervention, particularly those that construct impairment as inevitably a loss. Indeed, in their introduction to a book which includes several personal narratives of disabled people, Corker and French (1999a) state emphatically that they are not inviting their oppressors to say: '"We told you so!" for we are *not always writing with them in mind*' (p. 10, emphasis in original).

The issue for those of us working in the human services is that we are often in the position to impose models of disablement, and therefore we need to be aware of the extent to which certain approaches can be the source of oppression. If we wish to do more than simply manage the purchase and provision of health and welfare services, and to engage in helpful ways with the psychosocial dimensions of disablement, we need to learn from the experience of disabled people, rather than make assumptions based on a non-disabled perception of what impairment might mean. Feminist theorizing within disability studies has sought to extend the social model to include not only the material barriers that prevent people with impairments from participating in society, but also the personal experience of impairment and disability. Thomas (1999) emphasizes the importance of:

making *analytical* distinctions between: the experiences and restrictions of activity, or limitations to social action, which are the result of disability (understood in its social relational sense); the experiences of the psycho-emotional consequences of disablism, or limitations to social being; and the experiences of living with impairment and impairment effects, which include both restrictions of activity and psycho-emotional consequences. (p. 81)

Within this framework it is possible to envisage that people may experience loss either from the responses of a non-disabled society towards them or as a result of their impairment. With the loss of family discussed above, it is clearly a result of responses to impairment rather than the impairment itself, but as Creek *et al.* (1987) have said, there are tragic consequences to impairment and these will be felt. However, Abberley's (1991) argument is that these may also be the result of responses to impairment to the extent that people are socialized into certain fears regarding disablement. That being the case, it is important for those involved in working with disabled people to make these distinctions and to respond appropriately, though it remains inappropriate to impose a non-disabled perception of what adjustment and change is necessary.

The issue raised earlier by Slack (1999), which concerned the way non-disabled people respond to impairment, also illustrates the extent to which disabled people may find their identities being determined by others. As a non-disabled person myself, I obviously cannot describe this process from first-hand experience, but last year I did spend a lot of time with a friend while he became increasingly impaired in the course of dying from a brain tumour. What struck me during this was the extent to which external factors, rather than the effects of the tumour, threatened his identity and therefore compounded the problems he faced. The simplest example of this psycho-emotional impact was when he reached a stage in which he was unable to walk very far and applied for a wheelchair.

The Disablement Services Centre provided him with one of the basic Remploy, attendant-controlled chairs. These are based on a design that is now about thirty years old and which is both technically and stylistically dated. The folding frame is estimated to require approximately a quarter extra energy to push than would a rigid frame, as is common in sports model wheelchairs, and the design has become synonymous with dependence. This, combined with their decision that he should have an attendant-controlled chair because of the weakness in his left arm, made him feel very reluctant to use it. During our conversations, what he was saying to me was that he could accept his physical limitations, which at times were increasing almost daily, but he felt that the wheelchair was symbolic of an expectation that he should behave differently. It was not as simple as him not wishing to use a wheelchair at all, but that the labelling inherent in the design of the one he had been given was a threat to his identity.

For Berger or Salzberger-Wittenberg this might be construed as his reluctance to accept his impairments, whereas the problem actually lay elsewhere, in the health and welfare systems that have constructed immobility as a purely functional issue, rather than as part of an individual's identity. Even the technical shortcomings of the chair he was provided with have been overlooked by a disability industry that chooses the budgetary levels it is prepared to spend on such functional assistance.

However, from a social model perspective, we can view this threat of loss on two levels. It is possible to see the causal relationship between the policies of the NHS and their wheelchair services, and the impact this had. However, it is also important to consider the extent to which people have been socialized into the ways they perceive themselves and how this contributes to the threat. In this sense, there are both internal and external factors that need to be considered. Our susceptibility to the psycho-emotional effects of disablism (I say 'our' here because all people may at sometime in their lives become permanently impaired, particularly in developed countries where increases in the numbers of disabled people – Oliver and Barnes, 1998 – could well be taken as a sign of advancement) is in part determined by our preparedness for physical changes during our lifetimes and, in part, by the strength and nature of disablist actions from elsewhere.

The criticism of non-disabled theorizing is that it fails to listen to the experiences of disabled people and constructs the problem from a perspective that is based on fear. It is therefore incumbent on non-disabled people to listen and to learn from what disabled people are saying. This appears to be that the onset of impairment will be experienced in as many different ways as there are people experiencing it, but that what has been common to that experience, is the imposition of particular models by welfare and rehabilitation professionals. A first step therefore, in developing a critical approach to practice within the human services, is for non-disabled people to reflect on their fears of disablement. Professionals who view impairment as necessarily resulting in a loss, which requires the individuals affected first to grieve and then to adjust, are unlikely to be able to provide help that is of value to disabled people. Instead, we need to begin to listen to the people affected and be open to the differences in the ways in which they experience these events.

10 Ill-health

Jeanne Katz

Introduction

Much has been written in this book and elsewhere about the impact of loss on human beings, as well as on many other species. The ultimate loss is, of course, death, but the loss of the individual is simply one of many losses encountered by dying people and those who survive them, both prior to and following the death. As other chapters in this book demonstrate, the kinds of losses we experience are multifarious. Every time one makes a change in life, there is a loss involved. This may be welcome, in so far as the future may look rosier, but at the same time, we may be sad to see the end of an era in our lives, bid farewell to a colleague or to a familiar routine.

This chapter explores two types of loss in relation to health. The first part investigates how temporary or chronic illness and disease lead to experiencing different kinds of loss. The ways in which bereavement may affect physical and mental health are explored in the second half of the chapter. The chapter concludes by drawing out implications for human services professionals when working with those who have suffered either or both kinds of loss.

What constitutes 'health' is a very complex subject and one which has evoked a great deal of debate amongst lay people, professional health workers as well as policy makers. For example, Jones (1997) compares and contrasts different definitions of health. She notes how in the WHO definition '[health] is a positive concept emphasizing social and personal resources as well as physical capabilities' (p. 19) and contrasts this with a narrow medical view that health is simply the 'absence of disease'. This latter definition assumes that anyone suffering from a chronic illness or disability is 'sick', even if they are generally healthy and functioning normally.

Health can be seen as both a very subjective concept and one which can be measured in order to ascertain, for example, ability to function normally (normality being defined by those who have developed the test, usually after considerable piloting and pre-testing). Usually the health of a population is measured through examining mortality and morbidity statistics, and this can provide information on many factors which influence how a society functions. For example, it might tell us how many hours of work are lost through illness and social gradients in mortality statistics.

This chapter focuses primarily on subjective experiences of ill-health which, in many ways, use both the social and medical definitions of health. What losses do we (in western societies) experience when we perceive ourselves to be unhealthy? What implications does ill-health have for individuals?

Loss, like health, is not a unitary construct, and loss of health has many ramifications. It impacts in a variety of ways not only on the individual him- or herself, but also his or her family, friends, work colleagues, possibly the community or even on whole nations or international stock markets (for example, the illnesses of Reagan, Pompidou and Yeltsin). As societies, we incorporate assumptions about health which, when absent, precipitate a whole new set of assumptions.

Most adults have experienced loss of health, both temporary and permanent. To see how often this has occurred you could draw a lifeline on which you put the most important events of your life (birth; starting school; birth of siblings; important events, such as holidays, marriages, divorces and deaths of close relatives, friends and colleagues). In a different colour you could draw onto the same lifeline periods of your life when your health was compromised, from childhood to the present day.

Looking over my own lifeline I note two occasions when changes in my health status had very different implications for me. As a child I sat on my hand on a trampoline and broke my thumb. What losses did I incur then? As a pre-adolescent I was unhappy about having to have help to get dressed. I could not ride my bicycle to school for six weeks while I was in plaster, so I had to walk there and back which trebled my journey time. Naturally, I could not join my friends on our regular weekend cycling outings, so I lost out there too. I could not swim, nor play tennis for six weeks, both of which were daily activities, and I could not cut up my food – small losses in the general scheme of things, but substantial in the life of a ten-year old striving for independence. By eighteen, I had had a few operations, which affected my performance at school. However, probably the most disturbing health event before adulthood was contracting Bell's Palsy just after finishing high school. This is (for most and luckily for me) a temporary paralysis of one side of the face and resembles a stroke. Despite little physical discomfort, this created considerable angst for me. Was it going to get better in time for me to go to university half way across the globe? Would I ever get back my muscle tone on the right side of my face? Would I ever be able to close both eyes? Would I ever be able to drink again without using a straw? Would I ever look normal again, and if I did not, would I ever be able to make new friends? Would my current friends abandon me because of the way I looked, if it were permanent? Was I more likely to contract this again having had it once?

These two examples draw out some of the themes that I want to illustrate in relation to health and loss. To what extent does loss of health influence one's ability to function physically and how does it affect one's mental state? How do these kinds of losses affect one's perception of oneself at a particular moment in time as well as one's perceptions of one's own future?

On the face of it, breaking a minor bone in one's body is not dissimilar to losing a possession. You have to endure some discomfort and inconvenience, but eventually you adjust to a slightly altered reality. If the possession you lost was, for example, your wedding ring, it might be insured, and you might even get one you like better with the insurance money. But it might be a treasured possession – the person who gave it to you may be dead, or it might be a family heirloom. In neither case would the insurance money compensate you for the emotional loss.

Reactions to breaking a bone are not dissimilar to many other expressions of loss that have been identified in this book – first of all, in my case disbelief that I could have done such a stupid thing, fury with myself; frustration and blame (shouldn't the instructor have told me not to put my hands down to steady me?). The long-term implications of breaking a thumb clearly differ depending on the way one earns one's livelihood and the aspirations we hold for our future – an aspiring musician would respond differently to breaking a bone in a hand from someone whose hands were not crucial to one's career path.

We also may respond differently to health losses if we feel that somehow we contributed to the outcome through our behaviour. For example, someone who is injured in a car accident may feel that they could have done something about the driving, not gone that route, and so forth. As practitioners, you will have encountered responses which you might have seen as self-blame and feel this may have contributed to anxiety or depression.

Different types of loss of health

So far we have touched upon one type of loss in relation to ill-health – that of a *temporary* loss as a result of an injury or an acute non-life-limiting illness. There are, of course, *permanent* physical losses as a result of life-limiting illnesses, acute illnesses or injuries. In these situations illness eventually becomes part of everyday life and the loss might be reinforced on a daily basis. Limiting, long-term illness was defined in the 1991 UK census as 'long-term illness, health problem or handicap which limits the daily activities or the work that a person can do' (Jordan *et al.*, 2000, p. 398).

Maguire and Parkes (1998) classify losses in health as either *bodily changes* (perceptions of body image) or *changes of function*, where the individual alters the activities and roles they can take on. We should consider these categories in relation to general health losses, such as mobility and sensory losses which most of us confront as we age. Fitzgerald and Parkes (1998) measured responses to the onset of loss of sight and loss of hearing. They draw parallels with the conventional wisdom in relation to reactions to loss. Thus, responses to increasing immobility or decreased sight include shock or disbelief, pining for what was lost and for what they could no longer see; depression was found in more than 85 per cent of their subjects and continued even once pining had stopped. What is unusual in this study is the authors' conviction that preparation for the loss is a major factor in the adjustment of the subjects. They suggest strategies for health care professionals which they believe will ameliorate the experiences of those facing loss of sight or hearing.

Charmaz (1995) has studied how people adjust to chronic ill-health, and her findings provide some insights into how people cope with loss in all health situations. She notes that serious chronic illness forces sufferers to acknowledge the conflicts between one's self and one's body. This vantage point integrates the concept which Maguire and Parkes divide into *bodily changes* (perceptions of body image) and *changes of function*. Charmaz sees chronic illness as impacting on people's identities as well as their health. This precipitates a re-evaluation of who they are and their aspirations. This is a constantly negotiated process as they develop what Charmaz (1987) calls identity goals as they try to create relatively normal lives. Charmaz suggests that, initially, people with chronic illness plan their lives as if they are not ill and have expectations that would have been unrealistic even before they contracted the illness. But, as the illness progresses, they make 'identity trade-offs' or lower their expectations until they reach realistic goals. But these are constantly changing; sometimes they can raise their expectations realistically and other times not: 'Both raised or lowered identity goals form an implicit identity hierarchy that ill people create as they adapt to bodily loss and change' (1995, p. 659).

Charmaz notes the variety of ways of living with impairment, one of which is adapting. Adapting means adjusting to the illness, rather than fighting it. She describes three primary stages:

1. experiencing and defining impairment;
2. making bodily assessments and subsequently identity trade-offs; and
3. surrendering to the sick self by relinquishing control over illness and by flowing with the experience of it. (p. 657)

She suggests that adapting is not a one-off process, but that people suffering from chronic illness are constantly having to adapt as they experience new losses in function and ability. Charmaz' findings can be usefully employed when looking at other types of health losses, including acute progressive illness and episodes which create a new reality. One well-researched area is that relating to the loss of a limb or other body parts. Maguire and Parkes (1998) cite findings by Parkes (1975) which noted the similarities of reactions to loss of limb to reactions to loss of another person. In the early 1970s, as a social work student, I explored the responses to loss of limb between two groups of male amputees in Israel − those who had lost their limbs during the six-day war of June 1967 and those who had lost their limbs in industrial or road traffic accidents (Katz and Strauss, 1974). Responses to the loss of their limbs included depression, loss of self-esteem, perceived loss of social relationships in the initial but not latter stages; the amputees were very aware that they were no longer able to do what they could do before, both in terms of physical ability and, in many cases, professionally; they had lost the ability to move around and undertake some daily domestic tasks, such as carry children or shopping, and also, in many cases, they lost income both temporarily, while they were on sick leave, and permanently, as their projected ability for long-term earnings had been compromised. All their accounts indicated the subjectivity of health-related loss. The range of losses expressed by our sample highlighted the danger of preconceived notions of what a particular loss would mean to an individual. Some amputees, regardless of how they lost their limb, focused on loss of function, loss of earnings, loss of role as the male head of the family, including primary breadwinner. Many mourned their perceived previous relationships with their wives; some were very concerned about their appearance (loss of body image), and particularly how this affected both physical and sexual functions.

A variety of progressive medical conditions cause both loss of body functions as well as changes in body image – for example, heart disease and cancer. Cardiovascular diseases are the primary cause of death and ill-health in western societies. Although sufferers might outwardly see little bodily change the psychological implications of heart disease are considerable. Many researchers have attributed the intense responses to heart disease (as opposed to kidney disease or restricted bowel functioning) to the psychological importance the heart is given in western societies. Maguire and Parkes (1998) write:

> [The heart] is experienced as the symbol and source of life, an internal clock that ticks our life away, until it stops, dead. It follows that *any interference with the heart is likely to undermine our sense of the world as a safe place and of our body as a stronghold.* (p. 51, emphasis in original)

Sufferers may experience gradual or even dramatic curtailment of normal activities. Previously active individuals may be transformed into what were previously known as 'cardiac cripples', whereby they are unable to function in a self-caring way, and often unable to work outside the home. Thus, one's self-perception as a strong, fit individual can be transformed instantaneously following a cardiac event.

Cardiac surgery revolutionized the experience of heart disease during the second half of the twentieth century. At the same time as providing hope of longer survival for cardiac patients, it is also accompanied with considerable stress and distress in relation to what types of activity are permitted or safe following surgery. Cardiac patients are concerned about sexual activities, even when surgery has resulted in good cardiac functioning.

Loss in relation to sexual activity as well as other types of functioning is equally of concern to people with cancer. Much has been written about losses of body image in relation to cancer – those with colostomy bags, or who have undergone mastectomies, or hysterectomies. For many cancer sufferers the treatment in itself leads to a variety of physical responses, including hair loss; bloated appearance as a result of steroids; lethargy and fatigue; depression; or other psychological reactions. These of themselves cause experiences of loss of body image and self-esteem.

Certain cancers deserve particular mention. In breast cancer, the impact on body image has attracted considerable research attention. In a similar way that the heart has a mystique in relation to life and living, breasts embody femininity, and mastectomy creates a sense of mutilation. Other cancers of the female reproductive organs also contribute to a sense of a loss of femininity and losses of a sexual type. As Maguire and Parkes (1998) note, studies of people with cancers associated with sexual reproduction show similarities. A third of respondents in a number of studies reviewed by them felt that they had become less attractive to their partners (like the amputees) and a similar percentage of respondents noted that their interest in sex had decreased.

Certain kinds of cancer affect basic functioning in relation to responses to the sufferer or the sufferer's ability to communicate. An example of this has been beautifully put into writing by the late John Diamond, a columnist who chronicled his cancer journey over several years in *The Times*. Some of the losses he described related to his inability to speak which, for a radio commentator, meant losses in relation to work and consequently earnings, also implications for everyday life, social interaction and communicating with his small children. He eloquently wrote about his long-term losses, assuming that he would not return to work on radio and more importantly, not see his children grown up. His short-term plans were disrupted each time another lump was found and required chemo- or radiotherapy.

Research studies have measured adjustment to certain types of cancers. Salander *et al.* (2000) undertook a longitudinal study of patients with malignant glioma to ascertain how they conceptualized life post-diagnosis and treatment. They determined that sufferers divided their functioning into sustaining life-continuity or simply related to experiencing their disease. Two thirds of the patients were able to re-experience what they perceived as everyday life, even if for a short period of time. Hence, in their case, the losses they experienced were less acute than the third who only experienced 'disease' after diagnosis.

These psychological considerations can be more important in the adjustment to the illness than the nature of the cancer. However, they must be balanced against the real concern of sufferers that their cancer has been treated.

The impact of bereavement on health

The relationship between pathology and bereavement has been debated by theorists, particularly during the 1990s and the beginning of the twenty-first century (Walter, 1999; Hockey *et al.*, 2001). The debates centre on the nature of bereavement and models of care. Some of these explore whether or not bereavement can be seen as pathological or whether discipline-bound models of grief are useful. Ways of enabling ourselves to resolve grief, if that is even an appropriate response, have been subjected to postmodern theoretical analysis. Different models of grief resolution, such as a dual process model propounded by Stroebe and Schut (1999), have been debated by researchers and theorists alike.

This second half of this chapter does not provide a theoretical model of physical and emotional responses to grief. It simply surveys these responses and provides some guidance in relation to predicting risk factors.

There is much evidence which suggests that experiencing a bereavement can affect both physical and mental health in survivors, regardless of the cause of death. The theory that emerges from these findings suggests that bereavement in itself (that is, the suffering of grief) leads to ill-health.

The first classic research which explored the relationship between bereavement and ill-health was undertaken by Parkes in the 1960s. Parkes and other researchers have been investigating the impact of bereavement on the health of survivors for many years – these survivors include the spouse, other members of family, people in the vicinity of where a disaster took place (for example, the Aberfan mining tragedy) or close friends.

His initial study reviews the evidence of a causal relationship between experiencing a death of a loved one and then developing physical and/or mental health problems. In particular, Parkes examines the 'broken heart syndrome' and investigates whether bereavement can lead to death. The findings differ for men and for women. Drawing on data emerging from his own study, Parkes notes that, for widowers there is 40 per cent raised mortality rate in the first six months after the death of their wives compared to the rate of matched married men (Parkes, 1997). He hypothesizes that bereavement may directly impact on cardiovascular functioning in men, but causal links to death are hard to prove. Stroebe and Stroebe (1993) also found a link between bereavement and death but, in this case, suicide. All close relatives are at risk, but widowers, and particularly young widowers, were found to be most at risk.

Although the stereotype of the broken-hearted person is Queen Victoria, in fact the consequences for women of losing husbands is less dire than that for men losing wives (in western societies where studies have taken place). Both Parkes and Stroebe and Stroebe found some increase in mortality for recently widowed women, but this data was far less convincing than in men.

Payne et al. (1999) surveyed the epidemiological evidence of mortality and physical morbidity following bereavement. First they suggest that, if bereavement is seen as a stressor, this could potentially cause neuro-physiological consequences and/or a compromise to the immune system. They note that reduced levels of immunological functioning could therefore make bereaved people susceptible to infection, and even at risk of developing certain forms of cancer. They quote Sherr (1995), who suggests that people with AIDS who themselves suffer bereavement could potentially experience a deterioration in their own conditions. However, they note that immunological changes are hard to separate out from the health impact of social changes resulting from bereavement, such as reduced sleep, poor nutrition or general self-neglect. Stroebe and Stroebe (1993) note that these more indirect responses to stressful life events, such as a bereavement, could lead to behaviours which in themselves create damage to health, such as increased alcohol consumption. It might be hypothesized that drug misuse is a risk for the younger age group.

Although, as noted above, death resulting from bereavement is hard to prove, many researchers are convinced that the death of a relative or close friend can affect one's physical as well as mental health. Parkes cites the work of Jacobs, suggesting: 'that a third of those most directly affected will suffer detrimental effects to their physical or mental health'. This work links in with findings of Parkes and Weiss' (1983) American study, known as the Harvard Bereavement Study, where findings revealed that bereaved men and women demonstrated an increase in a range of both psychological and somatic symptoms. These findings in themselves were not surprising. In the 1960s Holmes and Rahe (1967) constructed a stressful life events scale which has been subsequently modified in many societies and situations. This suggested that the most stressful life event was the death of a spouse. If this were exacerbated by other stressors, such as moving house, or changing one's living conditions, one was at risk of developing a range of diseases, both psychological and somatic.

There is a variety of well-documented physical responses to bereavement in a western culture. These may arise partly out of physical and emotional exhaustion following an intensive period of caring for the dying relative. Whatever the cause, these responses range from general debility (which includes increased susceptibility to common infections or other diseases) to increased levels of mortality in bereaved people.

The most common physical symptoms include fatigue, or changes in sleep patterns – for example, insomnia. Others might be various kinds of physical discomfort, including pain, such as headaches, chest discomfort or musculo-skeletal pain. Appetite changes, particularly a reluctance to eat (sometimes leading to anorexia), are well documented. A woman interviewed for an audiocassette accompanying the *Death and Dying* course at the Open University talks about how, not only did she not want to eat once her daughter was dead (and hence was not eating), she also found it difficult to shop for food and prepare meals for her surviving children. Others find comfort in food or experience gastrointestinal changes. Some bereaved people also experience symptoms similar to those of the deceased (Payne *et al.*,1999).

The impact of bereavement on mental health

The impact on the mental health of bereaved people has been well documented. This is especially true of older people and often linked to their physical health – a well-known example of this is Parkes' study of widowers which indicated increased mortality patterns in men whose wives were recently deceased (Parkes, 1998a). Stroebe (1998) suggests that, in national surveys, suicide is one cause of death which explains the high rate of widowers' deaths. In some cultures, notably in certain castes in India, self-inflicted death (suttee) was practised amongst widows by throwing themselves on their husbands' funeral pyres – in this case, it might not be seen as indicative of mental disorder.

Psychiatric disorders resulting from bereavement have been found in a variety of studies conducted over the past thirty years. Stroebe (1998), surveying this literature, noted that although raised levels of psychiatric disorder were found in widowed, as opposed to married, people, this varies across sexual, racial and cultural boundaries. Bereaved women are more likely to suffer from depression than men, although widowed men are more depressed than married men.

Psychological difficulties might be exacerbated by practical issues or physical problems. Clearly, older people are suffering more consistent losses which may accompany the death of a partner – for example, their social support, as well as an anxiety about their own vulnerability. An example of this might be that, having lost their spouse, the older person is now living alone and taking greater risks in their domestic environment.

Moving from what might be labelled psychiatric disorder to psychological responses to bereavement, one encounters what are usually perceived as normal and expected. Common psychological responses to bereavement resemble the various stages or phases theories in response to the threat of personal death initially posited by Kübler-Ross and, more recently, modified by a variety of theorists, including Robert Buckman (1998). These responses include the whole range of emotions which could be experienced as a result of any crisis or life event, such as anger, tearfulness, shock and pining.

Payne *et al.* (1999) review research findings about psychological responses to bereavement. They cite Wortman and Silver's (1989) uncertainty about whether 'there is a universal human response to loss' (p. 22) and anthropological evidence that there are unlikely to be typical expressions of loss amongst different societies. They note that physical and psychological responses to grief are closely associated with particular cultures. Much of the literature accessible to researchers and authors contributing to this book is likely to be western and Anglophone – this inevitably limits the range of evidence provided. It also means that an open-mindedness is essential when encountering reactions from clients from different societies, and particularly minority ethnic groups; in essence, responses listed above are simply examples of what reactions might be expected – of course, these could be most inappropriate or even unacceptable in certain societies.

Implications for practice

Parkes and Markus (1998) look at the implications of loss in a variety of medical conditions. Parkes (1998c, p. 133) notes: 'major losses are important experiences that can contribute to causing physical and psychiatric illness' (emphasis in original). That means: 'members of the caring professions need to take steps to acquaint themselves with the losses that afflict their patients' (ibid., emphasis in original).

They suggest that forewarned is forearmed, that, particularly in situations where bereavement is expected, sensitive handling of the situation by the appropriate professional through communication with the to-be-bereaved will reduce the likelihood of subsequent psychiatric and other problems.

At the same time as being open-minded about the range of responses to loss, there are several factors that might be considered when practitioners assess clients in terms of what could controversially be termed a health risk following bereavement. As we have seen above, there is a variety of possible health implications for survivors following bereavement. Parkes (1998a) and others identify factors that need to be considered during a bereavement risk assessment. Parkes (1998b) notes that it is difficult to generalize from the variety of studies which have explored these variables. However, there are several patterns that emerge. These include whether the death was that of a child or a spouse; whether it was sudden, unexpected or untimely; was one of multiple deaths, such as a disaster; a suicide or murder.

Parkes (1998b) notes that the age of the deceased is relevant; when an older person dies, regardless of whether this is sudden, we cope better with it. When a younger person dies, we tend to see this as an 'untimely death' and find it harder to rationalize. Other traumatic losses, where deaths are sudden, unexpected or associated with multiple losses or circumstances, where the survivor's survival had also been under threat, can precipitate patterns of behaviour where acknowledging the grief may be avoided. Examples of this are survivors of mass extermination activities, such as those from Cambodia, Rwanda and the Jewish Holocaust. In relation to the last, few survivors discussed their experiences until well over thirty years after the event. Yet, even when survivors choose to keep silent about their experiences, Parkes suggests that survivors of traumatic losses are likely to experience high levels of anxiety and tension which might be perceived as a form of post-traumatic stress disorder. Survivors might relive these experiences over and again.

Anticipated deaths may be easier to cope with unless the bereaved person has focused their primary activities on caring for the deceased. Parkes suggests that the relationship with the deceased:

> both reflects personal vulnerability and itself influences the outcome of bereavement. Relationships characterised by clinging or ambivalence are particularly important; the former is easily recognised by nursing staff who witness the intensity with which a family member clings to the dying patient. (Parkes, 1998b, p. 998).

A supportive family may be a predictor of a good bereavement outcome, but Parkes emphasizes that it is the bereaved persons' perception of the family after the death has occurred that is relevant. Only after the death has occurred does it become clear whether the family permits expressions of grief, and only then do some long-standing conflicts emerge.

Parkes suggests that some people are particularly vulnerable, such as those with low self-esteem, those who find it difficult to trust others, those with previous psychiatric problems, or who have attempted to commit suicide, and those without family support. Other people at risk are, for example, those who were ambivalent about the person who had died, or were particularly dependent on the deceased, or had had an insecure relationship with their parents during childhood (Parkes, 1999). These individuals may experience what he terms as conflicted grief (1998b), and it becomes apparent that the bereaved person is 'haunted' by memories of the deceased. He suggests that these conflicted responses to the death may mirror difficult relationships with other surviving family members.

Conclusion

This chapter has surveyed some of the literature exploring loss in relation to health and bereavement. Human services professionals working with people suffering from ill-health will want to acknowledge the wide range of immediate, as well as projected, losses experienced by all those involved. Losses are not necessarily limited to the individual suffering from the disease, but have ramifications for family members, friends and colleagues. There can be similarities in relation to lost aspirations and indeed material loss.

Eliciting accounts from those who have experienced traumatic loss as well as progressive loss of function should be done in as open-ended a way as possible. Preconceived notions of what this loss would mean for oneself is often not helpful to others – their concept of what constitutes normal functioning is likely to be quite different from one's own.

11 Older People

Sue Thompson

Introduction

This chapter seeks to highlight the relative lack of attention given to older people's experiences of loss and to explore the part that ageism plays in perpetuating a situation in which older people are assumed to be less affected by it than are their younger counterparts. Although loss through death will be a key issue, the discussion will be broadened out to include the myriad of other forms of loss experienced by older people, such as loss of physical or intellectual function, status, dignity, practical and emotional support, relationships, life-chances and so on.

Links will be drawn between Doka's (2001) concept of 'disenfranchised grief', as discussed in the Introduction to this volume, and the way in which ageism, as a form of discrimination, pushes older people's needs and perspective to the margins of mainstream thought and provision, and treats them differently, and often less favourably, than younger adults. This chapter will discuss how this process can serve to devalue older people's experiences of loss and grieving by suggesting that older people should be 'used to it' and therefore feel the emotions less keenly. I will argue that loss is an intense experience at any stage in the life course and to deny its significance in the lives of older people is to deny that old age is part of life and that older people experience emotions differently once they reach an arbitrarily defined age (Thompson and Thompson, 1999).

Given the centrality of ageism as an explanatory concept in this chapter, I begin by discussing its main features and implications before moving on to look at loss experiences.

Ageism

As with many other forms of discrimination, such as sexism, racism, disablism and heterosexism, ageism works to convince members of society that particular groups of people are 'less than' others – less deserving of respect and resources, for example. Reoch (1997) captures this very prevalent sense of negativity in the following comment:

> One of the most hurtful misconceptions about the process of ageing is the assumption that at some point in their lives people inevitably stop growing personally ... The result is that older people are all too often treated as if they had already stopped living. (p. 14)

By perpetuating the myth that older people are 'less than' younger adults, or what Midwinter (1990) describes as 'postadults', ageism serves to legitimate their being pushed to the margins of society, both in ideological and practical terms. Thompson (1998b) refers in detail to a number of other processes which are also strongly associated with inequality and discrimination and which interact with, and reinforce each other, to contribute towards oppression, not only in terms of ageism but also all other forms of discrimination. After all, older people are not, as ageist ideology would have us believe, an homogeneous mass of people defined only by their age, but a diverse group who can also be defined as being male/female, gay/straight, black/white, disabled/ablebodied and so on. Indeed, as a social group, older people will be as diverse and stratified as any other cohort by social divisions such as gender, sexual orientation, ethnicity, physical and intellectual ability, and so are likely to experience discrimination at more than one level (Bernard and Meade, 1993; Blakemore and Boneham, 1994; Zarb, 1993). But many of the processes discussed by Thompson are particularly relevant to the situation of older people, especially those of stereotyping, infantilization, and welfarism, to which I will return later.

Before exploring how ageism can be seen to invisiblize or trivialize older people's experiences of loss, I want again to underline the complexity of ageism by looking briefly at the way in which it can be seen to operate at different levels. Earlier in this volume, Thompson offers PCS analysis as an explanatory framework for understanding and challenging discrimination. When this framework is applied to older people, it is possible to identify examples of ageism operating at each of the three levels:

Personal – the level of personal prejudice, where individuals' actions and comments convey the assumption that they want to distance themselves from old age. Conceptualizing someone as different and inferior can work to this end. Barring an early death, older people are younger people's 'future selves' and, for many people, ridiculing or labelling older people as a problem serves to deflect attention from their own mortality. One effect of personal prejudice is the internalization of such attitudes by older people themselves, who come to believe that they are indeed unworthy of the same rights as their younger counterparts. Macdonald (1983) describes the pressure to accept a definition of herself as a person of lesser worth than in her younger days:

> Old is ugly, old is powerless, old is the end ... Old is what no one could possibly want to be. At sixty-nine, I take in these messages from the outside every day, and have had to learn ways of reacting to all the negative messages around me in order to survive. (Cited in Lustbader, 1994, pp. 118–19)

Cultural – the level of shared attitudes, assumptions and meanings. It is the level at which stereotypes operate and are disseminated by the media in their various forms. For example, although there has been some attempt of late to portray older people in films, adverts and television programmes as freethinking and ambitious people, all too often the images are of older people as confused, cantankerous and decrepit, if they are there at all (Midwinter, 1991). Increasingly, sexist and racist jokes and references are not being tolerated – it is becoming culturally unacceptable to demean people in this way. However, demeaning people on the grounds of age has yet to be culturally vetoed. For example, it is seen by many as acceptable practice to refer to older people by their first name, or to act protectively by making decisions which are felt to be in their best interests, without reference to their preference or permission. Hockey and James (1993) refer to this process as 'infantilization' and argue that it reinforces the link between old age and dependency. The link between old age and loss in general remains one that is high in the public consciousness, even in the face of evidence to suggest that there are very many vigorous, healthy and independent people in the over-65 age group. But, in societies where wealth and vitality are valued concepts, older people are not seen as useful, and so it suits a purpose to marginalize them by portraying them as not only different from, but also of a lower status than, younger adults. The process of conceptualizing and 'packaging' older people as a burden to society, rather than as an asset, can be referred to as 'welfarization' (Fennell *et al.*, 1988) and helps to strengthen the association between ageing and loss by focusing on dependency, rather than on strengths and positive contributions.

Structural – this is the level which explains how ageist attitudes and assumptions are not only to be found in individuals, but are also embedded within the structures of society. The distribution of power at a structural level reflects the social divisions of class, race, gender and so on. One such social division that forms part of the social structure and its underpinning relations of power which receives comparatively little attention is that of age. This partly explains why the association between old age and decrepitude is so rarely challenged – power relations at the S level reinforce, and are reinforced by, ageist assumptions at the C level.

In giving this overview of ageism I have presented only a brief outline of a very complex subject, which is explored in much greater depth by authors such as Hughes (1995). My intention here is to say enough to identify ageist ideology and practices as contributory factors in the trivialization of loss when it is experienced by older people, and the relatively low priority given to loss issues by educators of those people working with them in the human services. If we, as workers and educators, conceptualize older people as of a lower status than younger adults, and fall prey to the stereotyping of older people as dependent and powerless, then there is little hope of changing the status quo, whereby it is seen as acceptable to assume that we lose our capacity for feeling emotions as we enter the latter stages of our lives. As Thompson (1998b) comments:

> The existence of ageism and its harmful consequences for older people has important implications for human services practice. It requires practitioners, educators, and policy-makers to move away from traditional notions of care and dependency towards an ethic of empowerment. (p. 100)

The task, then, is to ensure that older people are treated as unique individuals, with unique experiences of loss and unique ways of coping with it, rather than basing our interventions on assumptions premised on ageist stereotypes. Corr *et al.* (1997) refer to the way in which ageism devalues the experience of old age, and argue that the experiencing of multiple, but devalued losses, can lead to a devaluing of self and self-worth by older individuals themselves. This internalization of ageist ideology can then be seen to contribute to a situation where loss is seen, not only by younger people but by older people themselves, as part and parcel of being old and something which one should be able to cope with without too much trouble. Therefore, when it is experienced as traumatic, it is not recognized as such. This is an example of Doka's (1989) concept of disenfranchised grief, in so far as the ensuing grief reaction is not socially sanctioned. As I shall note below, this is a common feature of loss in old age.

The experience of loss in old age

Death and bereavement in old age

Research and theory development into the particular experiences of older people is relatively small in both the general field of death studies and within the field of gerontology (Thompson and Thompson, 1999). This would seem to be the case even though, as Moss and Moss (1989) remind us, the majority of deaths are those of older people.

There is a prevailing tendency to assume that, because loss features so much in the lives of older people (the death of friends and family members, loss of physical or intellectual faculties, role, status, earning power, sexual function and so on) and the accumulated experience of loss over the years, it is necessarily easier to bear (see, for example, Scrutton, 1995). This is clearly not the case for everyone as, for some, multiple experiences of loss can compound the sense of grief, rather than make it easier to bear (Moss and Moss, 1989). One of the effects of ageist ideology is to hide the nuances of individual experience under 'blanket' assumptions, and to neglect the *meaning* that individual people attach to specific loss experiences. For example, we might consider two scenarios in which an 85-year-old man experiences the death of a younger sister:

> Jack Roberts has not been close to his family and is not aware of, or even particularly interested to know, how many of his eleven siblings are still alive. He has failing health but continues to have a reasonably good social life and a very supportive circle of friends and neighbours. He has financial security and is content in the knowledge that any future care needs can be provided for.

> Arthur Jones shared a dilapidated house with his sister, who was also his only friend and surviving relative. They had lived together all of their lives and she had compensated for his mild learning disability by helping him with self-care and decision-making at

every level. In the months prior to his sister's death, both had become increasingly frail, but had refused all offers of support. She had discharged herself from hospital against advice because she knew how distressed her brother had become about the possibility of having to enter residential care.

These examples serve to highlight that the same experience – that is to say, the death of a sister – can have very different implications for different individuals. For the first man, the loss experience may be one that he finds distressing for a time, but perhaps less so than the death of one of his close friends, who love and understand him in a way that she had not. However, for the second man, the loss of a sister who had been his emotional and practical 'prop' throughout his life is quite likely to signify the advent of his worst fears, thereby having devastating consequences and precipitating a personal crisis from which he might never recover. Neimeyer *et al.* (2000) remind us of how grief has to be understood in relation to the *meaning* that people attach to it (see also Chapter 3 of this volume). They advocate an approach to loss which recognizes the uniqueness of bereavement and focuses on helping individuals to create a new future which incorporates the loss, rather than one which insists that they 'get over it' within a socially determined timescale:

> From a social constructionist perspective, a useful theory of grief would need to meet a number of criteria which stand in contrast to traditional theories ... It would reveal the personal reality of death or loss for different individuals, instead of assuming that death holds a universal significance for human beings ... It would be flexible enough to illuminate highly idiosyncratic constructions of death and their changes over time (pp. 199–200)

The fluid nature of the grieving process is one that is also highlighted by Stroebe and Schut (1999) who urge us to accept the complexity involved in grief reactions (see the Introduction to this volume). According to dual process theory, it is possible to experience the two phases (loss and restoration) within the same timescale. That is to say, we oscillate between the two, rather than work through the first phase before moving on to the second. As with meaning reconstruction theory, the 'dual process' approach explains grieving in terms of the meaning attached to it. If we take this challenge to traditional 'stages' theories on board, it becomes possible to see how we might interpret a particular episode as indicating 'problematic' grieving, when it really signifies just a temporary flashback to a loss-orientation phase, within a broader sense of progress towards integrating the loss into a new perspective.

For example, we might visit 75-year-old Elizabeth Craig eighteen months after the death of her 90-year-old partner and be surprised to find her very distressed and dishevelled, holding his photograph to her chest and weeping bitterly. With just a snapshot view such as this, one might assume that she should not have been surprised at his death, and that to still be grieving in such a fashion is an indication of her individual failure to come to terms with an expected occurrence. However, if we were to return the following day, we might discover her to be well-dressed and competently going about her usual business of keeping house and organizing a carers' support group, the photograph back on the sideboard with those of their children and grandchildren. This second scenario would, in fact, have been much more indicative of her grief reaction than the previous one, when having seen the first rose appearing in the garden which had been Mr Craig's pride and joy, she had retreated with her memories and let the rest of the world and its new priorities pass her by for a few hours.

It should be clear, then, that considerable harm can be done if the uniqueness of grief reactions is not appreciated. If the nuances are overlooked, a grieving person may be treated in ways that are unhelpful or even destructive. However, it is important to emphasize that ageism does precisely that – it denies the uniqueness of loss and replaces it with a stereotypical view. An anti-ageist approach therefore needs to be based on taking time to explore issues, to validate feelings and to offer the level of support required by the specific situation.

Losses involved in entering residential care

Giving up one's own home, even in circumstances where one accepts the need to move into a residential or nursing home, must surely rank among the most traumatic events in a lifetime, and yet it is quite often dismissed in a cavalier way as being inevitable or 'for the best'. Practitioners and relatives involved may fail to appreciate that such a move, even if not an emergency admission, is none the less likely to constitute a crisis for the individuals concerned – that is, a turning point in their lives which may therefore have loss implications for them (Thompson, 1991). Financial and logistical practicalities can overshadow the feelings dimension, with the result that the move is not perceived as a loss experience at all – or, at best, the loss experience is minimized. Even when the decision has been taken on the grounds that the advantages outweigh the disadvantages, the loss experience can still be very considerable. Since the advent of the community care ethos and legislation, most older people entering residential or nursing care do so now because of physical frailty or intellectual decline, rather than because of loneliness or convenience, unless they have the financial means to make arrangements by choice, rather than be assessed according to need (Higgs and Victor, 1993). They are therefore likely to have already experienced losses associated with, for example, poor mobility, poor memory, lack of co-ordination or control of bodily functions, and so on. Any or all of these losses can signify to an individual person that they have lost, or are in danger of losing, their independence. When these deficits are noticed by human services practitioners, and help offered with various activities of daily living, the help is often refused, and the refusal interpreted as the individual being 'obstinate'. But, if one looks at the offer from the perspective of an older person who perceives it as a challenge to their self-identity as an independently coping person (Richards, 2000), it becomes easier to conceptualize it as a loss experience. Having to consider entering residential care entails having to face that message writ large – you are no longer capable of living an independent lifestyle – and yet the ethos in many residential and nursing homes is arguably one that encourages dependency, rather than one that promotes rehabilitation.

We can usefully break down the overarching theme of loss of independence into more specific loss experiences, such as:

- *Identity* – prior to reaching the level of dependency necessitating admission to residential care, older people will have built up identities based on personality and life experiences which are as varied as those in any other age cohort. Many, for example, will have raised families, maintained homes, held public office, carried out difficult or dangerous jobs or achieved academic distinction. In essence, prior to being perceived as incompetent, they will have been competent. Once again we can note infantilization as an aspect of ageism.
- *Control* – while many residential and nursing homes strive to offer as personalized a service as possible, choice is often limited due to organizational restraints. Few appear to be run on a model where the decision-making is shared by residents and staff. Consider, for example, how it must feel to have little or no say in how daily activities are structured, or how menus or decor are chosen.
- *Spontaneity* – associated with the above is a loss of spontaneity. Whilst some homes try to promote an ethos where residents

choose when, what, where and whether to eat, for example, it is often the case that low staff ratios do not allow for individual wishes to be respected. Few homes appear to provide fridges and tea-making facilities in residents' rooms, for example. Although hot drinks are often available on request, as well as at set times, this can present its own difficulties if residents see that staff are busy. Also, it does not give the individual resident any sense of control over his or her own circumstances. Similarly, in terms of the desire to walk outside, or go shopping, where an older person has internalized ageist messages about being 'a burden', he or she often chooses not to bother the staff for fear of being thought a nuisance. It therefore becomes very easy to lose the spontaneity previously enjoyed and fall into routinized practices largely dictated by others.

- *The right to take risks* – while it is part of our daily lives to make decisions based on balancing what we know to entail risk (travelling, eating, smoking and so on) with expediency and pleasure, this right is often denied older people in what is perceived to be their own best interests. For example, many establishments restrict access to their kitchens in the interests of protecting residents from the risk of injury, thereby denying a source of pleasure and the opportunity of reciprocation to residents who, with some supervision, could continue an activity which they found purposeful and rewarding prior to admission. Decisions such as whether to smoke, or to take note of government guidelines on dietary intake, are often made on behalf of residents and incorporated into policy decisions without reference to the lifestyle choices of the people using the service. These are issues which tend not to be seen as loss experiences, and yet I would argue that the loss of the right to make one's own decisions about risk, after a lifetime of daily making decisions about risk-taking, is a potentially devastating one.

Dependency and the caring relationship

Care in the community involves mostly care of an informal nature – that is, care provided by relatives, friends and neighbours. In relation to the community care of older people, a large percentage of carers are also advanced in years themselves. While the financial and physical hardships of providing such care are often recognized, far less attention is given to the losses involved – for example, the loss of independence and autonomy. All too often in the field of social and health care, we become immersed in the task of caring, without recognizing that, in trying to provide assistance and support, we may become insensitive to the feelings of dependency that our actions engender. This is understandable in the face of a very powerful ageist ideology which promotes the message that this is how it should be, that older people are not like other adults and are devoid of feelings, even in the face of devastating losses. Consider how seldom grief counselling is offered to older people who acquire a disability through strokes or falls, and yet it is often seen as an important part of the rehabilitation of younger people who become dependent as a result of accidents (Scrutton, 1992). Lustbader (1994) challenges this by promoting *inter*dependence and the role that reciprocity can play in helping people cope with the losses that often accompany the ageing process. She refers, in the passage below, to the need to be 'of use', and explores how carers can alienate those for whom they provide assistance by not recognizing the impact that their actions are having on an individual's self-esteem:

> Frail people are generally denied chances to give something back to their helpers or to their communities. Their offers are refused with statements like, 'You don't have to do that. We'll take care of everything.' Helpers mean well, without realising how urgently people in their care crave a tangible counterbalance to their dependency. (p. 29)

A further aspect of loss experience in old age is that of the impact of the caring role on future hopes and the sacrifice of an expected quality of life. Many of us, particularly those who have reached middle-age, will have formed a vision of ourselves and our partners and friends once we have retired. We might have plans for travel if health and finances permit, or for spending more time in leisure pursuits or education. Projecting our thoughts into the future, we would probably expect to feel devastated if those dreams had to be abandoned because we took on the role of being a full-time carer of a dependent relative. Yet, so often those feelings are experienced in old age and go unrecognized or devalued, because it seems alien to assume that older people might have hopes and plans for *their* futures – what Lustbader (1994) refers to as 'unlived life'.

In addition to devaluing loss experiences in general, ageist thinking can also be seen to have an effect in terms of its tendency to portray older people as an homogeneous group, thereby 'invisiblizing' the diversity of life experience within it. People over sixty-five are as stratified by class, gender, ethnicity and sexual orientation as any other, and these aspects of identity will have an impact on how loss is experienced. For example, Rose and Bruce (1995) highlight gender differences in how carers are perceived and suggest that women are particularly disadvantaged because, when a female partner becomes dependent, male carers are often seen as exceptional or heroic if they take on the carer role, and at least have social esteem to help them through the sense of lost opportunities that they might feel. Commenting on their research into gender differences in caring, Rose and Bruce use the following analogy to make their point:

> Caring was what was expected of them [women] and only failure to care brought attention. While respecting the very real suffering of these men and their dedicated caring, we began to think of men's caring as a pet rabbit relationship. A pet rabbit's survival requires conscientious care; indeed its condition is a source of pride for its carer, and the well cared for pet, or rather its owner, receives much admiration. For women ... Their equally conscientious care – which gave them little or no respite – produced little of the real, if subdued, sense of pride that the men displayed. (pp. 126–7)

These comments should help us to recognize the dangers of not acknowledging the importance of carers' feelings, particularly of anger, frustration and so on. In some cases, such unacknowledged and unresolved feelings may be a factor in elder abuse. Such issues can also apply to paid carers in, for example, residential care, as institutional abuse is, of course, not unheard of (Peace *et al.*, 1999).

Finally, we should not underestimate the loss of individuality that can arise as a result of, for example, needing help with even one small task, an experience which can be devastating for some people (Scrutton, 1995). We need to see loss in the context of individual experience and thus resist the temptation of overemphasizing the commonalities of loss experiences.

Conclusion

In this discussion I have explored a number of issues which highlight the complex and fluid nature of loss and grief and argued that ageist stereotyping can obscure or invalidate the impact that loss experiences can have on older people. A consequence of not accepting that older people can experience loss traumatically is that we then tend not to offer therapeutic support. Both dual process theory and the meaning reconstruction approach talk of adapting to a new, albeit different, future and would seem to promise hope for those experiencing loss and grief at any stage of life. Adapting to loss necessarily has a future dimension to it, and so it is perhaps testament to the power of ageist ideology to deny the future, that older people tend to be perceived as different from their younger counterparts and largely excluded from helpful interventions.

Thompson (1998a) reminds us of Sartre's explanation of how our sense of self in the present is constructed through the interplay between our experience of the past and our ambitions for the future – the 'progressive-regressive' method. For older people, the implication of denying that they need to adapt to their futures can therefore be seen as denying their identities and their very humanity. If we continue to conceptualize the suffering experienced by older people as a form of disenfranchised grief and to exclude them from the understanding and help that we would see as valid forms of intervention when working with younger bereaved or traumatized adults, then we run the risk of perpetuating what is, arguably, ageism's most demeaning process – dehumanization. If we accept that loss is indeed part of life, and we accept that older people are not a group apart from 'adults', then surely to deny the impact of loss and grief in their lives is to treat them as if they were already dead.

It is obvious that each response to loss or a bereavement is different, and the meaning attached to the event by the client is crucial (see Chapter 3 in this volume). It is important to bear in mind that, while some bereaved people suffer from a variety of distressing symptoms following the death of a loved one, there are those who choose not to display nor express them to researchers, their family doctors or even other family members. For some people, a death is not a bereavement, there are no apparent losses involved, and as practitioners it is important not to ascribe feelings where they do not exist.

12 Losses and Justice: An Australian Perspective

John Dawes

Introduction

At one level the justice system can be understood as the major institutional way we deal with losses, largely around our expectations of how other people will behave towards us. These losses range from minor slights, where our sense of fairness is challenged, to more serious encounters where our homes are invaded, to severe assaults. This chapter discusses some of our ways of dealing with these losses, taking a narrative therapy approach. Narrative therapy is based on the idea that personal problems are created in social, cultural and political contexts (White and Epston, 1990).

Kelley describes narrative therapy as a major trend, similar to 'postmodern literary criticism, where the story line is deconstructed as the plot, characters and time line are reassessed for meaning' which 'helps clients through seeing other truths and other possible interpretations of events' (1996, pp. 463–4). This process is called *externalization*. Externalizing conversations 'attempt to move the process away from self-attack, recrimination, blame and judgement' (Monk, 1997, p. 6). Usually the client is an individual, although narrative approaches are 'especially useful with couples and families' and its use in groups and community work seems feasible. 'Narrative therapy is underpinned by a philosophy of language' where meaning is socially constructed and where we make sense of our lives in the context of our social history (Drewery and Winslade, 1997, p. 34).

There are parallels with narrative therapy at a national level. McKenna (1997) wrote of the 'fragmentation of the grand narrative' and the emergence of new histories of colonized indigenous peoples, women's history, environmental history and ethnic histories. Many of Australia's myths and stories are being 'reauthored' and new 'truths' discovered as we grapple with issues of national identity. Not all Australians identify with these changes and various reactionary movements have emerged, such as the One Nation Party.[1] Also, the 1999 referendum to change Australia to a Republic failed.[2] Changing our constitutional arrangements from a monarchy was seen by many as a way of reauthoring our founding stories to include indigenous people and be more sensitive to the notion that they are descendants of victims of an invasion. Landmark cases in the Australian High Court (*Mabo* and *Wik*) have added to the momentum, changing Australia significantly.[3] The *Mabo* decision ended the lie of 'terra nullius' – that is, that the Australian continent was unoccupied when Cook visited in 1770 (Bartlett, 1993) and claimed the whole of the East Coast (Hughes, 1987). This action and events in Britain paved the way for the First Fleet to arrive on 26 January 1788 (now Australia Day).

Australia's birth in 1788 as an outpost of European civilization and as a penal colony occurred when European countries were changing the way they punished their offenders. Punishment was, up to this point, directed at the body. Public torture and humiliation preceded execution. But soon punishment was directed at the mind (Foucault, 1977) and penitentiaries were built. However, in the interregnum between the ideas and their translation into public buildings (panopticons), transportation formed the solution. The 1776 United States Declaration of Independence closed off the US colonies to the reception of convicts and New South Wales became the destination. Those immigrant 'Australians', especially the convicts (736 in the first fleet) were exiled when the world was a bigger place than today (Hughes, 1987). Their losses are almost unimaginable now, as were the ensuing losses for Australia's indigenous peoples. Colonial expansion was about access to new economic resources including land and, in the inevitable march of 'progress', indigenous persons were victimized as their way of life, culture and lands were confronted by the brutality of the penal and colonial processes. And the losses for Australia's indigenous people are still having an impact today as we struggle with the idea of reconciliation.[4]

This chapter discusses some major reauthoring and the resultant discovery of new truths, including the losses experienced by many people and, for some, their disenfranchised grief (Doka, 2001). The growth in Australia's imprisonment rate, mandatory sentencing, deaths in custody and developments within the victims' movement all impact upon our understanding of loss.

Imprisonment in Australia

Australia, like many countries in the world, is experiencing significant growth in the use of imprisonment, with many unintended consequences, including substantial social and economic costs.

Rates of imprisonment

In June 1982, there were 9826 prisoners in Australia – an imprisonment rate of 89.8. In March 1999, there were 20,122 prisoners, with a national imprisonment rate of 141.5. The rate is calculated as the number imprisoned per 100,000 persons of imprisonable age and enables historical, intra- and cross-jurisdictional comparisons to be made. Within Australia, imprisonment rates vary substantially, with some below the national average and others well above. This intranational variation in the use of imprisonment, in itself, raises an important issue of justice. Is it just, for example, for young men in Queensland or in the Northern Territory to be between twice and four times more likely to go to prison for similar offences which in other states would be dealt with by some form of community option?

Retributive inflation

Retributive inflation has its origins in politicians' responses to citizen pressure resulting in an increase in tariffs. Carcach and Grant (1999) suggest that increasing the 'cost' to offenders of various crimes leads to increasing imprisonment rates. This approach widens the gate and leads to more persons being imprisoned, with the consequent loss of opportunities within the community through loss of social skills, employment, relationships and increasing stigmatization, as well as being exposed to more serious offenders and possible contagion. Also, more families are affected by the turmoil, shame and disruption caused when one of their members is imprisoned, with families often experiencing disenfranchised grief. How do you tell your neighbour that your son or daughter has been imprisoned?

Getting tougher

Getting tougher is another facet of retributive inflation. Carcach and Grant (1999) identify tougher sanctions on convicted criminals, such as longer prison terms, as a factor in the growth of imprisonment rates. Prison terms for serious offences such as murder, rape and armed robbery have been affected. Early release programmes have been curtailed due to increasing community pressure. In the 1970s, New South Wales, Victoria and South Australia introduced remission programmes that reduced not only the length of the sentence imposed, but also the amount of time actually served in prison. At the time these programmes were regarded as major reforms, designed to reward social behaviour and application to work – parallel with employment packages, especially bonuses, paid to free workers in the community (Nagle, 1978). The remission programmes, based on recommendations of Royal Commissions[5] and other similar inquiries,[6] were introduced following widespread turmoil, including riots and destruction of prison property. When these programmes were removed during the 1990s, their removal was described as *reform* and justified under the 'Truth-in-Sentencing' rubric.

System efficiencies

Carcach and Grant (1999) also identified changes in police policy in the way prisoners are processed which could lead to increased prison numbers. An example of this occurred when improved computerization, enabling speedier identification of outstanding warrants, led to more arrests. One successful response to the Royal Commission into Aboriginal Deaths in Custody (RCIADIC), aimed at reducing deaths, was speedier processing of prisoners and their removal from police to correctional custody (Dalton, 1999a). A common criticism of so-called 'community corrections' is that they widen the net of social control – that is, even if they reduce imprisonment rates, more people are actually under some form of supervision and control ('gaze'). Another aspect is 'net-widening', which occurs when people are placed on more intrusive and controlling programmes than are necessary (for example, community service rather than probation), because courts are responding to community pressures and sometimes it is just too difficult for the courts to determine the differences between programmes. The most severe form of net-widening occurs when people are imprisoned for technical breaches of non-custodial programmes, such as failure to pay a fine.

Increasing crime rates and greater willingness to report crime

Finally, Carcach and Grant (1999) identify variations in crime rates as a factor leading to increasing imprisonment. While the homicide rate has remained remarkably stable from 1915 to 1998 (below two persons per 100,000), the same is not true for other serious crime. Rates for crimes such as assault and robbery have increased dramatically, from about 20 incidents per 100,000 people in 1974 to near 100 per 100,000 for serious assault. Rates for more opportunistic crimes, such as stealing, break, enter and steal, motor vehicle theft and fraud have also escalated dramatically. Some of these crimes may also be linked to drugs. It is the apparent randomness of these crimes which concerns citizens. This is the dominant media story. But there is another story, as Mukherjee (2000) notes: about two thirds of Australia's homicides are committed by and against intimates and over 40 per cent of all assaults occur in private homes, with women and girls most frequently victimized. Of course, a more responsive criminal justice system may encourage more reporting of crime (Polk, 2000), especially by those victims who are supported.

Indigenous imprisonment rates

An examination of the indigenous imprisonment rates (ABS, 1999) points to the overrepresentation of indigenous people in prison and is a significant factor in the increasing numbers of prisoners. The highest imprisonment rate for Indigenous Australians was, for March 1999, in Western Australia (2920.5), followed by Queensland (1801.5), South Australia (1649.3) and the Northern Territory (1491.3). Even Victoria, with a moderate imprisonment rate of 78.9, had an indigenous rate of 917.9. The highest proportion of indigenous persons in custody was recorded in the NT (76 per cent of all prisoners) followed by WA (34 per cent) and Qld (22 per cent). The earlier narrative suggested that Aboriginal people were more criminal and this was reflected in their overimprisonment. Today it is widely recognized that the overrepresentation of Aboriginal people in the criminal justice system is the result of underlying structural issues, including racism, poverty and destruction of their culture (Mukherjee, 2000; RCIADIC, 1991).

Imprisonment remains the only appropriate penalty in very serious crime, where the community's outrage cannot be dealt with in other ways and the imposition of a less severe penalty challenges the notion of fairness. The loss of liberty expressed in a sentence of imprisonment remains the most severe and intrusive way a modern democratic state can deal with those who offend, but it should be reserved for the most serious offences. However, proportionality (making the sentence fit the crime) is under threat. The major challenge to proportionality is inappropriate mandatory sentencing. The social and economic costs (losses), to the community in *demonizing* a greater number of offenders through imprisonment are incalculable.

Mandatory sentencing

Mandatory sentencing 'refers to the practice of parliament setting a strict penalty for the commission of a criminal offence' (Roche, 1999), thereby removing discretion, resulting in a loss of proportionality and consistency and affecting some groups more than others, especially Aborigines, young people and poor people. Mandatory sentencing came to public attention when a 15-year-old Aboriginal boy died in a youth facility, following a 21-day sentence for theft of some small items of stationery. Marcia Langton, an Aboriginal academic, has characterized the NT laws as *mandatory imprisonment* rather than *mandatory sentencing* and says these laws were motivated by retribution not justice (Langton, 2000).

Mandatory sentences are commonly used in areas such as driving offences. A formula is applied to all – millionaires and paupers – and you are guilty unless you challenge the matter in court. The offence is expiated by payment of the fine. The argument against mandatory sentences for offences such as theft and burglary is that such sentences, especially if they involve a prison term, impact equally on all, no matter what the motivation for the offence or the quantum of goods stolen. This results in more Aboriginal people being imprisoned (Schetzer, 1998). It is the greater impact on Aborigines which has led Langton (2000) and others to describe the laws as racist. The argument about equal impact has superficial appeal and it is only when a number of cases are compared that the glaring loss of proportionality becomes obvious.

In the Northern Territory, an adult first-time offender convicted of a designated property offence must receive a minimum prison sentence of 14 days and, for a second offence, a minimum of 90 days. Offenders convicted of a third offence will receive a sentence of one year (Roche, 1999). Under amendments to the Juvenile Justice Act (NT), a Magistrate or Judge must impose a 28-day sentence of detention upon offenders aged 15 or 16 who have committed a second offence after the legislation became operational.

While Roche (1999) claims evidence suggests that mandatory sentencing can deliver modest but expensive crime prevention, discretion is displaced elsewhere – usually upon police and prosecutors. The Western Australian 1996 amendments to the Criminal Code (WA) require that a juvenile or adult offender, convicted for a third time or more of a home burglary, must receive a 12-month sentence of imprisonment or detention.

The arguments for mandatory sentencing are claimed to be crime prevention, incapacitation, deterrence and that such laws are enacted by democratically elected parliaments (Roche, 1999). Critics of mandatory sentencing argue that such sentences are not cost-effective, that they reduce the capacity for discretion by the court and therefore diminish or eliminate proportionality. Finally, politicians use mandatory sentencing and the fear of crime in the community, together with the community's superficial understanding of the law, as a way of ensuring their election and re-election to parliament (Hood, 1999; Dixon, 1995). A secondary impact has been to strengthen the hand of those who argue that such laws are in breach of Australia's responsibilities to the United Nations and are racist because of their disproportionate impact upon Aborigines. These laws, it has been suggested, take us back to when some of Australia's convicts arrived in this country after being transported for equally trivial offences (Robson, 1965; Hughes, 1987). Mandatory sentencing can be understood as a powerful, institutional and dominant reaffirmation of the 'stories' of one group – that is, the victims of petty crime – who say crime is out of control and the only response to crime must be tougher sanctions. Their way of life, possessions and comfort have been upset by acts of small-time crime, committed by young people, predominantly Aborigines. Although many voices have been raised in opposition to these laws, including that of the UN, the only concession won from the Chief Minister of the Northern Territory has been to lift the age of operation of the adult laws to those 18 years and over rather than 16.

The stolen generations

On 2 August 1995, the Commonwealth Attorney-General commissioned The Human Rights and Equal Opportunity Commission to trace the history of the forcible removal of indigenous children from their families; to examine current child welfare laws, practices and policies as they impact upon indigenous families; whether principles might emerge which would support the payment of compensation and to examine the causes of removal of indigenous children from their families today and whether such removal might be prevented (1997a). The report traces the history of forcible removal of indigenous children from their parents, a practice grounded in the racist, supremacist and assimilationist past, although there were also legitimate interventions in accordance with child welfare policies. The outcome of this investigation is the *Bringing Them Home* report in which grief and loss are major themes (1997b).

Social workers have been part of the reauthoring of the past, as their roles (for example, in child protection, especially among Australia's Aboriginal peoples) have become better known (AASW, 1997a; see also Tilbury, 1998) and practices more culturally sensitive. The Australian Association of Social Workers has acknowledged that 'social workers were involved in the forced separation of Aboriginal and Torres Strait Islander children from their families in every state and territory of Australia this century' (AASW, 1997a). In 1997 the AASW was signatory to an apology to Aboriginal and Torres Strait Islander peoples (AASW, 1997b):

> The Australian Council of Social Service (ACOSS) and our undersigned members deeply regret the damage caused by the forcible removal of Aboriginal and Torres Strait Islander children from their families. We acknowledge that the removal of children devastated individuals, families and entire communities. We acknowledge the finding of the Human Rights and Equal Opportunity Commission that a major intention of this official policy was to assimilate the children so that Aborigines as a distinct group would disappear. Hence, as the Commission found, it was a genocidal policy. We further acknowledge that the resulting loss of land, language and identity is a key cause of the intolerable levels of disadvantage currently faced by indigenous Australians. (AASW, 1997a, p. 4)

Later in 1997 the National President of the AASW committed the AASW to fully supporting the reconciliation process and to adequately dealing with our past as social workers by establishing a Task Group to prepare a statement about relinquishing mothers and adoption (Dodds, 1997). Thus social workers have been lending their support to causes of justice and the reauthoring of stories to enable different 'truths' to emerge.

Not all Australians have acclaimed the *Bringing Them Home* report. Some suggest the past practices of government agencies should be allowed to remain in the past where they belong. To examine past policies and practices through the lens of our current understanding is reasonable and, while we should not be held responsible for the actions of our European predecessors in this country, it is important that the full history be known. Those critical of this position invite us to consider the possibility that, in future, our cherished views and practices might suffer the same fate as those now being re-examined. Even the Prime Minister has spoken about rejecting the 'black armband' view of history (Howard, 1996; McKenna, 1997), suggesting that more emphasis should be placed on the positive aspects of Australian history and its achievements as a nation.

Others, the AASW among them, suggest that understanding the past is central to the idea of reconciliation and is crucial in the ongoing development of an inclusive, vibrant democracy. A leaked version of the Commonwealth Government's response was made available to the media and on 1 April 2000 headlines such as 'Sorry, You Don't Exist' appeared in the daily press. The Commonwealth Government's strategy has been to deny that a 'stolen generation' ever existed and that the allegations about thousands of Aboriginal children being stolen from their homes are 'grossly exaggerated'. The report suggested that no more than 10 per cent of Aboriginal children were forcibly separated from their families, including those separated for good reason under child welfare policies. The Aboriginal Affairs Minister also ruled out compensation. The Prime Minister has expressed 'deep and sincere regret' for the removal of Aboriginal children but, despite requests from the community, has refused to say sorry. Dealing with the report and with mandatory sentencing have proved to be extremely difficult and have threatened the stability of the Government, with some backbench members of the Government parties threatening to cross the floor of Parliament and vote with the Opposition.

Deaths in custody

Australia remains the only western (Anglophone) country to have established a national inquiry (RCIADIC) into deaths in custody. One of the major determinants behind the push for the RCIADIC was the awareness of a rapid increase in Aboriginal deaths in custody in 1987. Whilst there had been 11 in 1985 and 9 in 1986, in 1987 there were 21 (Biles et al., 1992). The total custodial deaths in Australia in 1987 were 93 (21 Aboriginal and 72 non-Aboriginal – Biles et al., 1992).

A key recommendation of the RCIADIC was that deaths in custody be monitored and data published on a regular basis. Since 31 May 1989 and up to September 1999, another 147 Aboriginal deaths in custody have occurred throughout Australia (Dalton, 1999b). Unlike the pattern of Aboriginal deaths in the 1980s, where about one third occurred in prisons, a large majority (66 per cent) were prison deaths. Australian police agencies have been successful in reducing the number of deaths in police lockups but not in custody-related operations such as high-speed chases (Dalton, 1999b).

The RCIADIC found that 'Aboriginal people do not die at a greater rate than non-Aboriginal people in custody', but 'what is over-whelmingly different is the rate at which Aboriginal people come into custody, compared with the rate of the general community' (RCIADIC, 1991, Vol.1, Findings 1.3.1 and 1.3.2). The RCIADIC has been described as a waste of money (thought to have cost taxpayers about $40 million) and as a 'lawyers' picnic'. These criticisms mask the reality that had better statistics about the use of imprisonment and deaths in custody been available in 1987, there might have been no Royal Commission at all, or a Royal Commission into *all* deaths in custody. However, much more than the raw statistics emerged and again the themes of loss and grief, especially disenfran-chised grief, can be found on every page of the Royal Commission's reports. Moreover, much of the RCIADIC's work could be regarded as doing again the work that was often poorly executed in the first place by the police, correctional agencies and coroners. The RCIADIC produced 99 reports of the deaths of individual Aborigines, an interim report and a final report in five volumes together with a number of regional reports.[7]

In my detailed study of 39 deaths in the SA prison system from January 1980 to March 1993 (Dawes, 1997) the Coroners' Reports were analysed and, where a death was subsequently investigated by the RCIADIC, the Commission's reports also considered. Many deficiencies emerged: some police investigations were inadequate, as were some pathologists' reports. Also, some families were not advised of the death of a family member and, later, that a coronial inquest was to be held into the death of a loved one. Some coronial inquests were brief and lacked thoroughness. Deficiencies emerged in much correctional practice. In some cases in the early 1980s the coroner did not conduct formal inquests. Under the law as it was the coroner exercised a discretion. The coroner examined most of the deaths, a postmortem examination was held, and, of course, the coroner had access to the police reports of the deaths. But inquests were not held, especially for those prisoners who died of natural causes (Dawes, 1997; Pounder, 1986).

Inquests

Inquests have many functions such as affirming the importance of each person, establishing the identity of the deceased person, assisting in the production of accurate mortality statistics, providing leads and evidence where malpractice is suspected and, very importantly, publicly identifying what was not involved in the death (Bray, undated, circa 1987). Inquests are also critical in assisting survivors come to terms with violent, unexpected deaths, including deaths in custody (Raphael, 1986; note Worden's, 1991, first and second tasks). When someone dies, there is always a sense in which it has not happened. Having knowledge of the *facts* of the death is important for the survivors. Prisons are closed environments and it is not always possible to allow family members to see the place of death. I was only asked once to allow this. I did this personally and believe it was helpful to the family. The coroner's report, after an inquest, is an important way in which the facts of the loss can be made explicit, although the value of this can be diminished by the delays in reporting.

The lack of an inquest may be a public statement that the life of a prisoner is not valued – the dominant narrative. At least, that is how some of the relatives may have seen the failure to hold formal inquests. In some RCIADIC cases, relatives were not contacted and only learned of the death at some later date (Dawes, 1997). An inquest may provide a message to relatives that, although their loved one was a prisoner, the death should be properly scrutinized and the authorities asked to account for their actions under the legal doctrine of 'duty of care'. The holding of an inquest, especially soon after the death, allows relatives more opportunity to complete a chapter of the grieving process and move forward with their lives (Raphael, 1986).

Where inquests were not held or were inadequate, at least the RCIADIC completed such work and probably assisted many Aboriginal families. While we may never forget the deceased person, especially a family member, effective coping requires adjustment to the deceased person no longer being present in the everyday sense. This adjustment may be more difficult in the case of children. We invest emotionally in our children. For parents of adult children who are imprisoned, those children may (nearly always do?) represent unfulfilled promise, shattered dreams and a profound sense of loss. Prisoners are *demonized* in the press, but they remain sons, fathers, husbands and partners. In fact they probably remain 'sons', longer than they remain in other roles, as long-term imprisonment tends to break up other relationships. Survivors need to speak about the loss (sometimes idolizing the deceased). The 99 RCIADIC reports of individual Aboriginal prisoners are successful in that they *un-demonize* those prisoners, painting a more human picture of each individual, thus allowing new truths to be discovered by reauthoring the past.

Staff and other prisoners may also grieve for the deceased prisoner who was a significant part of their daily lives, but whose loss is little acknowledged (Dawes, 1997). Disenfranchised grief means that other prisoners may not be able to show their grief and participate in the funeral (Dawes, 1997). The same restrictions may apply to prison officers, especially males. Gender differences are important and can contribute to disenfranchised grief (Thompson, 1997). Some male officers told me they felt sad at a prisoner's death, but could not show their feelings because they felt that these would be misinterpreted and their colleagues would perceive them as weak. The death of a prisoner is a stigmatized death, with homicides and suicides more stigmatized than deaths from natural causes. Deaths in custody also represent concurrent losses for other prisoners in addition to the cumulative losses of freedom, status, hope and life.

How then should we respond to the losses these deaths represent? While a comprehensive discussion of how deaths in custody might be reduced is beyond the scope of this chapter, many deaths could be prevented by reducing the number of persons in custody (Biles, 1994). Police and prison custody does provide some protection from death (Biles, 1994) and research has shown that offenders supervised on community orders 'are more likely to die than were persons of similar age in prison' (p. 25).

The difficulty for survivors of deaths in custody is that their relatives are in the total care of the state – removed from society to where the authorities meet nearly all of their needs. There is an expectation that such deaths should not occur, that the person is being looked after and supervised. The shock of hearing about the death is made more acute by its unexpected nature and that the deceased person is away from their family's care. The death may also trigger feelings of guilt and regret about commissions or omissions in the past which may result in the losses seeming more acute.

The treatment of victims

A common catchcry suggests that victims are the forgotten actors in the criminal justice system (Gardner, 1990), based on the fact that victims were not active participants in the criminal justice system once their statements had been made and their evidence heard. Perhaps there is an element of truth in the statement, but victims today are not forgotten, although their emotional needs and desire for information on the processes may not be addressed. Much of the apparatus of the criminal justice system has been established to prosecute and punish those who offend. What is important is how the system assists victims, not only in obtaining justice, but also psychologically, by creating the opportunity for resolution of the trauma-associated victimization. The impact of the offence and its aftermath upon a victim of crime is captured at a point of time and 'frozen' into the victim's statement and evidence incorporated into the case against the accused. Traditionally the victim's experience and trauma were 'framed' or captured by the way the investigating officers went about their work, their prejudices about what constitutes being a good or bad victim and the culture of the particular police agency. The victim's situation was captured in the police 'lens' as a snapshot. The dynamic experience of the victim after statements had been taken and the victim's ongoing struggle to make meaning of the experience and the objective 'costs' of the crime (such as the ongoing impact and physical suffering) was sometimes not known to the court, or if known, the extent of the court's deliberations on this material are often hidden.

Much of the work of law reform in response to the victims' movement tried to improve outcomes for victims and reduce or eliminate 'secondary victimization' – that is, 'first by the crime and the criminal and then by the poor treatment they receive in the criminal process' (Elias, 1993, p. 6). It is through listening to the victims' narratives that we have developed a richer understanding of what it means to be a victim. People who are victims of personal crime speak about losses – loss of the person murdered, or of a sense of security, or fairness. As Bard and Sangrey (1986, p. xvi) state: 'every victim of a personal crime is confronted with a brutal reality: the deliberate violation of one person by another.' It is critical that the victim's total experience is conveyed to the court, not only in the interests of justice, but also to assist in the victim's recovery and aid well-being. The major strategic approach enabling the victim's story to be told directly and not framed or captured by the police, is through the provision of a victim impact statement, especially if the victim makes the statement.

In 1981 an SA Government report recommended, amongst other things, the abolition of the unsworn statement and that courts should be advised of the effects of the crime upon the victim (*Victims of Crime Review: Report One*, 1999). This principle was later incorporated as Principle 14 of the Declaration of Rights for Victims of Crime. The Declaration was adopted in 1985 and contains 14 principles (*Information for Victims of Crime*, 2000). Victim impact statements were implemented by police gathering additional information about any financial, social, psychological and physical harm suffered by the victim including 'any other information that may aid the court in sentencing including restitution and compensation needs of the victim' (p. 107). This was a substantial and welcome reform but the victim's story was still mediated by and heard through the police or prosecutor. A modification to the victim impact statement programme was implemented through a questionnaire which was regarded by some victims as a significant improvement (*Victims of Crime Review: Report One*, 1999). The Criminal Law (Sentencing) Act 1988 codified Principle 14 and allows for a victim to refuse to provide such information if that is their wish.

A further amendment to the Criminal Law (Sentencing) Act S 7A was passed providing for victims of an indictable offence who suffer as a consequence of any injury loss or damage, to read a victim impact statement to a sentencing court. Victim support organizations have been a significant force in promoting the hearing of victims' narratives.

In trials all narratives need to be heard. A number of writers have cautioned against rights for victims being won at the expense of offenders (Daly, 1998; Harding, 1994; Sumner, 1994; Fattah, 1991) and the challenge for policy makers is to structure victims' rights in such a way as to not swamp those of offenders, especially if a retributivist, perhaps even vengeful climate exists.

Conclusion

Narrative therapy is based upon different discourses or stories that enable the creation of alternative empowering explanations of events. This process in individuals, groups or communities can help heal losses. Identified in this chapter have been different narratives surrounding the growth of Australia's prison population, the stolen

generations of Aboriginal children, deaths in custody and the treatment of the victims of crime. The narratives suggest alternative and
sometimes more challenging interpretations of phenomena than the
commonly understood explanations. The exploration of losses and
alternative empowering narratives offers a perspective which can be
extrapolated to other settler nations and marginalized populations.

Notes

1. See www.onenation.com.au
    One Nation Party (ONP): a political party formed by Pauline
    Hanson in 1997 after winning the Federal seat of Oxley as an
    Independent the previous year.
2. In November 1999, Australians voted in a national referendum
    about whether they wanted a Republican style of government,
    to sever the link with the Monarchy and for a new preamble to
    the Constitution. The results were: 43.5 per cent voted for the
    Republic and 54.7 per cent against and 39.5 per cent for the
    preamble and 60.5 per cent against (see www.abc.net.au and
    www.parliament.new.gov.au/gi/library/auscon.htm). The fol-
    lowing section of the preamble was contested by many
    Aborigines and Torres Strait Islanders as well as others who
    wanted to see included prior recognition of the ownership of the
    lands by indigenous Australians:

    > honouring Aborigines and Torres Strait Islanders, the nation's first
    > People, for their deep kinship with their lands and their ancient
    > and continuing cultures which enrich the life of our country;

3. High Court Decision on Mabo 3 June 1992:

    1. Upon the annexation of the Murray Islands to Queensland,
        the radical title to all the land in those islands vested in the
        Crown in right of Queensland.
    2. The traditional title of the Meriam people to the Murray
        Islands, being their rights to possession, occupation, use
        and enjoyment of the Islands, survived annexation of the
        Islands to Queensland and is preserved under the law of
        Queensland.
    3. The traditional title of the Meriam people to the lands in
        the Islands has not been extinguished by subsequent legis-
        lation or executive act and may not be extinguished

without the payment of compensation or damages to the traditional titleholders of the Islands.

4.   The land in the Murray Islands is not Crown land within the meaning of that term in s.5 of the Land. In the case of the *Wik Peoples* v *The State of Queensland and Others* (B8/96) one of the main issues to arise was the nature of the pastoral lease and its effect on the native title rights and interests of Aboriginal people. The *Native Title Act 1993* was enacted to deal with the consequences of *Mabo* and recognized and protected native title which had not been extinguished. Pastoral leases presented more complex issues for settlement – see www.nntt.gov.au.

4.   At the core of the concept of reconciliation is the formal recognition, by way of treaty, of the prior occupation and ownership of Australia by Aboriginal and Torres Strait Islander peoples. A *Council for Aboriginal Reconciliation* was established (Council for Aboriginal Reconciliation Act 1991) to consult Aborigines and Torres Strait Islanders and the wider community to determine whether reconciliation would be advanced by such a document. A draft Declaration for Reconciliation has been prepared but has not won government support (see www.austlii.edu.au /au/org/car/docref/draft/index.htm).

5.   *Report of the Commission into New South Wales Prisons, Nagle, J. Royal Commissioner, April 1978:* Sydney, New South Wales Government Printer.
Clarkson, G. *Report of the Royal Commission on Allegations in Relation to Prisons under the Charge, Care and Direction of the Director of the Department of Correctional Services and Certain Related Matters, 11 December 1981*: Adelaide, Government Printer.

6.   *Report of the Board of Inquiry into Several Matters Concerning H. M. Prison Pentridge and the Maintenance of Discipline in Prisons (the Jenkinson Inquiry) 5 September 1973:* Melbourne, Government Printer.

7.   The reports of the Royal Commission into Aboriginal Deaths in Custody can be found at www.aic.gov.au/index.htm.

Part Three

Working with Loss

13 Teaching and Learning About Loss

Jeremy Weinstein

Introduction

This chapter seeks to reach two audiences: students and lecturers. As students, having been provoked by some of the ideas in this text, you will now want to learn more but may have no formal taught courses available. This chapter attempts to provide some ideas for self-directed learning, identifying themes, further reading and some experiential exercises for you to undertake on your own or with the support of friends and colleagues.

For lecturers, I suggest some ideas about the core knowledge, values and skills that apply to teaching about loss and grief to students on professional courses wanting to improve their practice, both with individual clients and within their organizations.

My ideas are based on my own work as a lecturer in an inner-city, multiracial university where I teach about loss and bereavement to a range of professional groups at various academic levels. This includes one-off sessions to social workers or nurses studying courses such as 'Adaptation to Long-term Illness' or counselling skills, as well as a full unit on 'Loss: Social, Cultural and Professional Issues'. This is part of an interprofessional Master's degree in Professional Practice, with students comprising social workers, radiographers, midwives and nurses.

How issues arise: 'living psychologically beyond our means'

In a counselling skills class a neonatal nurse describes joining a mother who is standing over the incubator where her tiny baby lies. The mother then comments: 'It's so strange looking down at Lucy in her coffin ... Oh God, I meant to say cot.' The two women stay standing in silence until, after a few minutes, the nurse makes her excuses, saying that she has other babies to attend to. The class, in their response, are also still and shocked. When I try to encourage some thoughts about how the student might have responded differently, the group, uncharacteristically, stays silent, and I feel them willing me to move on and away from this painful vignette.

In a unit on 'loss', a social worker in a multidisciplinary student group describes the aftermath of a ten-day court action where a mother fought, unsuccessfully, against an adoption order on her youngest daughter, Sarah. The girl's fourth birthday is the last contact meeting, and so the celebration is 'a bitter-sweet occasion'. Sarah, who knows she will be having 'a new mummy and daddy', plays with her new toys, ignoring her tearful mother and older sister. Again, the students need time to absorb the many levels of loss faced by each and every member of that family, and the complexities for the professional whose role is to facilitate and work with the feelings, while also being responsible for them, since she had initiated the court action.

In another session, a white care worker describes the funeral of a young Afro-Caribbean killed in a car accident. She comments on the congregants filing past the open coffin in the church, and then the scenes in the cemetery where family members and friends heap earth onto the coffin, not leaving it to the anonymous labourers. Around the grave one group holds a prayer meeting, another supports the grief-stricken girlfriend, yet another gathers round to comfort the parents. The care worker, who had previously only attended rather perfunctory cremations, is moved by this very different ceremony, with its sustained emotion, its openness to a whole range of different ways of mourning, but all supported within one containing community of mourners. This story is richly resonant and helps others in the group share their own varied and deeply felt experiences of what loss and mourning mean in their own cultures and how rituals can help healing.

Moments like this are sharp reminders of how, as Freud once put it, in our attempts to cope in a 'civilized' manner with the reality of death (and loss): 'we are living psychologically beyond our means' (in Meghnagi, 1993, p. 38). As the examples cited above illustrate, human services professionals are not immune from the pressures and the raw emotions that are engendered by confronting loss. And there is a possibility of reaching resolution through opening ourselves up to the experience. What we need to find is the delicate balance between allowing for the feelings, but in ways that contribute to, rather than detract from, the professional tasks and understanding. I will shortly offer a discussion of the major themes and the suggested reading and exercises, but first I give an outline of a unit on loss, social, cultural and professional issues for which I am responsible.

The course details

The unit 'Loss: Social, Cultural and Professional Issues' has as its aims:

(a)   To give detailed attention to, and analysis of, differing cultural needs at times of loss.
(b)   To explore further meanings and responses in a wide range of loss situations.
(c)   To analyse the constructions of care in response to loss and the relevancy for different groups of people.

And, as learning outcomes, by the completion of the units students should be able to:

(a)   Analyse and evaluate the definitions of loss, their variations over time and within differing cultural groups and settings, including European and international perspectives.
(b)   Identify, through continuing exploration, the meaning and responses of a wide range of loss situations, taking cultural variations into account.
(c)   Critically evaluate a variety of theoretical perspectives relating to loss.
(d)   Examine how these theoretical perspectives have influenced policy and practice development, in both the statutory and voluntary sectors in the human services.
(e)   Explore the effects these might have on influencing the way an experience is constructed, and the ethnocentricity of help offered.
(f)   Analyse how discourses on loss are legitimized in relation to time, power and dominant ideologies.

(g)   Consider how future needs at time of loss might be assessed, provided and evaluated, taking account of individuality and cultural issues, specific to the student's area of practice.

The indicative content is:

(a)   Definitions of loss:
- cultural meanings and differences;
- loss through death of a person;
- loss of self and any part of self;
- other losses; and
- losses which remain taboo and which are high profile.

(b)   Death, loss and bereavement across cultures:

- what is 'normal' and 'abnormal'?
- what are the healing rituals?
- managing difference and discrimination.

(c)   Different approaches:

- the medical, biological theories (Lindemann and Engel), intrapsychic theories (Freud, Klein and Pincus), attachment-disengagement, reconstitutive theories (Bowlby) and the historical/sociological theories (Durkheim, Aries and Walter);
- analysis of stage and phases models;
- development and use of assessment and outcomes tools in response to loss.

(d)   Structure and processes:

- historical analysis;
- construction of responses to loss and cultural comparisons;
- lay versus professional responses.

(e)   Loss from an international perspective:

- European, American and international models and policies;
- the relevance for the British experience.

(f)   Provision of care, health service, voluntary and lay caring:

- social services;
- voluntary organizations;
- the hospice movement and its impact on health care;
- future directions.

The assignment is a 4000-word case study which explores the degree to which the impact of loss for an individual and/or group can be assessed using current theories and models.

Opening ourselves up to understanding loss: the use of poetry, prose and film

The unit outline indicates the knowledge base, which provides a means of distinguishing between what many of the texts still refer to as 'normal' and 'pathological' responses to grief, in this and other cultures, and what we need to reformulate as patterns of behaviour, thoughts and feelings that may be more or less helpful for individuals and the wider community(ies). And this cognitive approach is necessary but not, in itself, sufficient, for there is also a need to open up to the experience of loss so that the theories can be fully appreciated and critiqued.

Poetry and prose are good ways of introducing, and then linking, the explicit and implicit knowledge base and the inherent values. Dinnage (1992) follows a very traditional path, drawing on the classical texts from *Beowulf* to Wilfred Owen, taking in Coleridge and Shakespeare along the way, and there are more current reference points.

Novels are a powerful medium and, of many possible examples, I would offer Swift's Booker Prize winner, *Last Orders* (1996), an exploration of a group of mainly working-class South London men marking the death of a friend and/or family member, while Alan Bennett's vignette, *Father! Father! Burning Bright* (2000) provides a poignant picture of a northern England middle-class man clumsily awaiting his father's death.

There is a growing genre of documentary accounts offering highly personalized and poignant accounts of individuals who are facing death and loss, either their own or those of their loved ones. This not an experience restricted to the UK and northern America, as is illustrated by the account of Lu Youqing. By posting letters on a website in his native China, describing his dying of cancer, he 'established a new standard for honesty in a society where reticence and considerations of face inhibit frank discussions of illness and death' (Gittings, 2000, p. 10). Examples from the UK of people openly documenting their daily experience of cancer are Diamond (1998) and Picardie (1998). In the latter there are important 'after words' by her partner, Matt Seaton, describing his struggles as a carer of someone who is dying, a perspective explored also by Widgery's (1989) essay 'Meeting Molly', a tribute to the short life of his baby daughter. Morrison's (1998) focus is on being with his father as he dies and the memories it brings up for him of this difficult father–son relationship. Bayley (1998) describes living with the dementia of his famous wife (Iris Murdoch) and Grant (1998) takes the same theme; this time the patient is her mother. The emphasis on essentially British responses to grief is challenged here, since she reflects on what this experience means for a whole generation of Jewish emigrants from Eastern Europe. The theme of loss through exile is taken up in Lamming's classic account (1954) of the Afro-Caribbean experience, and Anita Desai's more recent (2000) study of a young Indian caught, as a student in America, in a bewilderingly alien world.

The cinema can also have a considerable impact for, as I have written elsewhere (Weinstein, 1997), in a society where death, dying and grieving have become such sheltered and secretive occurrences, what we see on the big screen can provide some lessons in what the process of bereavement and recovery can be like. *Truly, Madly, Deeply* (1990), *Sleepless in Seattle* (1993), and *Four Weddings and a Funeral* (1994) famously featuring Auden's poem 'Stop all the Clocks', are all popular and influential films. And this perhaps rather idealized and middle-class perspective is complemented by recent films focusing on the rawer experiences of working-class families where resolution is less easy to find. Examples include the funeral at the climax of *My Name is Joe* (1998), the harsh comedy *Orphans* (1999) and *Under the Skin* (1997), portraying a young woman's descent into promiscuity and a form of madness, and then her precarious recovery, following the death of her mother and a bitter rivalry between two sisters. *Last Orders* is also now in the process of being filmed.

For some, this preoccupation with death is unhealthy. The above examples of confessional writing have been condemned as part of the sentimentalization of society (Anderson and Mullen, 1998). This is a useful reminder of the stoical or reserved tradition within British society, which also has to be acknowledged and understood. Nonetheless, depictions of death, dying and loss, which are deliberately written outside of the academic disciplines, are invaluable and challenging accounts that give us entry to the range of experiences and emotions that we need to know about before we can be fully available to our clients/patients.

Opening ourselves up to understanding loss: experiential exercises

And we can be further helped to access our own reactions through what Yalom (1980, pp. 174–5) terms 'existential shock therapy'. He cites examples of students being asked to:

(i)   write their own epitaph or obituary, contrasting the ideal one with the real one; or

(ii)   draw a straight line on a blank sheet of paper where one end represents birth and the other death (the student then marks the spot where they think they currently are and meditates upon this for five minutes); or

(iii) immerse themselves in a guided fantasy that has them imagining their own death, how and when it might occur, what the funeral might be like, who would come and what might they say?

(iv)   take part in a 'calling out' exercise: students gather together and have casual conversation. A name is called out at random and that student has immediately to stop talking and turn his or her back on the others who continue chatting as if undisturbed by the sudden absence of their colleague.

Yalom reports that many participants report an increased awareness of the arbitrariness and fragility of existence.

Jacobs (1991) provides detailed briefing sheets for his more elaborate exercises, intended to last between an hour and 75 minutes. These explore, in turn, reactions to ageing and illness, mini-role plays on loss, death and a community and, lastly, a role play based on a couple whose adolescent son dies.

I have used a worksheet on 'loss awareness' adapted from Irish et al. (1993) which focuses on ethnic variations and asks students to reflect on losses that they have experienced personally and what these have meant for them. These are listed as 'concrete losses' – for example, of money, personal possessions, stocks and shares, job. The second is 'development losses' – loss of fertility, hearing, hair and so on. The next is 'abstract losses' – such as the loss of dreams, faith, childhood, identity. 'Loss of self' includes illness, physical/emotional abuse, surgery and substance abuse. The last is 'Loss of other people', including death of parent, lover, child or friend, as well as loss through divorce or geographical moves. This is important in reminding us that death is only one sort of loss, and not always the most important.

Moving to death specifically, there is a choice of two other work-sheets. One, taken from Worden (1991), asks students to share, first in pairs and then feeding back to the large group, their thoughts about the first death they can remember, the most recent and the most painful and then they are asked about their primary style of coping and how they know their own grief is resolved. A final question is: 'When is it appropriate to share your own experience of grief with a client?' The other is, again, from Irish *et al.* (1993) and inquires into attitudes about 'normal' grief – for example, How long people 'should' mourn and how? Who of the mourners 'should' be the most affected? What sort of death is the most distressing? and so on.

Using any one, or more, of the above exercises sets the tone for the teaching, whether in a one-off session or in the longer unit. It enables students to share often very intimate experiences drawn from their experiences of different countries, cultures and communities. The group is introduced to the many introjects that are held, the values that we carry and where they originate – also, the whole host of different ways, all equally valid, that people mourn. Further, it allows that knowledge to be shared within the group; we learn not just about people who are patients/clients 'out there' but about us, here in the room.

Relating the work to clients: assessment

Drawing on all of the above, we then need to relate this work to clients, in all their diversity. Worden (1991) describes well the deter-minants of grief, and how these can contribute to uncomplicated, complicated or pathological grief. This draws, of course, on a medical model and other approaches allow us to see the issues more in terms of how different patterns of grieving emerge, and the degree to which they serve individuals. This is further elaborated by Eisenbruch (1984) who resists providing a list of the normative grieving patterns of different ethnic or religious groups (which can be misleadingly prescriptive and static), preferring instead a series of questions, such as who are the principal mourners and the percep-tion of the dead person and their spirit.

To explore more fully the influences on how individuals grieve I have devised some case studies:

1. John has died of an AIDS-related illness. Douglas, an ex-lover, moved back in during the later stages of his illness and was the primary carer. Two weeks before the death, however, John's

mother, Mary, came from the Irish Republic to look after him. She had not known about John's sexuality and refused to accept that he was 'really' gay, blaming Douglas, and city life in general, for leading him astray and causing his death. Douglas, and other gay friends, are banned from the house and denied any major role in the funeral.

2. Lou, 77, had been married to George for 61 years until he died six months earlier of Motor Neurone Disease. Lou had spent most of the last year of the illness nursing George at home, but eventually arranged for his respite care in a hospice where he died shortly afterwards. Lou now lives alone. Her four children all live locally but are preoccupied with their own families and do not spend as much time with Lou as she wishes. The son, Philip, especially is concerned that she is still very tearful and depressed and frequently tells her that it is time for her to 'pull herself together'. Lou has heart problems and arthritis, which limit her mobility.

3. Susan is 37 and pregnant. She has two sons (aged 10 and 8) from an earlier relationship. Despite the pregnancy being difficult Susan has taken as much care of herself as she can manage, given the demands of her family. The pregnancy has run its course and the family has prepared itself for the new arrival. Once admitted, however, the baby has to be delivered by a Caesarian operation and when Susan wakes up from the anaesthetic, in a side room on the maternity ward, she learns that the baby, a daughter, died shortly after birth.

4. Mahmood is an adolescent from Afghanistan where his family was terrorized by one of the warring factions. A group of fighters came looking for his father who was in hiding, and when the family insisted that they did not know his whereabouts, Mahmood's mother was shot in front of him. He was told that the fighters would be back for him next. Mahmood fled over the border to Pakistan where he was helped by relatives to fly on to London where he was placed in care.

In each of these cases we consider the individuals and their possible grieving responses, given what we know from Worden and Eisenbruch. In some cases details can be changed to see how this might influence the processes and the impact of difference, discrimination and disadvantage. Thus, in the first scenario, how might it be if John had died as a result of injecting drug use rather than sexual activity or if John was Afro-Caribbean or Asian?

The emergence of other themes

The importance of gender

Inevitably other themes emerge to be developed, depending on the time that is available. One of these is the importance of gender, and it is significant that, in the case studies outlined above, there are ample opportunities to explore how men and women might grieve differently, sometimes in ways that can be complementary and sometimes confrontational. Thus, there is Mary, John's mother, versus the male lover Douglas, Lou the wife as compared to Philip the son, Susan the pregnant wife and the anonymous husband.

Gender is a sensitive and contested issue, in this as in many other areas (see Riches, Chapter 5 in this volume). Cline (1995) argues that she is the first to expose the sexual politics of death and challenge the silence surrounding women's relationship to grief and loss. She is especially important in bringing to the fore the experiences of black and Asian women, also lesbians. In direct contrast, Walter (1999) argues that the predominant model of what is successful grieving, with its emphasis on encouraging the expression, rather than the containment, of feelings, and based on research predominantly of widows: 'privileges a characteristically female form of grief' (p. 168). Certainly, what seems important is that these gender dimensions are now explicit rather than implicit, a process further encouraged by the increasingly cited 'dual process' model (Stroebe and Schut, 1999). This delineates the (mainly male) practical and the (mainly female) expressive grief responses, and acknowledges the importance of both.

The importance of ritual, religious and spiritual beliefs

A further debate is the important role of rituals and how they can serve to help integrate the dead into the life of the living, on individual, community and societal levels. As Walter (1999) puts it so clearly, if 'society cannot integrate its dead, then it loses touch with its past, it has no history' (p. 20).

This argument is elaborated by news footage of events such as the death of Princess Diana, the disaster at Hillsborough or the extended coverage of the murder of Stephen Lawrence and the continuing campaign by his parents, all of which provide important insights into the dimensions of race, class and gender.

Inextricably linked to rituals are religious and spiritual beliefs. These are important for, as Lynch (1998) puts it: 'funerals press the noses of the faithful against the windows of their faith' (p. 91). And yet students are often readier to argue race or be out with their sexuality, than to openly express their beliefs about religion (see Moss, Chapter 2 in this volume). This is reflected in Danbury's (1996) findings that clients of bereavement counsellors felt constrained or discouraged from talking about their feelings about life after death although they 'frequently needed reassurance that it is normal, for example, to have hallucinations of the dead' (p. 103).

This issue needs, then, careful integration. If we are secular, atheistic or agnostic, we might need help to accept religious beliefs or rituals and/or the search for a deeper meaning to existence. If religious, we have to acknowledge that religious practices and beliefs can help heighten feelings, and can also deflect emotions and thoughts away from the loss. And both groups might need to struggle to stay nonjudgmental of the 'wilder fringes' – see Picardie's (2000) account of her own struggle with herself when planning to visit a medium. There is an increasing number of recent texts addressing these issues (Stein, 1999; Aldridge, 2000; West, 2000) while the following questionnaire (developed from a student presentation) provokes further reflection:

1. What, for you, are the differences between 'religious belief' and 'spirituality'?
2. How is/has your life, either negatively or positively, been affected and influenced by religious belief and/or spiritual feelings?
3. What might be the impact of religious belief and/or spiritual feelings on service users?
4. What do you think constitutes a religious perspective?
5. What do you think constitutes a spiritual perspective?

The importance of the organization

'Ritual' also includes identifying the various rites of passage that organizations use to manage, or fail to manage, loss. This is 'a death system' (Kastenbaum, 1972), the manner in which we live our dying, and that of other people, and which is the sum total of the persons, places, ideas, traditions, acts, omissions, emotions and statements that are thought or told out loud about death.

- It is cognitive, in that it teaches us what to think about death and dying.

- It is affective, in that it teaches us how to feel about death and dying.
- It is behavioural, in that it teaches us how to act in response to death and dying.

Menzies (1961) identified, in her classic text, the defensiveness that underlies many professional settings and various writers have sought to update her analysis. The case studies in Sutcliffe *et al.* (1998), particularly the chapter by Cornish on the death of a school pupil, are especially helpful in developing this thinking into a systemic understanding. There is also Lawton's (2000) provocative ethnographic study of a hospice which captures the contrast between the stated philosophy of an agency and how this is perceived by users. Drawing on these studies, we can then consider how this applies to our own organizations where the loss might be working as a nurse with physically disabled people or social workers who have removed a child from their family of origin. In the unit, the interprofessional nature of the student group is especially helpful here in both appreciating and challenging each other's accepted professional norms.

Skills

In any teaching, whether self-directed or in a formal taught unit, the best learning comes from shared discussion of experiences which will reveal the very real existing skills, and they are also likely to reflect the concerns identified in the literature. For example, a hospital social worker describes how, although in constant contact with dying patients, she deferred to the prevailing medical norms and so stayed 'largely unaware of my potential role in helping them' (Smith, 1982, p. 3).

Another social work perspective, but, again, with a wider relevance, describes how:

> traditional social work aims may seem, at first sight, to be useless in the face of such remorseless finality ... what the social worker might elsewhere attempt to achieve needs not so much to be reversed as set aside ... activity and optimism are not required but rather pain and sorrow, even despair ... have to be worked with. (Philpot, 1989, pp. 11–12)

Other commentators are clear about the importance, in this work, of being a 'stranger, who understands grief in general, and stands in an acknowledged therapeutic role' and who 'can probably give more support to the working out of grief' (Marris, 1974, p. 153). Also, the professional who can 'stay with the process and listen, not push for outcomes, show respect for what is there, see the usefulness and even the beauty of the way others express their mourning and sense of loss and allow oneself to be the firm ground on which the other stands' (Zinker, 1994, p. 262).

To move towards turning these words into practice, it is important to identify and develop the appropriate skills, while also acknowledging how contested an issue this is. Walter (1999) chastens professionals who take on the role of the 'emotional police', working to a fixed ideal of what good mourning should consist of, and following a crude tasks or stages approach that is too prescriptive and systematically misunderstands the needs of the bereaved.

None the less, I argue that there are a number of core and interrelated skills which can be summed up broadly under the headings of (a) assessment; (b) communication/counselling; and (c) understanding organizations.

Assessment skills

These consist of:

1. Being open to understanding and accepting of whatever ways loss is expressed.
2. Understanding the indicators for predicting the experience of loss, such as the nature of the attachment, the mode of death, social factors and so on.
3. Understanding the ethnic and cultural variations.
4. Being able to see not just the individual patient/client but the whole family system.
5. Knowing about other agencies and the help they offer, whether this is formal counselling or befriending or self-help.

Communication/counselling skills

The listening skills underpinned by Rogers' (1965) core conditions, empathy, congruence and acceptance, will be familiar to students from their initial professional training (see also Mearns and Thorne, 1999).

In terms of how to work with grief, the most widely accepted model is that of Worden (1991) who seeks to shift the focus away from phases, which he sees as implying a certain passivity, to 'tasks' which emphasize that grief work is a process that demands something more active. These are:

1. *For the bereaved:* to accept the reality of the loss.
   For the counsellor: to increase the reality of the loss.
2. *For the bereaved:* to work through to the pain of grief.
   For the counsellor: to help deal with both expressed and latent affect.
3. *For the bereaved:* to adjust to an environment in which the deceased is missing.
   For the counsellor: to help overcome various impediments to readjustment after a loss.
4. *For the bereaved:* to emotionally relocate the deceased and move on with life.
   For the counsellor: to encourage the individual to say an appropriate goodbye and to feel comfortable reinvesting in life.

And we need to take care to check this final point, given Walter's (1999) criticism as previously cited.

Organizational skills

1. Understanding the rites of passage that organizations use to manage, or fail to manage, various forms of loss.
2. Tracking the theories that, explicitly or implicitly, influence the policies and practices of their employing organization.
3. Identifying how the organization can support them, as professionals, to build on the knowledge and skills they have in working with loss and bereavement.
4. Identifying what the organization can do to support clients/patients and their carers in coping with loss and bereavement.
5. Helping to develop strategies to change, if and where necessary, the practices of the organization.

Some conclusions

This chapter seeks to contribute to the debate about loss and bereavement and I indicate how and why these are controversial. I focus on a programme that can be formally taught or self-led, which promotes a list of learning outcomes linked to specific skills in the areas of assessment, communication/counselling and working within organizations. I argue that professionals working with loss and grief need greater assurance in distinguishing between those approaches to grieving that help healing processes and those that might hinder. Linked to this are issues of gender, ritual, religion and spiritual beliefs and the impact of the wider organization. Discussions of issues of race and ethnicity have been incorporated throughout, as these can be seen to be central to the experience of loss. I have also given prominence to the experiences of nonprofessionals, whether in their own written accounts, or reported in research studies, who have been caught up in these literally life or death dramas.

In all of this what becomes apparent is a cycle by which, while seeking to come to grips with this important topic, we mirror the problems of the wider society in honestly confronting the painful feelings that surround loss and death. It is to be hoped that the discussion above provides some degree of confidence, while also allowing for a continuing curiosity in the whole complex process, helping to square this circle and, by working through resistances, personal and professional, identify good practice.

14 A Framework for Working with Loss

Margaret Lloyd

Introduction

It is commonly stated that loss is a pervasive theme in human services and that many recurrent users of welfare services have cumulative and often poorly resolved experiences of loss (Lloyd, 1992; Currer, 2001). Indeed, the primary purpose of this book is to explore that very assertion. Equally common for mainstream practitioners is the experience that they do not know how to accommodate loss work within their overall remit, nor does the available theory seem to 'fit' many of the situations with which they are working. It does, however, ring bells with their personal bereavements or relationship losses, sometimes with disturbing accuracy. This mismatch is frustrating. If loss is fundamental to human existence, then an understanding of the experience and the appropriate offer of help, should be integral to everything that human services practitioners do. This chapter explores some of the tensions and dilemmas posed in health, social care and pastoral settings, for multi-task and multiple role practitioners seeking to recognize the significance, and work with the consequences, of loss for users of their service. It then suggests a framework which purports to encompass the range of loss experiences, and which might enable the practitioner to connect working with the implicit or explicit loss with those aspects of their intervention which are ostensibly the primary focus.

Theoretical revision

The glaringly obvious statement on the utility of the available grief theories is that both the original formulations (for example, Lindemann, 1944; Parkes, 1970) and more recent alternative models (for example, Stroebe and Schut, 1999) start from a study of the grief which attends bereavement, and identify loss as a psychological and emotional phenomenon occurring within grief. There has been a widespread tendency amongst trainers and practitioners in the human services to conflate a range of losses and assume theoretical conformity to the bereavement model (for example, Ainsworth-Smith and Speck, 1982; Lendrum and Syme,1992). This is made all the more tempting because anecdotal evidence suggests that, for many people, the experiences of divorce and radical surgery, to name two of the most frequently occurring examples, parallel the grief of bereavement. Moreover, the favoured practice model, unchallenged until relatively recently, has been to help people to adjust to, and recover from, the loss as it manifests itself in the progressive 'stages' of grief. Whole areas of practice in childcare services have been developed around recognizing the significance of loss in the lives of vulnerable and damaged children, and using a range of interventions to help them express the pain of grief and eventually let go and move on emotionally. Undoubtedly, much valuable work has been done from this perspective but not, I suggest, without the practitioners adjusting the theory as they went along.

This process of 'theoretical modification on the hoof' is a familiar one to practitioners and forms the basis of reflective practice (Thompson, 2000b). I have discussed elsewhere the shortcomings of the dominant grief theories as a generic tool for mainstream practitioners, where organizational constraints and competing professional agendas seriously limit the transferability of clinical models of intervention, and the grief itself may be neither the primary nor sole focus of the intervention, nor the reason for the referral (Lloyd, 1992). Even where grief surrounding death and dying is the legitimate focus, the emphasis in the training literature on individual, psychological processes at the expense of sociological and existential perspectives leaves the practitioner ill-equipped (Bhaduri, 1990; Lloyd, 1997).

Other theoretical formulations have similarly been offered as catch-all frameworks, despite concerns about their theoretical shortcomings which are particularly relevant when uncritically applied to the varied experiences of loss. Both O'Hagan (1986) and Thompson (1991) are critical of the narrow psychological focus of 'classical crisis theory' (Caplan, 1961; Rapoport, 1970). Crisis theory must be revisited to incorporate the multidimensional character and situational elements which most practitioners recognize. Thompson places more emphasis on the intrapersonal nature of crisis, whilst similarly arguing for a sociological axis to be added, but suggests that these 'crises of misery and loneliness' (Gorer, 1965, p. 110) have an existential base which crisis theory completely ignores. Attachment theory, and the corresponding experiences of separation and loss, most notably developed by Bowlby (1969) has been hugely influential in many branches of human services. Grief theorists such as Parkes (1996) explicitly draw on the process observed by Bowlby in developing the 'phases' of grief. We now recognize that attachment theory is limited by its Eurocentric formulation and gendered application. Yet the response to loss as a universal psychological phenomenon and emotional experience, whose problematic impact both stems from, and results in, complicated attachment behaviour, endures amongst practitioners. Commonly, practitioners are ill-at-ease with the theory but desperately cling to some guide, lest they also flounder in the chaos and despair of the other person's loss.

Changing contexts

One reason for the continuing adherence to established models, however, lies in the fact that they also seem to be 'true'. It is not that the theory is inherently problematic, practitioners may reason, but that things have changed. No longer does the worker in mainstream services have time to spend with people on emotional problems, or conversely, there is no longer the need, because as a society we have become much more open to acknowledging feelings of loss in general and talking of death in particular. There are two particular contexts which have a bearing on this question: first, the multicultural society; second, the postmodern human services workplace. Our framework for working with loss must be capable of accommodating both.

A multicultural context

The seminal works on grief as an emotional and psychological phenomenon, such as Lindemann (1944) and sociological analyses of the treatment of death, such as Gorer (1965) were theorized from study of Anglo-Saxon, North American and North European societies whose religious roots were predominantly Protestant

Christian. Consequently, there is a failure in the theoretical modelling to accommodate social and cultural difference, which has only recently begun to be addressed. 'Culture', in postmodern theorizing, has emerged as a concept which embraces sociological, psychological and philosophical dimensions, denoting a dynamic interplay between identity and meaning, organizational constructs and organized practices. Thus it is highly significant when seeking to understand and work with experiences of loss. However, there are three separate strands within the discussion: social traditions and rituals; individual experience and behaviour; and ontological assumptions. When practitioners talk about ethnically sensitive practice in a multicultural context, they tend to be referring only to the first of these. We cannot, however, develop an adequate theoretical framework without integrating all three.

Knowledge of traditional practices attending the dying process, preparation and disposal of the body and patterns of mourning in the major religious and cultural traditions and minority groups is now recognized to be essential for the practitioner working with dying and bereavement (Parkes *et al.*, 1997). The diversity, and sometimes opposing nature, of these leads to the immediate conclusion that one model cannot suffice for all. However, as we have noted, culture is a dynamic concept, and its operation in a multicultural society still more so. The rituals surrounding death and dying have developed to serve a social purpose and, where different traditions rub shoulders, it is not only inevitable, but also desirable, that some integration which incorporates the essential purposes and helpful practices of different cultures should emerge. In their discussion of the development of psychosocial approaches to palliative care amongst the Hong Kong Chinese community, Chan *et al.* (2000) discuss how the failure to integrate the holistic principles of Chinese medicine with western technological advances in the treatment of cancer, has resulted in cancer being the most highly stigmatized and least talked about illness, despite it being the most common cause of death. The conflict experienced by many children of immigrant parents, expected to mark the death of an elder with full attention to the requirements of the root culture when their own inclinations have been significantly shaped by the adopted home, provides another example.

The consequences of this failure to develop the sociological perspective are seen most immediately by the practitioner in trying to respond sensitively to the needs of individuals and families. The social traditions represent rites of passage for individuals in transition, whether from living to dying, or the social status of a wife to a widow. Despite numerous anthropological studies of the making and employing of death rituals within and across cultures, we still lack the empirical research which investigates subjective meaning for the individual, experienced within particular cultural context (Eisenbruch, 1984, provides a minor, though valuable exception). The integration of individual and social perspectives is increasingly important in a world of not only cultural diversity, but also individuals straddling cultures and traditions and experiencing major social transition. Gunaratnam (1997) is scathing in her attack on 'cultural reductionism' and 'cultural and religious prescription', leading to:

> a tendency to project and confuse private feelings with public behaviour ... [and] oversimplified assumptions about the relationships between ritual behaviour, social support and subjective grief. (p. 177)

The implications of this yawning gap in our understanding are even greater when we consider the broader dimension of loss. 'Stage theory', developed from studies of dying and bereaved individuals, with its emphasis on psychological process and emotional adjustment, has been translated into explanations of how individuals react to loss in general. This assumes firstly, that dying and bereavement are all about loss, and secondly that loss is a homogeneous experience. Without a more sophisticated framework which allows for differing representations of 'loss', the range of significance attached to what is superficially the same experience, and the culturally diverse and complex relationship between loss, dying and bereavement, this theoretical connection is limiting and may be misleading. If an individual belongs to a culture which is life-affirming, but longs for death as they mourn their progressive loss of life, their psychological task may be quite different from that of someone whose culture accepts the continuity of life and death but who, as an individual, is overwhelmed by the desolation of the disruption of emotional bonds. Similarly, the particular framing of one's sense of order, and the degree to which that contributes to one's emotional well-being, will determine what experiences represent loss, and the significance attached to that loss.

Much of this has to do with the ontological assumptions which determine how each person approaches death and form the basis for their dealing with loss. Ontological assumptions are also an important shaping influence on the cultural prescription of patterns of dying and mourning (Clark and Seymour, 1999). Thus, a person who finds their beliefs and assumptions threatened by an experience of loss, or who is trapped in a prescribed pattern whose assumptions they do not wholly share, faces an existential crisis. This is a dimension which has been almost entirely neglected by human services practitioners in the west (Thompson, 1992, 1997) although it forms an integral part of the understanding of similar professionals in the African and Indian sub-continents (Gokam, 1994; Sacco, 1994). In a paper discussing the impact of the religious and philosophical east–west divide on social work practice, Bhaduri (1990) argues that nowhere is the reliance of social work in the west on psychological and social structural theories more transparently inadequate than when dealing with dying and bereavement. Hospital social workers in a study conducted by myself confirmed this assertion, identifying existential issues as a key distinguishing feature of their work with dying and bereaved people and amongst the most problematic (Lloyd, 1997).

The postmodern human services context

There has been increasing concern amongst professionals in mainstream services for more than a decade, about their capacity to provide the counselling support which people who are struggling with loss are presumed to need. The policy changes of the 1990s in the UK and their impact on the delivery of health and social care services – most particularly the drive for measurable outcomes and the restrictions imposed by managers on the professional task – have added to this dilemma. Studies of the early implementation of the National Health Service and Community Care Act 1990 indicated that experienced staff were much concerned with the issue of the loss of their counselling role and skills (Lewis and Glennerster, 1996). The issue is not confined to the UK, however. Neither is the problem a direct result of UK policy and trans-Atlantic service developments such as care management. Cowen (1999) argues that global forces, such as marketization tendencies, increasing bureaucratization and managerialism, combined in the UK with the loss of the public sector ethic, have 'served to downgrade the status of holistic models and ethical caring in social work practice' (p. 101). The problem appears to be that, in the face of the profound changes in health and social care delivery, practitioners have been unable to show how work with loss and grief can be accommodated within the care management system, except for those very few workers in specialist settings. Moreover, the debate about service quality initially developed as a preoccupation with easily quantifiable outputs and performance indicators based on such measures. In a scenario dominated by a managerial culture of cost-effective task division and outcomes-focused accountability, attention to anything other than practical and physical need is perched with ever-increasing fragility within service provision. As one team leader remarked to the author, 'If someone's inner pain is eased, it's not particularly measurable' (Lloyd, 1997). Both Brearley (1995) and Seden (1999) identify the threats to the continuance of the counselling element in statutory social work settings.

A second tension arises from the uncertainty about professional identity which has attended these changes in the model of service delivery. Effective multidisciplinary working and holistic care require the different workers to be confident of their particular contribution and clear about their role. Moreover, workers must be able to justify their existence, as chaplains in health care settings are increasingly aware (Lloyd, 1995). The confusion about what is counselling, and who should do it, has contributed to a hesitance on the part of many non-specialist workers to address questions of loss. They may deal with the referral without probing the underlying problem which stems from an unresolved or poorly resolved loss (Lloyd, 1992). The form of 'counselling' offered by many traditional caseworkers has been shaped by their organizational contexts and, as these contexts have become less hospitable, and the counselling movement has become increasingly professionalized, many such workers have lost confidence in their ability to offer this 'down-beat counselling' (Seden, 1999). When added to the tendency amongst practitioners loosely to equate loss work with counselling (Bevan and Thompson, 2000), and of training courses in counselling skills to rely heavily on illustrative case material where loss is the central feature, it becomes increasingly likely that workers in mainstream settings will no longer see loss as part of their remit.

In summary, there must be two linked responses to a workplace context which appears to threaten the survival of work with loss. The theoretical underpinnings must be developed so as to underpin an approach which is relevant to the needs of the postmodern world, extending the limited counselling model on which practitioners have for too long relied.

A revised framework

Reflective practice needs both a conceptual framework and guidance as to the task. This is especially important because practitioners in human services have to negotiate their individual practice within the organizational and policy frameworks. This book brings together a rich and diverse range of perspectives on loss. What does the practitioner make of this when faced with a specific situation with someone struggling with the impact of loss? We know that it has been the psychologically-based stage theory models which have dominated the thinking of practitioners and been applied to all experiences of loss, and the socio-psychological analyses of the interactionists which have influenced the development of palliative care practices. There has been little research, however, into the conscious use of theoretical underpinnings by these professionals in their practice. My own work (Lloyd, 1995, 1997) has attempted to identify the knowledge bases and academic disciplines employed by social workers and chaplains and to analyse the way in which these shape their practice. Sadly, there is little evidence of these workers explicitly using theoretical resources to negotiate the dilemmas which loss practice so frequently presents.

My research leads me to the conclusion that four principles about the integration of theory and practice may guide the development of a framework for working with loss:

1. Practitioners are generally more comfortable with the implicit use of concepts rather than their explicit application; they do not want to offer a template which appears to deny the uniqueness of individuals and their experienced situations.
2. Challenge to these implicit assumptions, however, creates some of the sharpest dilemmas in practice and engenders a feeling of helplessness in the practitioner; thus our conceptual foundation needs conscious exploration to be secure.
3. Adoption of broad concepts facilitates a more holistic understanding.
4. A 'reflective practice' model must provide practitioners with a guide to draw on theoretical resources *in the immediate and everyday situation*, where commonly practitioners make individual and ad hoc accommodations to deal with the dilemmas.

Our task, then, is firstly, to develop a conceptual map, and, secondly, to work out how to use it.

Mapping the concept of loss

If we take an interdisciplinary approach to the literature on death and dying, we discover a rather broader and more transferable approach to loss in general than in the psychologically-based theories which practitioners have tended to adopt. Three main clusters emerge, each of which has sociological, psychological and philosophical aspects. First, *attitudes to death and dying* are explored in sociological, psychological and theological/philosophical discourse. Second, *constructions of life and death* are similarly analysed, and the third cluster is concerned with the *process of adjustment*. If we generalize this framework to incorporate loss not necessarily connected with death, it translates as: attitudes to loss; assumptions about human existence; and incorporating loss into ongoing experience.

The theoretical revision of 'modern death', sometimes referred to as 'postmodern death', has begun the task of integrating perspectives. There are a number of facets to this, which can be outlined only briefly within the constraints of this chapter. The most frequently rehearsed argument is that postmodern societies have broken the silence on death, as evidenced by its extensive featuring in the news and entertainment media. Counterarguments suggest that our fascination is with shocking and public or fictitious death (Pickering *et al.*, 1997), and the implications of death for life and the personal impact on the living continue to be taboo (Lloyd, 2000). An example of these ambiguous attitudes to death is to be found in the experience reported by hospice patients, that it is acceptable to talk about cancer, and making the most of life, but not about death (Lloyd, 1997). Continuing this theme, developments from the original social interactionist analysis of 'awareness contexts' (Glaser and Strauss, 1965) suggest that disclosure of the diagnosis must take account of both emotional and ontological considerations concerning personhood, since to destroy hope is to destroy the essential person (Twycross, 1997). The spectrum of 'helplessness' and 'hope' as a way of reaching out to the dilemmas of both dying and bereaved persons and practitioners, is offered by Rumbold (1986), connecting the notion of hope with the psychological and emotional distress in such a way as to see the former rising out of the latter.

One element of 'modern death' which was vividly illustrated in the practices of western secularized societies was 'privatized death' – that dying and bereaved people encountered impersonal bureaucracies and distanced professionals rather than being nurtured by a community. Recent work suggests that people in late modernity are concerned that dying should take place 'in community', both in the sense that individual deaths are recognized and accommodated by the wider community in an orderly fashion (Seale, 1995b) and in the sense of a continuing influence on the present of what has gone before – what Young and

Cullen (1996) term 'a collective immortality'. However, Elias (1985) argues that it is the necessity for individuals to *make sense of their experiences alone*, rather than physical and social isolation, which is critical in this discussion of 'privatized' or 'in community' death. 'Making sense' in an existential void is our key to the transferability of these concepts to the broader arenas of loss.

The pursuit of meaning is also an important linking concept between all three of the conceptual clusters which I have identified, both for individuals and social groupings, and it is one which lends itself most directly to the helping task (see Chapter 3 in this volume). It facilitates a more complex understanding of the nature and importance of belief systems, spirituality, the importance of tradition and culture, the development of personally significant rituals and their interrelationships. The significance of *meaninglessness* and the disruption of order and meaning, is a recognized trigger for loss crises and alienation in both individuals and societies (for example, Marris, 1974). This psychological and social alienation can also be linked to the ontological quest which is initiated when fundamental ontological assumptions appear no longer to hold true. Both alienation and social exclusion are contained in the notion of 'social death' – where individuals or communities cease to exist in the consciousness of mainstream society long before physical death or extinction of a minority culture takes place. Here we have another useful concept to transfer to our understanding of certain forms of loss.

Lastly, Walter (1994) uses evidence of technological advancement to argue that the boundaries between life and death are becoming more diffuse; hence, in postmodern death, individuals desire to control their own dying (Walter, 1994). The fact that medical intervention in the shape of life support may now obscure the moment of death, has actually complicated this control, however. The complexity of ethical decision-making faced by postmodern health care systems, has highlighted the fact that satisfactory resolution of the dilemmas cannot be realized without the incorporation of a philosophical ethics discourse within sociolegal considerations. Moreover, the prescribed pattern of 'the good death' is seriously challenged by this fragmented dying. This in itself is no bad thing since, as with the use of stage theory, the crude application of the notion of the good death in the hands of well-meaning practitioners has come to exercise something of a tyranny (Lloyd, 1995). In fact, the roots of the good death are multifaceted: there is facilitating symbolism and ritual (Grainger, 1998); control of pain and easing of discomfort (Twycross, 1997); respect for autonomy and dignity (Finlay, 1996);

the maintenance of social status (Sheldon, 1997). Recognition of difference and plurality of meaning, which poststructural analysis has contributed, should lead us to a position where 'dying well' and 'losing well' for each individual requires a careful negotiation of these elements, such that the process is personally acceptable and the event has social meaning.

The central point to be made, which runs through all this more recent theorizing, is that in order to further understanding of the phenomenon, and to enhance the appropriateness of the caring response, integration of sociological, psychological and philosophical perspectives is required. Important as the theoretical development has been, however, it has yet to be translated into a framework for practice which appears to offer the clarity and certainty of the favoured psychological models. This uncertainty should also be seen as a strength, however. A longstanding theoretical problem and practice dilemma for the human services professions is their adherence to an action/change philosophy and a problem-solving orientation. Loss, as we have explored it, is not directly amenable to such construction.

Using the guide

Despite the popularity of stage theory, it seems to me that the really interesting idea put forward by Parkes (1975, 2000) is to understand grieving as a way of negotiating the psychosocial transition occasioned by bereavement. Parkes proposes that the individual's existence is structured by an internal world, made up of a series of assumptive models which is used to understand his or her life, and the external world, which influences the nature of and impact of outside events. When the interaction of these two worlds is disrupted, as in an event such as bereavement, the individual is in psychosocial transition and their assumptive models either in need of revision or redundant. Parkes does not expand this model to incorporate the breadth of perspective which we are seeking, but it is not hard to see how it offers an all-embracing framework. Put simply, it offers the potential to understand and respond to loss as *the loss within and the loss without*. This encompasses the social construction of loss, the psychological impact and the philosophical search. The relative significance of each of these will vary across individuals and social groups, but each is contained within that inner/outer framework. Thus, the task of the practitioner is to help the person dealing with loss to reconstruct their inner world so as to re-establish order and consonance with the outer world, where currently they experience chaos and dissonance.

It is crucial that this is not regarded as some luxury reframed counselling model, but integrated with the core tasks of mainstream practice. Many people become users of health, social care, criminal justice or other human services *because* their assumptive worlds have been shattered or eroded, or becoming a service user *causes* them to be shattered or eroded, or *in the course of* the intervention, their models are shown to be redundant or needing revision. This book has explored many of these situations and contexts. I suggest that the link with the core task and primary responsibility of the mainstream worker has to do with one or more of the following; the examples belong to the 'bread-and-butter' of work in mainstream settings.

- *Redefining roles.*   When a person becomes a carer, they may experience loss in connection with both the role(s) relinquished and the role assumed. Equally, the cared-for person may struggle with the redefined role imposed upon them. Inability to deal with this for both will threaten the caring relationship and may be at the centre of conflicts and difficulties which the worker is obliged to address.
- *Rebuilding identities.*   Experiences such as illness, the onset of disability, addiction or imprisonment may all require the person to rebuild their identity and sense of self. Within this task is the need to accommodate the loss or relinquishing of a former identity, without which they are unable to make use of the service or support being offered to move forward.
- *Negotiating transition.*   The experience of transition – social, psychological, geographical – is a fundamental part of the lives of many service users. Recognizing and helping to deal with the losses involved in relocating into the community or another foster home, of becoming a teenage parent, or of entering residential care are essential if the worker is to assist the service user to engage positively with the 'new life'.
- *Surviving abuse.*   The preoccupation of professionals may be the protection of a vulnerable party from a powerful abuser, but survivors frequently focus on their struggles to regain trust and their essential self. Unless this loss is accommodated into a rebuilt sense of personhood, the damage will be perpetuated with spiralling consequences for the abused person and those around him or her.
- *Maintaining the spirit.*   In situations of continuous hardship and stress, such as those arising from socioeconomic deprivation, pain,

discrimination and oppression, it may be the ability to understand the loss and trauma in a wider framework which allows the person to come through. Every human services practitioner is only too aware that those who do not come through break down, or become trapped in cycles of bitter loneliness, self-neglect, criminal and other problematic behaviours.

Conclusion

This chapter has developed the integration of sociological, psychological and philosophical perspectives on loss. A framework for practice which holds these together in a conceptual model which understands loss as an experience of psychosocial and ontological transition is suggested. The practitioner's task is thus to facilitate the reconstruction of inner and outer worlds and the synergy between them. It is argued that such an approach is relevant and feasible for human services practitioners in a range of settings.

References

Abberley, P. (1991) *Three Theories of Abnormality*, Occasional Papers in Sociology No. 10, Bristol, Bristol Polytechnic Department of Economics and Social Science.

Abbot, P and Sapsford R. (1987) *Community Care for Mentally Handicapped Children*, Milton Keynes, Open University Press.

Acheson, D. (1998) *Independent Inquiry into 'Inequalities in Health' Report*, London, The Stationery Office.

Adams, R., Dominelli, L. and Payne, M. (eds) (1998) *Social Work: Themes, Issues and Critical Debates*, London, Macmillan – now Palgrave.

Aguilera, D. C. and Messick, J. M. (1986) *Crisis Intervention: Theory and Methodology*, St Louis, Mosby.

Ahmed, S. (1987) 'Racism in Social Work Assessment', in BASW Social Work and Racism Group (1987).

Ahmed, S., Cheetham, J. and Small, J. (eds) (1986) *Social Work with Children and their Families*, London, Batsford.

Ainsworth-Smith, I. and Speck, P. (eds) (1982) *Letting Go. Caring for the Dying and Bereaved*, London, SPCK.

Aldgate, J. (1988) 'Work with Children Experiencing Separation and Loss: A Theoretical Framework', in Aldgate and Simmonds (1988).

Aldgate, J. and Simmonds, J. (eds) (1988) *Direct Work with Children*, London, Batsford Academic.

Aldridge, D. (2000) *Spirituality, Healing and Medicine: Return to the Silence*, London, Jessica Kingsley.

Allan, G. (ed.) (1999) *The Sociology of the Family*, Oxford, Blackwell.

Altschuler, J. (1993) 'Gender and Illness: Implications for Family Therapy', *Journal of Family Therapy*, 15, 381–401.

Anderson, J. M., Blue, C. and Lau, A. (1991) 'Women's Perspectives on Chronic Illness: Ethnicity, Ideology and Restructuring Life', *Social Science and Medicine*, 33(2).

Anderson, D. and Mullen, P. (eds) (1998) *Faking It, the Sentimalisation of Modern Society*, Harmondsworth, Penguin.

Angus, L. and Hardke, K. (1994) 'Narrative Processes in Psychotherapy', *Canadian Psychology*, 35, 190–203.

Angus, L., Levitt, H. and Hardke, K. (1999) 'Narrative Processes and Psychotherapeutic Change', *Journal of Clinical Psychology*, 55, 1255–70.

Arber, S. and Evandrou, M. (eds) (1993) *Ageing, Independence and the Life Course*, London, Jessica Kingsley.

Arber, S. and Ginn, J. (eds) (1995) *Connecting Gender and Ageing: A Sociological Approach*, Buckingham, Open University Press.

Arroba, T. and James, K. (1987) *Pressure at Work: A Survival Guide*, London, McGraw-Hill.

Attig, T. (1996) *How we Grieve: Relearning the World*, New York, Oxford University Press.

Attig, T. (2001) *The Heart of Grief*, New York, Oxford University Press.

Attorney-General's Department (1990) J. Gardner, *Victims and Criminal Justice, Research Report* No. 5, Adelaide: SA Government Printer.

Attorney-General's Department, Justice Strategy Unit (1999) *Victims of Crime Review: Report One*, Adelaide, Government of South Australia.

Attorney-General's Department (2000) *Information for Victims of Crime*, Adelaide, Government of South Australia.

Auden, W. H. (1969) *Collected Shorter Poems, 1927–1957*, London, Faber and Faber.

Austin-Baker, J. (1996) Personal communication.

Australian Association of Social Workers (1997a) *National Bulletin*, 7(1), February.

Australian Association of Social Workers (1997b) *National Bulletin*, August.

Australian Bureau of Statistics (1999) *Corrective Services Australia: March Quarter 1999*, Canberra, Australian Bureau of Statistics.

Australian Bureau of Statistics (2000) *Australian Social Trends 1999*, Canberra, Australian Bureau of Statistics.

Badham, P. and Ballard, P. (eds) (1996) *Facing Death*, Cardiff, University of Wales Press.

Bailey, R. (1988) 'Poverty and Social Work Education', in Becker and Macpherson (1988).

Baldwin, J. A. (1995) 'African Self-consciousness and the Mental Health of African-Americans', *Journal of Black Studies*, 15(2).

Bard, M. and Sangrey, D. (1986) *The Crime Victim's Book*, Secaucus, NJ, Citadel.

Barnes, J. (2000) 'Murder Followed by Suicide in Australia, 1973–1992: A Research Note', *Journal of Sociology*, 36(1).

Barnett, R., Blend, J., Cavet, J. *et al.* (2000) *Jewish Issues in Social Work and Social Care: A Resource Pack for Educators and Practitioners*, Newcastle, University of Northumbria at Newcastle.

Barrett, R. K. (1998) 'Sociocultural Considerations for Working with Blacks Experiencing Loss and Grief', in Doka and Davidson (1998).

Bartlett, R. (1993) *The Mabo Decision*, Sydney, Butterworths.

BASW Social Work and Racism Group (1987) *Racism and Social Work Practice: Time For A Change*, Birmingham, BASW.

Bayley, J. (1998) *Iris, A Memoir of Iris Murdoch*, London, Duckworth.

Beck, A. T., Steer, R. A. and Garbin, B. G. (1988) 'Psychometric Properties of the Beck Depression Inventory: Twenty-five Years of Evaluation', *Clinical Psychology Review*, 8, 77–100.

Becker, E. (1975) *Escape from Evil*, New York, Collier Macmillan.

Becker, S. (1988) 'Poverty Awareness', in Becker and Macpherson (1988).

Becker, S. and Macpherson, S. (eds) (1988) *Poor Clients: The Extent and Nature of Financial Poverty Amongst Consumers of Social Work Services*, Nottingham, Nottingham University Benefits Research Unit.

Beliappa, J. (1991) *Illness or Distress? Alternative Models of Mental Health*, London, Confederation of Indian Organizations (UK).

Bennett, A. (2000) *Father! Father! Burning Bright, A Story*, London, Profile Books in association with London Review of Books.

Benzeval, M. (1995) *Tackling Inequalities in Health: An Agenda for Action*, London, King's Fund.

Berger, P. (1966) *Invitation to Sociology*, Harmondsworth, Penguin.

Berger, R. (1988) 'Learning to Survive and Cope with Human Loss', *Social Work Today*, 28 April.

Berkowitz, L. (ed.) (1989) *Advances in Experimental and Social Psychology*, San Diego, CA, Academic Press.

Bernard, M. and Meade, K. (eds) (1993) *Women Come of Age*, London, Edward Arnold.

Bernstein, B. (1973) *Class, Codes and Control*, London, Routledge and Kegan Paul.

Bevan, D. (1998) 'Death, Dying and Inequality', *Care: The Journal of Practice and Development*, 7(1).

Bevan, D. and Thompson, N. (2000) 'Death, Dying and Bereavement', in Davies (2000).

Bhaduri, R. (1990) 'Crossing the Divide', *Social Work Today*, 29 March, p.28.

Biles, D. (1994) 'Deaths in Custody: the Nature and Scope of the Problem', in Liebling and Ward (1994).

Biles, D. and McDonald, D. (eds) (1992) *Deaths in Custody Australia, 1980–1989*, Canberra, Australian Institute of Criminology.

Biles, D., McDonald, D. and Fleming, J. (1992) 'Research Paper No. 7, Australian Deaths in Custody, 1980–88: An Analysis of Aboriginal and Non-Aboriginal Deaths in Prison and Police Custody', in Biles and McDonald (1992).

Billington, R., Hockey, J. and Strawbridge, S. (1998) *Exploring Self and Society*, London, Macmillan – now Palgrave.

Bivens, A. J., Neimeyer, R. A., Kirchberg, T. M. and Moore, M. K. (1994) 'Death Concern and Religious Belief Among Gays and Bisexuals of Variable Proximity to AIDS', *Omega*, 30, 105–120.

Blakemore, K. and Boneham, M. (1994) *Age, Race and Ethnicity*, Buckingham, Open University Press.

Bowlby, J. (1951) *Maternal Care and Mental Health*, Geneva, World Health Organization.

Bowlby, J. (1969) *Attachment and Loss*, London, Hogarth.

Bowlby, J. (1988) *A Secure Base: Clinical Application of Attachment Theory*, London, Routledge.

Bowlby, J. (1991) *Loss: Sadness and Depression (Volume 3 of 'Attachment and Loss')*, Harmondsworth, Penguin.

Brabant, S. (1994) 'Defining the Family After the Death of a Child', *Death Studies*, 18, 197–206.

Bradshaw, P. (1998) 'An Emotive Fight to the Death for Columnists', *Evening Standard*, 3.2.

Brah, A. (1996) *Cartographies of Diaspora: Contesting Identities*, London, Routledge.

Brandon, D. (2000) *Tao of Survival: Spirituality in Social Care and Counselling*, Birmingham, Venture Press.

Brandon, M., Schofield, G. and Trinder, L. (1998) *Social Work with Children*, London, Macmillan – now Palgrave

Braun, M. J. and Berg, D. H. (1994) 'Meaning Reconstruction in the Experience of Parental Bereavement', *Death Studies*, 18, 105–29.

Bray, C. (undated, circa 1987) *Needs of Families with a Death Reported to the Coroner: Possible Social Work Responses*, Sydney, NSW Department of Health.

Brearley, J. (1995) *Counselling and Social Work*, Buckingham, Open University Press.

Brodzinsky, D. M. and Marshall, D. S. (1990) *The Psychology of Adoption*, New York, Oxford University Press.

Bryant, C. (1989) 'Fathers Grieve Too', *Journal of Perinatology*, 9(4).

Buber, M. (1957) *I and Thou*, Edinburgh, T. and T. Clark.

Buckman, R. (1998) 'Communication in Palliative Care: A Practical Guide', in Doyle *et al.* (1998).

Bullock, R., Little, M. and Millham, S. (1993) *Going Home: The Return of Children Separated from their Families*, Aldershot, Dartmouth Publishing.

Burke, A. (1984) 'Racism and Psychological Disturbance Among West Indians in Britain', *International Journal of Social Psychiatry*, 30(1/2).

Burnett, P., Middleton, W., Raphael, B. and Martinek, N. (1997) 'Measuring Core Bereavement Phenomena', *Psychological Medicine*, 27, 49–57.

Burr, V. (1995) *An Introduction to Social Constructionism*, London, Routledge.

Byrne, G. J. A. and Raphael, B. (1997) 'The Psychological Symptoms of Conjugal Bereavement in Elderly Men Over the First 13 Months', *International Journal of Geriatric Psychiatry*, 12(2), 241–51.

Calman, K. C. (1984) 'Quality of Life in Cancer Patients: An Hypothesis', *Journal of Medical Ethics*, 10, 124–7.

Campbell, S. and Silverman, P. (1996) *Widower: When Men are Left Alone*, Amityville, NY, Baywood.

Canda, E. and Furman, L. (1999) *Spiritual Diversity in Social Work Practice*, New York, Free Press.

Caplan, G. (1961) *An Approach to Community Mental Health*, London, Tavistock.

Carcach, C. and Grant, A. (1999) 'Imprisonment in Australia: Trends in Prison Populations and Imprisonment Rates 1982–1998', *Trends and Issues in Crime and Criminal Justice*, No 130, Canberra, Australian Institute on Criminology, www.aic.gov.au

Cashmore, E. (ed.) (1996) *Dictionary of Race and Ethnic Relations*, 4th edn, London, Routledge.

Central Statistics Office (1994) *Social Trends*, 24, London, HMSO.

Chailand, G. and Rageau, J.-P. (1995) *The Penguin Atlas of Diasporas*, London, Viking.

Chan, C., Law, M. and Leung, P. (2000) 'An Empowerment Group for Chinese Cancer Patients in Hong Kong', in Fielding and Chan (2000).

Chappell, D. and Wilson, P. (eds) (2000) *Crime and the Criminal Justice System in Australia: 2000 and Beyond*, Sydney, Butterworths.

Charmaz, K. (1987) 'Struggling for a Self: Identity Levels of the Chronically Ill', in Roth and Conrad (1987).

Charmaz, K. (1995) 'The Body, Identity and Self: Adapting to Impairment', *Sociological Quarterly*, Fall 36(4), 657–81.

Chen, L. C., Kleinman, A. and Ware, N. C. (eds) (1993) *Health and Social Change in International Perspective*, Boston, MA, Harvard University Press.

Chief Medical Officers' Expert Advisory Group on Cancer (1995) *A Policy Framework for Commissioning Cancer Services (the Calman–Hine Report)*, London, Department of Health.

Chodorow, N. (1989) *Feminism and Psychoanalytic Theory*, New Haven, CT, Yale University Press.

Clark, D. (ed.) (1991) *Marriage, Domestic Life and Social Change, Writings for Jacqueline Burgoyne 1944–1988*, London, Routledge.

Clark, D. (1999) 'Cradled to the Grave? Terminal Care in the United Kingdom, 1948–67', *Mortality*, 4(3).

Clark, D. and Malson, H. (1995) 'Key Issues in Palliative Care Needs Assessment', *Progress in Palliative Care*, 3, 53–5.

Clark, D. and Seymour, J. (1999) *Reflections on Palliative Care*, Buckingham, Open University Press.

Clarkson, G. (1981) *Report of the Royal Commission on Allegations in Relation to Prisons under the Charge, Care and Direction of the Director of the Department of Correctional Services and Certain Related Matters, 11 December*, Adelaide, Government Printer.

Cline, S. (1995) *Lifting the Taboo, Women, Death and Dying*, London, Little, Brown.

Cockett, M. and Tripp, J. (1994) *The Exeter Family Study: Family Breakdown and its Impact on Children*, Exeter, University of Exeter Press.

Cook, J. A. (1983) 'A Death in the Family: Parental Bereavement in the First Year', *Suicide and Life-Threatening Behaviour*, 13, 42–61.

Cook, J. A. (1984) 'Influence of Gender on the Problems of Fatally Ill Children', *Journal of Psychosocial Oncology*, 2, 71–9.

Cook, J. A. (1988) 'Dad's Double Binds: Rethinking Father's Bereavement from a Men's Studies Perspective', *Journal of Contemporary Ethnography*, 17(3).

Cordell, A. and Thomas, N. (1990) 'Fathers and Grieving: Coping with Infant Death', *Journal of Perinatology*, 10(1).

Corden, A., Sainsbury, R. and Sloper, P. (2001) *Financial Implications of the Death of a Child*, York, Joseph Rowntree Foundation.

Corker, M. and French, S. (1999a) 'Reclaiming Discourse in Disability Studies', in Corker and French (1999b).

Corker, M. and French, S. (eds) (1999b) *Disability Discourse*, Buckingham, Open University Press.

Corr, C. A. (1993) 'Coping with Dying: Lessons We Should and Should Not Learn from the Work of Elisabeth Kübler-Ross', *Death Studies*, 17, 69–83.

Corr, C. A., Nabe, C. M., Corr, D.M. (1997) *Death and Dying, Life and Living*, Pacific Grove, CA, Brooks/Cole.

Costain Schou, K. C. and Hewison, J. (1999) *Experiencing Cancer*, Buckingham, Open University Press.

Cowen, H. (1999) *Community Care, Ideology and Social Policy*, London, Prentice-Hall.

Creek, G., Moore, M., Oliver, M. Salisbury, V., Silver, J. and Zarb, G. (1987) *Personal and Social Implications of Spinal Cord Injury: A Retrospective Study*, London, Thames Polytechnic.

Crompton, M. (1996) *Children, Spirituality and Religion: A Training Pack*, London, CCETSW.

Currer, C. (2001) *Responding to Grief. Dying, Bereavement and Social Care*, Basingstoke, Palgrave.

Curtis, J. and Ellis, V. (1996) *Where's Daddy?*, London, Bloomsbury.

Dalton, V. (1999a) 'Australian Deaths in Custody and Custody Related Police Operations', *Trends and Issues in Criminal Justice Number 105*, Canberra, Australian Institute of Criminology.

Dalton, V. (1999b) 'Aboriginal Deaths in Prison 1980 to 1998: National Overview', *Trends and Issues in Criminal Justice Number 131*, Canberra, Australian Institute of Criminology

Daly, K. (1998) Restorative Justice: Moving Past the Caricatures, Paper prepared for Seminar on Restorative Justice, Institute of Criminology, University of Sydney Law School, 8 April.

Danbury, H. (1996) *Bereavement Counselling Effectiveness: A Client-opinion Study*, Aldershot, Avebury.

Daniel, B., Wassell, S. and Gilligan, R. (1999) *Child Development for Child Care and Protection Workers*, London, Jessica Kingsley.

Das, V. (1993) 'Moral Orientations to Suffering', in Chen *et al.* (1993).

Davies, M. (ed.) (2000) *The Blackwell Encyclopeadia of Social Work*, Oxford, Blackwell.

Davies, R. (ed.) (1998) *Stress in Social Work*, London, Jessica Kingsley.

Davis, C. G., Nolen-Hoeksema, S. and Larson, J. (1998) 'Making Sense of Loss and Benefiting from the Experience: Two Construals of Meaning', *Journal of Personality and Social Psychology*, 75, 561–74.

Davis, C. G., Wortman, C. B., Lehman, C. B. and Silver, R. C. (2000) 'Searching for Meaning in Loss: Are Clinical Assumptions Correct?', *Death Studies*, 24, 497–540.

Dawes, M. J. (1997) *Dying in Prison: A Study of Deaths in Correctional Custody in South Australia*, unpublished PhD Thesis, The Flinders University of South Australia.

Department of Health (2000) *The NHS Cancer Plan: A Plan for Investment, A Plan for Reform*, London, DoH.

Desai, A. (2000) *Fasting, Feasting*, London, Vintage.

Diamond, J. (1998) *C. Because Cowards Get Cancer Too*, London, Vermillion.

Dickenson, D., Johnson, M. and Katz, J. (eds) (2000) *Death, Dying and Bereavement*, 2nd edn, London, Sage.

Dinnage, R. (1992) *The Ruffian on the Stair: Reflections on Death*, Harmondsworth, Penguin.

Dixon, D. (1995) 'Crime, Criminology and Public Policy', *Australian and New Zealand Journal of Criminology*, Special Supplementary Issue.

Dodds, I. (1997) 'Norma Parker Address', *National Bulletin*, October, Canberra, Australian Association of Social Workers.

Doka, K. J. (ed.) (1989) *Disenfranchised Grief: Recognising Hidden Sorrow*, Lexington, MA, Lexington.

Doka, K. J. (ed.) (2001) *Disenfranchised Grief*, 3rd edn, New York, Lexington.

Doka, K. J. and Morgan, J. D. (eds) (1993) *Death and Spirituality*, Amityville, NY, Baywood.

Doka, K. J. and Davidson, J. D. (eds) (1998) *Living with Grief: Who We Are, How We Grieve*, Philadelphia, PA, Brunner/Mazel.

Doka, K. J. and Martin, T. (2001) 'Take It Like A Man: Masculine Responses to Loss', in Lund (2001).

Donaghy, B. (1997) *Leaving Early*, Sydney, Harper Health/Harper Collins.

Donald, J. and Rattansi, A. (eds) (1992) *'Race', Culture and Difference*, London, Sage.

Douglas, J. and Johnson, J. (eds) (1977) *Existential Sociology*, Cambridge, Cambridge University Press.

Dowling, E. and Gorell Barnes, G. (2000) *Working with Children and Parents through Separation and Divorce*, London, Macmillan – now Palgrave.

Doyle, D., Hanks, G. W. and MacDonald, N. (eds) (1993) *The Oxford Textbook of Palliative Medicine* (2nd edn 1998), Oxford, Oxford University Press.

Drewery, W. and Winslade, J. (1997) 'The Theoretical Story of Narrative Therapy', in Monk *et al.* (1997).

Duncombe, J. and Marsden, D. (1995) 'Workaholics and Whinging Women: Theorising Intimacy and Emotion Work – the Last Frontier of Gender Inequality?', *Sociological Review*, 43(1).

Duncombe, J. and Marsden, D. (1999) 'Love and Intimacy: the Gender Division of Emotion and "Emotion Work": A Neglected Aspect of Sociological Discussion of Heterosexual Relationships', in Allan (1999).

Durkheim, E. (1964) *The Division of Labour in Society* (1893), London, Macmillan – now Palgrave.

Edelstein, S., Burge, D. and Waterman, J. (2000) 'Loss and Grief in Foster Carers', *Child Welfare*, LXXX, Child Welfare League of America.

Eisenbruch, M. (1984) 'Cross-Cultural Aspects of Bereavement I and II', *Culture, Medicine and Psychiatry*, 8, 283/309 and 315/347.

Elias, N. (1985) *The Loneliness of the Dying*, Oxford, Basil Blackwell.

Elias, R. (1993) *Victims Still: The Political Manipulation of Crime Victims*, Newbury Park, CA, Sage.

Ender, M. G. and Hermsen, J. M. (1996) 'Working With the Bereaved: US Army Experiences with Nontraditional Families', *Death Studies*, 20(6).

Esterling, B. A., L'Abate, L., Murray, E. J. and Pennebaker, J. W. (1999) 'Empirical Foundations for Writing in Prevention and Psychotherapy: Mental and Physical Health Outcomes', *Clinical Psychology Review*, 19, 79–96.

Fahlberg, V. I. (1994) *A Child's Journey Through Placement*, London, BAAF.

Fattah, E. (1991) *Towards a Critical Victimology*, London, St. Martin's Press.

Feifel, H. (ed.) (1977) *New Meanings of Death*, New York, McGraw-Hill.

Fennell, G., Phillipson, P. and Evers, H. (1988) *The Sociology of Old Age*, Milton Keynes, Open University Press.

Field, D., Hockey, J. and Small, N. (eds) (1997) *Death, Gender and Ethnicity*, London, Routledge.

Fielding, R. and Chan, C. (eds) (2000) *Psychosocial Oncology and Palliative Care in Hong Kong*, Hong Kong, Hong Kong University Press.

Finch, J. and Morgan, D. (1991) 'Marriage in the 1980s: A New Sense of Realism?', in Clark (1991).

Finkelstein, V. (1980) *Attitudes and Disabled People: Issues for Discussion*, New York, World Rehabilitation Fund.

Finlay, I. (1996) 'Ethical Decision-making in Palliative Care', in Badham and Ballard (1996).

Fitzgerald, R. and Parkes, C. M. (1998) 'Loss of Sensory and Cognitive Functions', in Parkes and Markus (1998).

Fleming, S. J. and Belanger, K. (2001) 'Trauma, Grief, and Surviving Childhood Sexual Abuse', in Neimeyer (2001b).

Foster, Z. P. (1965) 'How Social Work Can Influence Hospital Management of Fatal Illness', *Journal of National Association of Social Workers*, 10(4).

Foucault, M. (1977) *Discipline and Punish: The Birth of the Prison*, translated from the French by Alan Sheridan, Harmondsworth, Penguin.

Frantz, T., Farrell, M. M. and Trolley, B. C. (2001) 'Positive Outcomes of Losing a Loved One', in Neimeyer (2001b).

Fratter, J. (1996) *Adoption with Contact*, London, BAAF.

Freiberg, A. (2000) 'Working Together to Improve Policies for Victims of Crime', paper presented at Victims of Crime Conference, Adelaide.

Gabe, J., Calman, M. and Bury, M. (eds) (1991) *The Sociology of the Health Service*, London, Routledge.

Gardner, J. (1990) *Victims and Criminal Justice*, Attorney-General's Department Research Report No 5, Adelaide, SA Government Printer.

Gibson, F. (2001) 'No Strings Attached', in Britain Uncovered: *The Observer*, 18 March. pp 25–31.

Gilbert, R. (ed.) (2000) *Health Care and Spirituality: Listening, Assessing, Caring*, Amityville, NY, Baywood.

Gittings, J. (2000) 'Last Testament', *The Guardian* 2, 19 December.

Glaser, B. and Strauss, A. (1965) *Awareness of Dying*, Chicago, Aldine Publishing.

Gokam, W. (1994) 'Social Work and Spirituality', paper presented at the 27th *Congress of the International Schools of Social Work*, Amsterdam.

Goldman, L. (1981) *Death and the Creative Life*, Springer, New York.

Goldman, L. (1994) *Life and Loss: A Guide to Helping Grieving Children*, New York, Accelerated Development.

Gonçalves, O., Korman, Y. and Angus, L. (2000) 'Constructing Psychopathology From a Cognitive Narrative Perspective', in Neimeyer and Raskin (2000).

Gorer, G. (1965), *Death, Grief and Mourning in Contemporary Britain*, London, Cresset Press.

Grainger, R. (1998) *The Social Symbolism of Grief and Mourning*, London, Jessica Kingsley.

Grant, G. (2001) 'Older People with Learning Disabilities: Health, Community Inclusion and Family Caregiving' in Nolan *et al.* (2001).

Grant, L. (1998) *Remind Me Who I Am Again*, London, Granta Books.

Green, J. (1989) *Death with Dignity: Meeting the Spiritual Needs of Patients in a Multi-cultural Society, Vol.1*, London, Macmillan – now Palgrave.

Greenberg, L. S. (1992) 'Task Analysis', in Toukmanian and Rennie (1992).

Grollman, E. (ed.) (1995) *Bereaved Children and Teens*, Boston, Beacon Press.

Guidano, V. F. (1995) 'Self-observation in Constructivist Psychotherapy', in Neimeyer and Mahoney (1995).

Gunaratnam, Y. (1997) 'Culture is Not Enough: A Critique of Multiculturalism in Palliative Care', in Field *et al.* (1997).

Gutierrez, G. (1973) *A Theology of Liberation*, New York, Maryknoll.

Gutierrez, G. (1984) *We Drink From Our Own Wells*, New York, Maryknoll.

Hall, S. (1990) 'Cultural Identity and Diaspora', in Rutherford (1990).

Hall, S. (1992) 'New Ethnicities', in Donald and Rattansi (1992).

Harding, R. (1994) 'Victimisation, Moral Panics, and the Distortion of Criminal Justice Policy: A Review Essay of Ezzat Fattah's "Towards A Critical Victimology"', *Current Issues in Criminal Justice*, 6(1).

Harding, S. (ed.) (1987) *Feminism and Methodology*, Milton Keynes, Open University Press.

Harper, J. (1993) 'What Does She Look Like? What Children Want to Know about their Birth Families', *Adoption and Fostering*, 17(2).

Hart, B. (1996) 'The Construction of the Gendered Self', *Journal of Family Therapy*, 18(43).

Harvey, J. H. (ed.) (1998) *Perspectives on Loss: A Sourcebook*, Philadelphia, Brunner Routledge.

Haworth, M., Lennard, R., Sadiq, A. and Smith, M. (1997) 'Asian Interpreters and Palliative Care', *Palliative Medicine Research Abstracts*, 11,77.

Hearn, J. (1987) *The Gender of Oppression*, Hemel Hempstead, Harvester Wheatsheaf.

Helmrath, T. A. and Steinitz, E. (1978) 'Death of an Infant: Parental Grieving and the Failure of Social Support', *Journal of Family Practice*, 6(4).

Hemmings, P. (1995) 'Social Work Intervention with Bereaved Children', *Journal of Social Work Practice*, 9(2).

Hester, M., Pearson, C. and Harwin, N. (2000) *Making An Impact: Children and Domestic Violence*, London, Jessica Kingsley.

Hicks, S. and McDermott J. (eds) (1999) *Lesbian and Gay Fostering and Adoption: Extraordinary Yet Ordinary*, London, Jessica Kingsley.

Higgs, P. and Victor, C. (1993) 'Institutional Care and the Life Course', in Arber and Evandrou (1993).

Hill, M. and Shaw, M. (eds) (1998) *Signposts in Adoption: Policy, Practice and Research Issues*, London, BAAF.

Hockey, J. (1997) 'Women in Grief', in Field *et al.* (1997).

Hockey, J. and James, A. (1993) *Growing Up and Growing Old*, London, Sage.

Hockey, J., Katz, J. and Small, N. (eds) (2001) *Grief, Mourning and Death Ritual*, Buckingham, Open University Press.

Hollinger, R. (1994) *Postmodernism and the Social Sciences*, London, Sage.

Holmes, T. H. and Rahe, R. H. (1967) 'The Social Readjustment Rating Scale', *Journal of Psychosomatic Research*, 11, 213–18.

Holroyd, R. and Sheppard, A. (1997) 'Parental Separation: Effects on Children and Implications for Services', *Child Care, Health and Development*, 23(5).

Hood, R. (1999) 'Penal Policy and Criminological Challenges in the New Millennium', An Address to the 14th Annual Conference of the Australian and New Zealand Society of Criminology, Perth, University of Western Australia.

Howard, J. (1996) *Weekly House Hansard*, 30 October.

Howarth, G. and Jupp, P. (eds) (1996) *Contemporary Issues in the Sociology of Death, Dying and Disposal*, London, Macmillan – now Palgrave.

Howe, D. (1995) *Attachment Theory for Social Work Practice*, London, Macmillan – now Palgrave.

Howe, D., Brandon, M., Hinings, D. and Schofield, G. (1999) *Attachment Theory, Child Maltreatment and Family Support*, London, Macmillan – now Palgrave.

Howe, D. and Feast, J. (2000) *Adoption, Search and Reunion: The Long Term Experience of Adopted Adults*, London, The Children's Society.

Hughes, B. and Logan, J. (1993) *Birth Parents: The Hidden Dimension*, Manchester, University of Manchester.

[ ]   Buckingham, Open

[ ]   sportation of Convicts

[ ]   997a) *Report of the Torres Strait Islander* Sydney, Australian

[ ]   97b) *Bringing Them the National Inquiry r Children from their* Service.

[ ]   its: Choice versus

Irish, D. (1995) 'Children and Death: Diversity in Universality', in Grollman (1995).

Irish, D. P., Lundquist, K. F. and Nelson, V. J. (eds) (1993) *Ethnic Variations in Dying, Death and Grief*, Washington, Taylor and Francis.

Israel, M. (1999) 'Victims and Justice', in Sarre and Tomaino (1999).

Ivaldi, G. (2000) *Surveying Adoption: A Comprehensive Analysis of Local Authority Adoptions 1998–1999 (England)*, London, BAAF.

Jackson, S. and Thomas, N. (1999) *On the Move Again? What Works in Creating Stability for Looked After Children*, Ilford, Barnardos.

Jaco, R. M. (2001) 'Distinguishing Features of Social Support, Counselling and Therapy', in J. D. Morgan (ed.), *Social Support: A Reflection of Humanity*, Amityville, NY, Baywood.

Jacobs, M. (1991) *Insight and Experience, A Manual of Training in the Technique and Theory of Psychodynamic Counselling and Therapy*, Buckingham, Open University Press.

Jacobs, S., Hansen, F., Kasl, S. and Ostfeld, A. (1989) 'Depressions of Bereavement', *Comprehensive Psychiatry*, 30(3), 218–24.

Janoff-Bulman, R. and Berg, M. (1998) 'Disillusionment and the Creation of Values', in Harvey (1998).

Jewett, C. (1982) *Helping Children Cope with Separation and Loss*, Guildford, Batsford Academic.

Johnston, E. (1991) *Royal Commission into Aboriginal Deaths in Custody, National Report, Volumes 1 to 5*, Canberra, Australian Government Publication Service.

Jones, A. and Kroll, B. (1998) 'The Eyes and Ears of the Court: Tightrope Walking in a Strong Wind', in Davies (1998).

Jones, C. and Novak, T. (1999) *Poverty, Welfare and the Disciplinary State*, London, Routledge.

Jones, L. J. (1994) *The Social Context of Health and Health Work*, London, Macmillan – now Palgrave.

Jones, L. J. (1997) 'What is Health?', in Katz and Peberdy (1997).

Jordan, B (2000) 'Conclusion: Tough Love: Social Work Practice in UK Society', in Stepney and Ford (2000).

Jordan, K., Ong, B. N. and Croft, P. (2000) 'Researching Limiting Long-term Illness', *Social Science and Medicine*, 50, 397–405.

Kastenbaum, R. (1972) *The Psychology of Death*, New York, Springer.

Kastenbaum, R. (1995) *Death, Society and Human Experience*, 5th edn, Boston, Allyn and Bacon.

Katz, J. and Peberdy, A. (eds) (1997) *Promoting Health: Knowledge and Practice*, London, Macmillan – now Palgrave.

Katz, J. and Strauss, R. (1974) 'The Social Consequences of Amputation: Those Injured in Industrial Accidents and Those in Military Service', unpublished BA (Social Work) dissertation, Bar Ilan University, Israel.

Kelley, P. (1996) 'Narrative Theory and Social Work Treatment', in Turner (1996).

Kelly, G. A. (1955) *The Psychology of Personal Constructs*, New York, Norton.

Kelly, L. E., Knox, V. J. and Gekoski, W. L. (1998) 'Women's Views of Institutional versus Community-based Long-term Care', *Research on Ageing*, 20(2).

Klass, D. (1996) 'The Deceased Child in the Psychic and Social Worlds of Bereaved Parents During the Resolution of Grief', in Klass *et al.* (1996).

Klass, D., Silverman, P. R. and Nickman, S. L. (eds) (1996) *Continuing Bonds, New Understandings of Grief*, London, Taylor and Francis.

Koffman, J. and Higginson, I. J. (2001) 'Accounts of Satisfaction with Health Care at the End of Life: A Comparison of First Generation Black Caribbeans and White Patients with Advanced Disease', *Palliative Medicine*, 15(4).

Kotara, J. (1977) 'The Chronic Pain Experience', in Douglas and Johnson (1977).

Kroll, B. (1994) *Chasing Rainbows: Children, Divorce and Loss*, Lyme Regis, Russell House Publishing.

Kroll, B. (1998) *Children of Divorce: Helping Your Child to Cope*, London, BBC Education.

Kroll, B. (2000a) 'Not Intruding, Not Colluding: Process and Practice in a Contact Centre', *Children and Society*, 14(3).

Kroll, B. (2000b) 'Milk Bottle, Messenger, Monitor, Spy: Children's Experience of Contact', *Child Care in Practice*, 6(3).

Kübler-Ross, E. (1969) *On Death and Dying*, New York, Macmillan.

Lambert, M. J. and Cattani-Thompson, K. (1996) 'Current Findings Regarding the Effectiveness of Counseling: Implications for Practice', *Journal of Counseling and Development*, 74, July/August, 601–8.

Lamming, G. (1954) *The Emigrants*, London, Michael Joseph.

Langton, M. (2000) 'Does Mandatory Sentencing Cause Fundamental Damage to the Legal System?', Elliot Johnston Tribute Lecture, National Law Week, Adelaide, Flinders University of South Australia.

Laungani, B. (1997) 'Death in a Hindu Family', in Parkes *et al.* (1997).

Lawton, J. (2000) *The Dying Process: Patients' Experiences of Palliative Care*, London, Routledge.

Lendrum, S. and Syme, S. (1992) *The Gift of Tears*, London, Routledge.

Lewis, J. and Glennerster, H. (1996) *Implementing the New Community Care*, Buckingham, Open University Press.

Liebling, A. and Ward, T. (eds) (1994) *Deaths in Custody: International Perspectives*, London, Whiting and Birch.

Lindemann, E. (1944) 'Symptomotology and Management of Acute Grief', *American Journal of Psychiatry*, 101, 141–8.

Lloyd, M. (1992) 'Tools for Many Trades: Reaffirming the Use of Grief Counselling by Health, Welfare and Pastoral Workers', *British Journal of Guidance and Counselling*, 20(2), 151–64.

Lloyd, M. (1995) *Embracing the Paradox: Pastoral Care with Dying and Bereaved People*, Contact Pastoral Monographs No.5, Edinburgh, Contact Pastoral Limited Trust.

Lloyd, M. (1996) 'Philosophy and Religion in the Face of Death and Bereavement', *Journal of Religion and Health*, 35(4).

Lloyd, M. (1997) 'Dying and Bereavement, Spirituality and Social Work in a Market Economy of Welfare', *British Journal of Social Work*, 27(2), 175–90.

Lloyd, M. (2000) *Holistic Approaches to Health and Social Care in the UK in the 1990s*, PhD Thesis, University of Manchester.

Lowe, N., Murch, M., Borkowski, M., Weaver, A. and Beckford, V. with Thomas, C. (1999) *Supporting Adoption: Reframing the Approach*, London, BAAF.

Ludlow, M. (2000) 'Sorry You Don't Exist: Government Rules On Stolen Generation', *Advertiser*, Adelaide, 1 April.

Lund, D. (ed.) (2001) *Men Coping with Grief*, Amityville, NY, Baywood.

Lupton, D. and Barclay, L. (1997) *Constructing Fatherhood: Discourses and Experiences*, London, Sage.

Lustbader, W. (1994) *Counting on Kindness: The Dilemmas of Dependency*, New York, Free Press.

Lynch, T. (1998) *The Undertaking, Life Studies from the Dismal Trade*, London, Vintage Books.

Macdonald, B. (1983) *Look Me in the Eye: Women, Aging and Ageism*, San Francisco, Spinsters' Ink.

Macmillan, J. (2001) *Adoption: A Birth Mother's Perspective*, unpublished dissertation, University of Wales, Swansea.

Macpherson, W. (1999) *The Stephen Lawrence Inquiry: Report of an Inquest*, London, The Stationery Office.

Maguire, P. and Parkes, C. M. (1998) 'Surgery and Loss of Body Parts', in Parkes and Markus (1998).

Malkinson, R., Rubin, S. and Wiztum, E. (eds) (2000) *Traumatic and Non-traumatic Loss and Bereavement*, Madison, CT, Psychosocial Press.

Mallon, B. (1998) *Helping Children to Manage Loss*, London, Jessica Kingsley.

Marlow, A and Loveday, B. (eds) (2000) *After Macpherson*, Lyme Regis, Russell House Publishing.

Morris, P. (1974) *Loss and Change*, London, Routledge and Kegan Paul.

Mascolo, M. F., Craig-Bray, L. and Neimeyer, R. A. (1997) 'The Construction of Meaning and Action in Development and Psychotherapy: An Epigenetic Systems Approach', in Neimeyer and Neimeyer (1997).

Mason, K. and Selman, P. (1998) 'Birth Parents' Experience of Contested Adoption', in Hill and Shaw (1998).

Masson, J., Harrison, C. and Pavlovic, A. (1997) *Working With Children and Lost Parents, Findings: Social Care Research 98*, York, Joseph Rowntree Foundation.

Masters, W. H., Johnson, V. E. and Kolodny, R. C. (1994) *Heterosexuality*, London, Thorsons/HarperCollins.

Maxime, J. (1986) 'Some Psychological Models of Black Self-Concept', in Ahmed *et al.* (1986).

McGee, M. (1995) 'Do We Need Additional Models of Grieving? The Argentine Mothers of the Plaza de Mayo', *Illness, Crisis and Loss*, 4(3/4).

McGreal, D., Evans, B. J. and Burrows, G. D. (1997) 'Gender Differences in Coping Following the Loss of a Child Through Miscarriage or Still Birth: A Pilot Study', *Stress Medicine*, 13(3).

McKenna, M. (1997) 'Different Perspectives on Black Armband History', *Australian Parliamentary Library, Research Paper 5*, 1997–98.

Mearns, D. and Thorne, B. (1999) *Person-Centred Counselling in Action*, 2nd edn, London, Sage.

Meghnagi, D. (ed.) (1993) *Freud and Judaism*, London, Karnac Books.

Mellor, P. and Shilling, C. (1993) 'Modernity, Self-identity and the Sequestration of Death', *Sociology*, 27(3).

Menzies, I. (1961) 'A Case Study in the Functioning of Social Systems as a Defence Against Anxiety', *Human Relations*, 13(2).

Midwinter, E. (1990) 'An Ageing World', *Ageing and Society*, 10.

Midwinter, E. (1991) 'Forgotten Army', *Social Work Today*, 7 November.

Milo, E.M. (1997) 'Maternal Responses to the Life and Death of a Child with Developmental Disability', *Death Studies*, 21, 443–76.

Mitchell, A. (1985) *Children in the Middle: Living through Divorce*, London, Tavistock.

Mohan, J. (1991) 'Privatisation in the British Health Sector: A Challenge to the NHS?', in Gabe *et al.* (1991).

Monk, G. (1997) 'How Narrative Therapy Works', in Monk *et al.* (1997).

Monk, G., Winslade, J., Crocket, K. and Epston, D. (eds) (1997) *Narrative Therapy in Practice: the Archaeology of Hope*, San Francisco, Jossey-Bass.

Morgan, J. D. (1993) 'The Existential Quest for Meaning', in Doka and Morgan (1993).

Morgan, J. D. (1995) 'Living Our Dying and Our Grieving: Historical and Cultural Attitudes', in Wass and Neimeyer (1995).

Morgan J. D. (2000) 'Dying and Grieving are Journeys of the Spirit', in Gilbert (2000).

Morris, J. (1991) *Pride Against Prejudice: Transforming Attitude to Disability*, London, The Women's Press.

Morris, J. (1997) 'Gone Missing? Disabled Children Living Away from their Families', *Disability and Society*, 12(2).

Morrison, B. (1998) *And When Did You Last See Your Father?*, London, Granta Books.

Moss, M.S. and Moss, S.Z. (1989) 'Death of the Very Old', in Doka (1989).

Mukherjee, S. (2000) 'Crime Trends: A National Perspective', in Chappell and Wilson (2000).

Mulday, M. and Ernst, J. (1991) 'The Changing Profile of Social Death', *Archives of European Sociology*, 32, 172–96.

Mullender, A. (ed.) (1991) *Open Adoption*, London, BAAF.

Mullender, A. (ed.) (1999) *We are Family*, London, BAAF.

Murphy, S. A., Johnson, C., Cain, K. C., Das Gupta, A., Dimond, M. and Lohan, J. (1998) 'Broad-spectrum Group Treatment for Parents Bereaved by the Violent Deaths of Their 12- to 28-year-old Children: A Randomized Controlled Trial', *Death Studies*, 22, 209–35.

Nadeau, J.W. (1997) *Families Making Sense of Death*, Newbury Park, CA, Sage.

National Council for Hospice and Specialist Palliative Care Services (NCHSPCS) (1993) *Needs Assessment for Hospice and Specialist Palliative Care Services: From Philosophy to Contracts*, Occasional Paper No 4, London, NCHSPCS.

National Council for Hospice and Specialist Palliative Care Services (NCHSPCS) (1995) *Opening Doors: Improving Access to Hospice and Specialist Palliative Care Services by Members of the Black and Ethnic Minority Communities*, London, NCHSPCS.

National Council for Hospice and Specialist Palliative Care Services (NCHSPCS) (1998) *Promoting Partnership: Planning and Managing Community Palliative Care*, London, NCHSPCS.

Neale, B. and Wade, A. (2000) *Parent Problems! Children's Views on Life when Parents Split Up*, Surrey, Young Voice.

Neimeyer, G. J. (ed.) (1993) *Constructivist Assessment: A Casebook*, Newbury Park, CA, Sage.

Neimeyer, G. J. and Neimeyer, R. A. (eds) (1997) *Advances in Personal Construct Psychology*, Greenwich, CT, JAI Press.

Neimeyer, R. A. (1993) 'Constructivist Approaches to the Measurement of Meaning', in Neimeyer, G. J. (1993).

Neimeyer, R. A. (1998) 'Social Constructionism in the Counselling Context', *Counselling Psychology Quarterly*, 11, 135–49.

Neimeyer, R. A. (2000a) 'Narrative Disruptions in the Construction of Self', in Neimeyer and Raskin (2000).

Neimeyer, R. A. (2000b) 'Searching for the Meaning of Meaning', *Death Studies*, 24, 541–58.

Neimeyer, R. A. (2001a) 'The Language of Loss: Grief Therapy as a Process of Meaning Reconstruction', in Neimeyer (2001b).

Neimeyer, R. A. (ed.) (2001b) *Meaning Reconstruction and the Experience of Loss*, Washington, DC, American Psychological Association.

Neimeyer, R. A. (2001c) *Lessons of Loss: A Guide to Coping*, New York, Brunner Routledge.

Neimeyer, R. A. and Jordan, J. R. (2001) 'Disenfranchisement as Empathic Failure', in Doka (2001).

Neimeyer, R. A., Keesee, N. J. and Fortner, B. V. (2000) 'Loss and Meaning Reconstruction: Propositions and Procedures', in Malkinson *et al.* (2000).

Neimeyer, R. A. and Levitt, H. (2001) 'Coping and Coherence: A Narrative Perspective on Resilience', in Snyder (2001).

Neimeyer, R. A. and Mahoney, M. J. (eds) (1995) *Constructivism in Psychotherapy*, Washington, DC, American Psychological Association.

Neimeyer, R. A. and Raskin, J. (eds) (2000) *Constructions of Disorder*, Washington, DC, American Psychological Association.

Neuberger, J. (1987) *Caring for Dying People of Different Faiths*, London, Austen Cornish and Lisa Sainsbury Foundation.

Nolan, M., Davies, S. and Grant, G. (eds) (2001) *Working with Older People and Their Families*, Buckingham, Open University Press.

O'Hagan, K. (1986) *Crisis Intervention in Social Services*, London, Macmillan – now Palgrave.

Oliver, M. (1988) Letter to the editor, *Social Work Today*, 19 May.

Oliver, M. (1990) *The Politics of Disablement*, London, Macmillan – now Palgrave.

Oliver, M. and Barnes, C. (1998) *Disabled People and Social Policy: From Exclusion to Inclusion*, Harlow, Addison Wesley Longman.

Oliver, M. and Sapey, B. (1999) *Social Work with Disabled People*, 2nd edn, London, Macmillan – now Palgrave.

Owen, M. (1999) *Novices, Old Hands and Professionals*, London, BAAF.

Owusu-Bempah, J. and Howitt, D. (1997) 'Socio-genealogical Connectedness, Attachment Theory and Child Care Practice', *Child and Family Social Work*, 2, 199–207.

Parkes C. M. (1975) 'Psychosocial Transitions: Comparison Between Reactions to Loss of a Limb and Loss of a Spouse', *British Journal of Psychiatry*, 127, 204–10.

Parkes, C. M. (1970) 'The First Year of Bereavement: A Longitudinal Study of the Reaction of London Widows to the Death of their Husbands', *Psychiatry*, 33, 444–67.

Parkes, C. M. (1975) 'What Becomes of Redundant World Models? A Contribution to the Study of Adaptation to Change', *British Journal of Medical Psychology*, 48, 131–7.

Parkes, C. M. (1993) 'Psychiatric Problems Following Bereavement by Murder or Manslaughter', *British Journal of Psychiatry*, 162, 49–54.

Parkes, C. M. (1996) *Bereavement: Studies of Grief in Adult Life*, 3rd edn (1st edn published 1972, Harmondsworth, Penguin) London, Routledge.

Parkes, C. M. (1997) 'Attachments and Losses in Cross Cultural Perspectives', in Parkes *et al.* (1997).

Parkes, C. M. (1998a) 'Bereavement in Adult Life', in Parkes and Markus (1998).

Parkes, C. M. (1998b) 'Bereavement', in Doyle *et al.* (1998).

Parkes, C. M. (1998c) 'Assumptions About Loss and Principles of Care', in Parkes and Markus (1998).

Parkes, C. M (1999) 'Coping with Loss: Consequences and Implications for Care', *International Journal of Palliative Nursing*, 5(5), 250–6.

Parkes, C. M. (2000) 'Bereavement as a Psychosocial Transition: Processes of Adaptation to Change', in Dickenson *et al.* (2000)

Parkes, C. M. (2001) *Bereavement*, 4th edn, London and New York, Routledge.

Parkes, C. M., Laungani, P. and Young, B. (eds) (1997) *Death and Bereavement Across Cultures*, London, Routledge.

Parkes, C. M. and Markus, A. (eds) (1998) *Coping with Loss*, London, BMJ Books.

Parkes, C. M. and Weiss R. S. (1983) *Recovery from Bereavement*, New York, Basic Books.

Parsons, T. and Bales, R. F. (eds) (1956) *Family, Socialisation and Interaction Process*, London, Routledge and Kegan Paul.

Patel, N. (1990) *A 'Race Against Time?' Social Services Provision to Black Elders*, London, Runnymede Trust.

Patel, N., Humphries, B. and Naik, D. (1998) 'The 3 "R's in Social Work" Religion, "Race" and Racism in Europe', in Williams *et al.* (1998).

Patel, N., Naik, D. and Humphries, B. (1997) *Visions of Reality*, London, CCETSW.

Pavlovic, A. and Mullender, A. (1999) 'Adult Birth Siblings – Who Are They and Why do They Search?', in Mullender (1999).

Payne, S., Horn, S., and Relf, M. (1999) *Loss and Bereavement*, Buckingham, Open University Press.

Peace, S., Kellaher, L. and Willcocks, D. (1997) *Re-evaluating Residential Care*, Buckingham, Open University Press.

Peberdy, A. (2000) 'Spiritual Care of Dying People', in Dickenson *et al.* (2000).

Peddicord, D. J. (1990) 'Issues in the Disclosure of Perinatal Death', in Stricker and Fisher (1990).

Penketh, L. (2000) *Tackling Institutional Racism: Anti-racist Policies and Social Work Education and Training*, Bristol, Policy Press.

Pennebaker, J. W. (1989) 'Confession, Inhibition, and Disease', in Berkowitz (1989).

Pennebaker, J. W. (1997a) *Opening Up*, New York, Guilford.

Pennebaker, J. W. (1997b) 'Writing about Emotional Experiences as a Therapeutic Process', *Psychological Science*, 8, 162–9.

Pennebaker, J. W., Kiecolt-Glaser, J. K. and Glaser, R. (1988) 'Disclosure of Traumas and Immune Function: Health Implications for Psychotherapy', *Journal of Consulting and Clinical Psychology*, 56, 239–45.

Peto, R. (1998) *CancerBacup NEWS: Helping People Live with Cancer*, Issue 33 Autumn 1998.

Petrie, K. J., Booth, R. J., Pennebaker, J. W., Davison, K. P. and Thomas, M. G. (1995) 'Disclosure of Trauma and Immune Response to a Hepatitis B Vaccination Program', *Journal of Consulting and Clinical Psychology*, 63, 787–92.

Philpot, T. (ed.) (1989) *Last Things: Social Work with the Dying and Bereaved*, Wallington, Reed Business/Community Care.

Picardie, J. (2000) *If I Dream I Have You*, London, Granta, 'Shrinks' edition, 71.

Picardie, R. (1998) *Before I Say Goodbye*, Harmondsworth, Penguin.

Pickering, M., Littlewood, J. and Walter, T. (1997) 'Beauty and the Beast: Sex and Death in the Tabloid Press', in Field *et al.* (1997).

Polk, K. (2000) 'Changing Patterns of Violence', in Chappell and Wilson (2000).

Pounder, D. (1986) 'Death Behind Bars: An 11-Year Survey of Prisoner Deaths In South Australia', *Med. Sci. Law*, 27(3).

Prigerson, H. G. and Jacobs, S. C. (2001) 'Traumatic Grief as a Distinct Disorder: A Rationale, Consensus Criteria, and a Preliminary Empirical Test', in Stroebe *et al.* (2001).

Prigerson, H. G., Shear, M.K., Jacobs, S. C., Reynolds, C. F., Maceijewski, P. K., Pilkonis, P. A., Wortman, C., Williams, J. B. W., Widiger, T. A., Rosenheck, R. A., Davidson, J., Frank, E., Kupfer, D. J. and Zisook, S. (1999) 'Consensus Criteria for Traumatic Grief: A Preliminary Empirical Test', *British Journal of Psychiatry*, 174, 67–73.

Puddifoot, J. E. and Johnson, M. P. (1997) 'The Legitimacy of Grieving: the Partner's Experience at the Miscarriage', *Social Science and Medicine*, 45(6).

Radley, A. (1989) 'Style, Discourse and Constraint in Adjustment to Chronic Illness', *Sociology of Health and Illness*, 11, 230–52.

Rando, T. (1984) *Grief, Dying and Death: Clinical Interventions for Caregivers*, Champaign, IL, Research Press Company.

Raphael, B. (1983) *The Anatomy of Bereavement*, New York, Basic Books.

Raphael, B. (1986) *When Disaster Strikes: A Handbook For The Caring Professions*, London, Unwin Hyman.

Rapoport, L. (1970) 'Crisis Intervention as a Brief Mode of Treatment', in Roberts and Nee (1970).

Reoch, R. (1997) *Dying Well: A Holistic Guide for the Dying and their Carers*, London, Gaia.

Report of the Board of Inquiry into Several Matters Concerning H.M. Prison Pentridge and the Maintenance of Discipline (the Jenkinson Inquiry) 5 September 1973, Melbourne, Government Printer.

Report of the Commission into New South Wales Prisons, Nagle, J. Royal Commissioner, April 1978, Sydney, New South Wales Government Printer.

Richards, S. (2000) 'Bridging the Divide: Elders and the Assessment Process', *British Journal of Social Work*, 30, 37–49.

Richards, A. T., Acree, M. and Folkman, S. (1999) 'Spiritual Aspects of Loss Among Partners of Men with AIDS: Postbereavement Follow-up', *Death Studies*, 23.

Riches, G. and Dawson, P. (2000) *An Intimate Loneliness: Supporting Bereaved Parents and Siblings*, Buckingham, Open University Press.

Roberts, R. W. and Nee, R. H. (eds) (1970) *Theories of Social Casework*, Chicago, University of Chicago Press.

Robinson, L. (1995) *Psychology for Social Workers: Black Perspectives*, London, Routledge.

Robson, L. (1965) *The Convict Settlers of Australia*, Melbourne, Melbourne University Press.

Roche, D. (1999) 'Mandatory Sentencing', *Trends and Issues in Crime and Criminal Justice*, No. 138, Canberra, Australian Institute of Criminology.

Rodgers, B. and Pryor, J. (1998) *Divorce and Separation: The Outcomes for Children*, York, Joseph Rowntree Foundation.

Rogers, C. R. (1965) *Client-Centred Therapy*, London, Constable.

Roll, J. (1986) *Understanding Poverty*, London, Family Policy Studies Institute.

Rose, H. and Bruce, E. (1995) 'Mutual Care But Differential Esteem: Caring Between Older Couples', in Arber and Ginn (1995).

Rosenblatt, P. C. (1993) 'Cross-Cultural Variation in the Experience, Expression and Understanding of Grief', in Irish *et al.* (1993).

Rosenblatt, P. C. (1997) 'Grief in Small-Scale Societies', in Parkes *et al.* (1997).

Roth, J.A. and Conrad, P. (eds) (1987) *Research in the Sociology of Health Care: The Experience and Management of Chronic Illness*, Vol. 6, Greenwich, CT, JAI Press.

Roy, D.R. (1997) 'Palliative Care: A Fragment Towards its Philosophy', *Journal of Palliative Care*, 13(1).

Royal Commission Into Aboriginal Deaths In Custody, Interim Report (J. H. Muirhead) (1991), Canberra, Australian Government Publication Service.

Rubinstein, J. L, Hereen, T., Housman, D. *et al.* (1989) 'Suicidal Behaviour in 'Normal' Adolescents: Risk and Protective Factors', *American Journal of Orthopsychiatry*, 9(1).

Rumbold, B. (1986) *Helplessness and Hope: Pastoral Care in Terminal Illness*, London, SCM Press.

Rutherford, J. (ed.) (1990) *Identity: Community, Culture and Difference*, London, Lawrence and Wishart.

Rynearson, E. K. and McCreery, J. M. (1993) 'Bereavement after Homicide: A Synergism of Trauma and Loss', *American Journal of Psychiatry*, 150(2).

Sacco, T. (1994) 'Spirituality and Social Work Students in their First Year of Study at a South African University', paper presented at the *27th Congress of the International Schools of Social Work*, Amsterdam.

Salander, P., Bergenheim, A. T. and Henriksson, R. (2000) 'How Was Life After Treatment of a Malignant Brain Tumour?', *Social Science and Medicine*, 51, 589–98.

Salzberger-Wittenberg, I. (1970) *Psycho-Analytic Insights and Relationships: A Kleinian Approach*, London, Routledge and Kegan Paul.

Samwell-Smith, K. (2000) 'Meeting Our Needs: Some Proposals for Change', in Selman (2000).

Sarre, R. and Tomaino, J. (eds) (1999) *Exploring Criminal Justice: Contemporary Australian Themes*, Adelaide, Institute of Justice Studies.

Saunders, C. M. S. (1959) 'Care of the Dying 2: Should a Patient Know ...?', *Nursing Times*, 16 October.

Saunders, C.M.S. (1976) 'Care of the Dying 1: The Problem of Euthanasia' (2nd printing), *Nursing Times*, 72(26).

Saunders, C.M.S. (1977) 'Dying They Live – St. Christopher's Hospice', in Feifel (1977).

Sawbridge, P. (1991) 'On Behalf of Birth Parents', in Mullender (1991)

Schaffer, H. (1996) *Social Development*, Oxford, Blackwell.

Schetzer, L. (1998) *NT Mandatory Sentencing – 12 Months of Bad Policy*, Accessed on 27/05/2000.

Schneidman, E. (2000) *Lives and Deaths*, Philadelphia, Brunner Routledge.

Schwab, R. (1992) 'Effects of a Child's Death on the Marital Relationship', *Death Studies*, 16, 141–54.

Scrutton, S. (1989) *Counselling Older People – A Creative Response to Ageing*, London, Edward Arnold.

Scrutton, S. (1992) *Counselling Older People*, London, Edward Arnold.

Scrutton, S. (1995) *Bereavement and Grief: Supporting Older People Through Loss*, London, Edward Arnold.

Seale, C. (1995a) 'Heroic Death', *Sociology*, 29(4).

Seale, C. (1995b) 'Dying Alone', *Sociology of Health and Illness*, 17, 377–91.

Seale, C. and Addington-Hall, J. (1994) 'Euthanasia: Why People Want to Die Earlier', *Soc. Sci. Med.*, 39(5).

Seden, J. (1999) *Counselling Skills in Social Work Practice*, Buckingham, Open University Press.

Seidler, V. J. (1991) *Recreating Sexual Politics*, London, Routledge.

Selman, P. (ed.) (2000) *Intercountry Adoption: Developments, Trends and Perspectives*, London, BAAF.

Sheldon, B. and Chilvers, R. (2000) *Evidence-Based Social Care*, Lyme Regis, Russell House Publishing.

Sheldon, F. (1997) *Psychosocial Palliative Care: Good Practice in the Care of the Dying and Bereaved*, Cheltenham, Stanley Thornes.

Sherr, L. (ed.) (1995) *Grief and AIDS*, Chichester, John Wiley.

Sibeon, R. (1991) *Towards a New Sociology of Social Work*, Aldershot, Avebury.

Silverman, P. R. and Worden, J. W. (1992) 'Children's Reactions in the Early Months after the Death of a Parent', *American Journal of Orthopsychiatry*, 62, 93–104.

Singh, G. (2000) 'The Concept and Context of Institutional Racism', in Marlow and Loveday (2000).

Slack, S. (1999) 'I Am More Than My Wheels', in Corker and French (1999b).

Smaje, C. and Field, D. (1997) 'Absent Minorities?' in Field *et al.* (1997).

Smart, C. and Wade, A. (2000) *New Childhoods: Children and Co-parenting After Divorce*, Research Briefing No.7 ESRC.

Smirnoff, L. A. and Fetting, J. A. (1991) 'Factors Affecting Treatment Decisions for Life-threatening Illness: the Case of Medical Treatment of Breast Cancer', *Social Science and Medicine*, 32(7).

Smith, C. (1998) '"Men Don't Do this Sort of thing": A Case Study of the Social Isolation of Househusbands', *Men and Masculinities*, 1(2).

Smith, C. R. (1982) *Social Work with the Dying and Bereaved*, London, Macmillan – now Palgrave.

Smith, D. (1987) 'Women's Perspective as a Radical Critique of Sociology', in Harding (1987).

Snyder, R. (ed.) (2001) *Coping with Stress*, New York, Oxford University Press.

Spruyt, O. (1999) 'Community-based Palliative Care for Bangladeshi Patients in East London: Accounts of Bereaved Carers', *Palliative Medicine*, 13, 119–29.

St Christopher's Hospice (1996) 'Mission Statement', London, St Christopher's Hospice.

Stanworth, R. (2000) The Search for Sources of Meaning and Sense of Self in People who are Dying, PhD Thesis, Heythrop College, University of London.

Stein, S. M. (ed.) (1999) *Beyond Belief, Psychotherapy and Religion*, London, Karnac Books.

Stepney, P. and Ford, D. (eds) (2000) *Social Work Models, Methods and Theories: A Framework for Practice*, Lyme Regis, Russell House Publishing.

Stricker, G. and Fisher, M. (eds) (1990) *Self-Disclosure In The Therapeutic Relationship*, New York, Plenum Press.

Stroebe, M., Stroebe, W. and Hansson, R. O. (eds) (1993) *Handbook of Bereavement: Theory, Research and Intervention*, Cambridge, Cambridge University Press.

Stroebe, M. S. (1998) 'New Directions in Bereavement Research: Exploration of Gender Differences', *Palliative Medicine*, 12, 5–12.

Stroebe, M. S., Hansson, R. O., Stroebe, W. and Schut, H. (eds) (2001) *Handbook of Bereavement Research: Consequences, Coping, and Care*, Washington, DC, American Psychological Association.

Stroebe, M. and Schut, H. (1995) 'The Dual Process Model of Coping with Loss', paper presented at the International Work Group on Death, Dying and Bereavement, St Catherine's College, Oxford, UK.

Stroebe, M. and Schut, H. (1999) 'The Dual Process Model of Coping with Bereavement: Rationale and Description', *Death Studies*, 23(3).

Stroebe, M. S, Schut, H. and Abakoumkin, G. (1996) 'The Role of Loneliness and Social Support in Adjustment to Loss: A Test of Attachment versus Stress Theory', *Journal of Personality and Social Psychology*, 70(6).

Stroebe, W. and Stroebe, M. (1987) *Bereavement and Health*, New York, Cambridge University Press.

Stroebe, M. and Stroebe, W. (1993) 'The Mortality of Bereavement: A Review', in Stroebe *et al.* (1993)

Strong, R. (2001) *Re: Disability and the Sufferer*, message to Disability Research discussion group, disability-research@jiscmail.ac.uk, 6 February.

Sumner, C. (1994) 'Introduction: President's Opening Address', in Sumner *et al.* (1994).

Sumner, C., Israel, M., O'Connell, M. and Sarre, R. (eds) (1994) *International Victimology: Selected Papers from the 8th International Symposium*, proceedings of a symposium, Adelaide.

Sutcliffe, P., Tufnell, G. and Cornish, U. (eds) (1998) *Working with the Dying and the Bereaved*, London, Macmillan – now Palgrave.

Sutton, C. (1994) *Social Work, Community Work and Psychology*, Leicester, BPS Books.

Swan-Jackson, A. (1996) *Caught in the Middle: Teenagers Talk about their Parents' Divorce*, London, Piccadilly Press.

Swift, G. (1996) *Last Orders*, London, Picador.

Tedeschi, R., Park, C. and Calhoun, L. (eds) (1998) *Posttraumatic Growth: Positive Changes in the Aftermath of Crisis*, Mahwah, NJ, Lawrence Erlbaum.

Tehrani, N. and Westlake, R. (1994) 'Debriefing Individuals Affected by Violence', *Counselling Quarterly*, 7(3).

Thomas, C. (1999) *Female Forms: Experiencing and Understanding Disability*, Buckingham, Open University Press.

Thomas, C. and Beckford, V. with Lowe, N. and Murch, M. (1999) *Adopted Children Speaking*, London, BAAF.

Thompson, N. (1991) *Crisis Intervention Revisited*, Birmingham, Pepar.

Thompson, N. (1992) *Existentialism and Social Work*, Aldershot, Avebury.

Thompson, N. (1995) *Age and Dignity: Working with Older People*, Aldershot, Arena.

Thompson, N. (1997) 'Masculinity and Loss', in Field *et al.* (1997).

Thompson, N. (1998a) 'The Ontology of Ageing', *British Journal of Social Work*, 28(5).

Thompson, N. (1998b) *Promoting Equality: Challenging Discrimination and Oppression in the Human Services*, London, Macmillan – now Palgrave.

Thompson, N. (1999) *Stress Matters*, Birmingham, Pepar.

Thompson, N. (2000a) *Understanding Social Work: Preparing for Practice*, Basingstoke, Palgrave.

Thompson, N. (2000b) *Theory and Practice in the Human Services*, 2nd edn, Buckingham, Open University Press.

Thompson, N. (2001a) *Anti-Discriminatory Practice*, 3rd edn, Basingstoke, Palgrave.

Thompson, N. (2001b) 'The Ontology of Masculinity: The Roots of Manhood', in Lund (2001).

Thompson, N., Murphy, M. and Stradling, S. (1994) *Dealing with Stress*, London, Macmillan – now Palgrave.

Thompson, N., Murphy, M. and Stradling, S. (1996) *Meeting the Stress Challenge*, Lyme Regis, Russell House Publishing.

Thompson, S. and Thompson, N. (1999) 'Older People, Crisis and Loss', *Illness, Crisis and Loss*, 7(2).

Thorns, A. and Sykes, N. (2000) 'Opioid Use in Last Week of Life and Implications for End-of-life Decision Making', *The Lancet*, 356, 398–9.

Tilbury, C. (1998) 'Child Protection Policy and Practice in Relation to Aboriginal and Torres Strait Islander Children in Queensland in the 1990s', *Australian Social Work*, 51(2).

Toukmanian, S. G. and Rennie, D. L. (eds) (1992) *Psychotherapy Process Research*, Newbury Park, CA, Sage.

Townsend, P. (1979) *Poverty in the UK*, Harmondsworth, Penguin.

Townsend, P. and Davidson, N. (1988) 'The Black Report' in Townsend *et al.* (1988).

Townsend, P., Davidson, N. and Whitehead, M. (1988) *Inequalities in Health*, Harmondsworth, Penguin.

Townsend, J., Frank, A. O., Fermont, D., Dyer, S., Karan, O. and Walgrave, A. (1990) 'Terminal Cancer Care and Patients' Preference for Place of Death: A Prospective Study', *British Medical Journal*, 301, 415–27.

Triseliotis, J., Sellick, C. and Short, R. (1995) *Foster Care: Theory and Practice*, London, Batsford.

Tugendhat, J. (1990) *What Teenagers Can Tell Us about Divorce and Stepfamilies*, London, Bloomsbury.

Turner, F. (ed.) (1996) *Social Work Treatment: Interlocking Theoretical Approaches*, 4th edn, New York, The Free Press.

Twycross, R. (1997) *Introducing Palliative Care*, 2nd edn, Abingdon, Radcliffe Medical Press.

UK National Standards for Foster Care (1999) National Foster Care Association, London, NFCA.

Viney, L. L. (1991) 'The Personal Construct Theory of Death and Loss', *Death Studies*, 15, 139–55.

Walczak, Y. and Burns, S. (1984) *Divorce: The Child's Point of View*, London, Harper and Row.

Walker, J. (1996) *Being There: Fathers After Divorce*, Newcastle, Relate Centre for Family Studies, Newcastle University.

Walker, C. and Walker, A. (1998) 'Social Work and Society', in Adams *et al.* (1998).

Wall, P.D. (1986) '25 Volumes of Pain', *Pain*, 25, 1–4.

Wallerstein, J. S. and Blakeslee, S. (1989) *Second Chances*, London, Corgi.

Wallerstein, J. and Kelly, J. (1980) *Surviving the Breakup: How Children and Parents Cope with Divorce*, London, Grant McIntyre.

Walsh, F. and McGoldrick, M. (1991) *Living Beyond Loss*, New York, Norton.

Walter, T. (1994) *The Revival of Death*, London, Routledge.

Walter, T. (1996) 'A New Model of Grief: Bereavement and Biography', *Mortality*, 1(1).

Walter, T. (1999) *On Bereavement: the Culture of Grief*, Buckingham, Open University Press.

Wass, H. and Neimeyer, R. A. (eds) (1995) *Dying: Facing the Facts*, 3rd edn, London, Taylor and Francis.

Watson, L. and McGhee, J. (1995) *Developing Post-Placement Support: A Project in Scotland*, London, BAAF.

Webb-Johnson, A. (1991) *A Cry for Change: An Asian Perspective on Developing Quality Mental Health Care*, London, Confederation of Indian Organizations (UK).

Weinstein, J. (1997) 'A Dramatic View of Bereavement', *Counselling*, November.

Weiss, R. S. (1975) *Loneliness: The Experience of Emotional and Social Isolation*, Cambridge, MA, MIT Press.

Weiss, R. S. (1990) *Staying the Course: The Emotional and Social Lives of Men Who do Well at Work*, New York, Free Press.

West, W. (2000) *Psychotherapy and Spirituality, Crossing the Line between Therapy and Religion*, London, Sage.

Westwood, S., Couloute, J., Desai, S., Matthew, P. and Piper, A. (1989) *Sadness in My Heart: Racism and Mental Health: A Research Report*, Leicester Black Mental Health Group and University of Leicester.

White, M. and Epston, D. (1990) *Narrative Means to Therapeutic Ends*, New York, Norton.

Who Cares? Trust (1993) *Not Just a Name: The Views of Young People in Foster and Residential Care*, London, National Consumer Council.

Widgery, D. (1989) *Preserving Disorder: Selected Essays 1968–88*, London, Pluto Press.

Williams, C., Soydan, H. and Johnson, M.R.D. (eds) (1998) *Social Work and Minorities: European Perspectives*, London, Routledge.

Worden, W. J. (1991) *Grief Counselling and Grief Therapy: A Handbook for the Mental Health Practitioner*, 2nd edn, London, Routledge.

Wortham, S. (2001) *Narratives in Action*, New York, Teachers College Press.

Wortman, C. and Silver, R. (1989) 'The Myths of Coping with Loss', *Journal of Consulting and Clinical Psychology*, 57(3).

Yalom, I. D. (1980) *Existential Psychotherapy*, New York, Basic Books.

Young, M. and Cullen, L. (1996) *A Good Death*, London, Routledge.

Zarb, G. (1993) '"Forgotten But Not Gone": The Experience of Ageing with a Disability', in Arber and Evandrou (1993).

Zinker, J. (1994) *In Search of Good Form*, San Francisco, Jossey Bass.

Zohar, D. and Marshall, I. (1999) *SQ: Connecting with Our Spiritual Intelligence*, London, Bloomsbury.

Zulli, A. P. (1998) 'Healing Rituals: Powerful and Empowering', in Doka and Davidson (1998).

Index